The Middle School Student's Guide to
Study Skills

Student Workbook

Illustrations by Zapp!

by Susan Mulcaire

This book belongs to:

_____

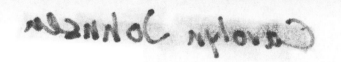

Tween Publishing acknowledges Zapp Illustrations: pages 2, 3, 6, 10, 11, 15, 16, 23, 26, 32, 33, 44, 45, 48, 53, 66, 67, 78, 79, 88, 89, 98, 99, 110, 111, 124, 125, 135, 144, 145, 151, 156, 157, 166, 167, 176, 177, 186, 187, 198, 199, 210, 211, 225, 238, 239, 250, 251, 264, 265, 276, 277, 288, 289, 295, 302, 303, 314, 315.

Printed in the United States of America

ISBN 978-0-9785210-6-6

TABLE OF CONTENTS

WHAT ARE STUDY SKILLS?

Have you ever thought about what it takes to be a winning athlete? Is talent enough? Physical ability? Stamina? What about the mentality and attitude of a winning athlete? How much do those things play a part in success?

Athletic success doesn't happen by luck. Winning athletes practice techniques and skills over and over. They focus on perfecting their skills. They set goals. They identify and correct their mistakes. They are dedicated and ambitious. Hard work and focused practice make an athlete faster, more efficient, and more effective at their sport.

Being a successful student also takes practice, skills, and techniques. These are called *study skills*. Good study skills make you a faster, more efficient, and more effective student.

The term "study" skills is a bit misleading because it implies that these skills are just for studying — like reviewing for a test or quiz. Study skills are *not* limited to reviewing for tests and quizzes. Study skills apply to all aspects of learning. **How you learn is just as important as what you learn!**

Chapter 1 Learning Goals:

- [ ] state a simple definition of learning.
- [ ] recognize the broad application of study skills to all aspects of learning.
- [ ] describe the benefits of good study skills.

Study skills apply whether you are studying for a quiz or test, in class listening to your teacher, participating in a lab or other learning activity, taking a test, reading a textbook or doing homework. **Study skills are practices, strategies and techniques for all aspects of learning.**

What is learning?

1. Learning is the **acquisition** of knowledge.

What is *learning?* As a student, you spend much of your day trying to do it, but have you ever given any thought to what learning is and how it happens? Learning is a complex concept. There's a large body of psychology devoted to learning and how it happens. There are many ways people learn. Some learning is automatic. For example, when you were a small child you may have learned not to touch a hot stove by touching it once. (Ouch!) That's learning by *conditioning.* Other learning, like memorizing the names of the presidents, or how to find the area of a prism is not automatic. It takes time and often a great deal of effort. The end result of learning is the acquisition of knowledge. **Good study skills improve your ability to acquire knowledge.**

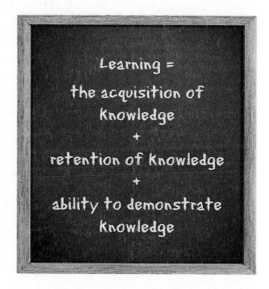

Learning =
the acquisition of
Knowledge
+
retention of Knowledge
+
ability to demonstrate
Knowledge

2. Learning is the **retention** of knowledge.

Have you ever spent hours studying, were sure you knew the material, but couldn't remember it when you needed to? Did you not learn it as well as you thought? Why did the knowledge slip away? Lots of things we learn are not meant to be remembered for a long time, so our brains quickly let go of the information. Other information, like the kind you learn in school, is meant to be remembered for a long time. If you forget information too soon after you learned it, you did not learn it successfully. Good study skills include practices and strategies for retaining information for a longer period of time. **Good study skills improve your ability to retain knowledge.**

3. Learning is the **ability to demonstrate** knowledge.

Learning is measurable, and an important part of learning is being able to successfully demonstrate what you've learned so it can be accurately measured (graded) by your teacher. As a student, you are always being asked to demonstrate your knowledge. Tests and quizzes, class participation, reports, essays, verbal reports, group presentations—even just answering your teacher's questions in class are all ways that your knowledge is demonstrated. You must be able to demonstrate knowledge in a variety of testing formats: *essay and short answer, multiple choice, true or false, fill-in-the-blanks, oral response, etc.* **Good study skills improve your ability to successfully demonstrate knowledge.**

What study skills will you learn in this book?

In this book you will explore study skills for all aspects of learning—not just to study for a test or quiz. **The goal is to improve your ability to acquire, retain, and demonstrate knowledge, so you can be a more successful student.** Besides, you won't be a middle school student for much longer. The skills you'll learn in this book will create a solid foundation for the skills you'll need for success in high school and college.

Let's start learning study skills!

You will begin your journey to good study skills by learning about the **process of learning** in chapters 1-4. It helps to know a little about the process of learning, thinking, and how your brain works in order to be able to reflect on and improve your own thinking and learning. In chapters 5-7 you'll expand your awareness of **learning styles, multi-sensory resources, and strategies** for developing your own unique abilities and compensating for your weaknesses. In chapters 8-11 you'll examine the benefits of establishing and sticking to a **pre-learning routine**. In chapters 12-14 you'll explore what it means to be an **active learner**. In chapters 15-17 you'll learn how (and why) to **take notes and outline** your textbook chapters. In chapters 18-23 you will explore practices and strategies that enable you to recall a lot more of what you learn, and tips for success on all kinds of **tests and assessments**. Finally, because you will be heading off to college in just a few short years, you will explore important skills for **college readiness** in chapters 24-28.

Do your best to complete the worksheets and activities in this book. Your teacher has the answer key in the Instructor's Guide. If you are an independent learner, reading this book to learn study skills on your own, you can check your answers at http://www.middleschoolguide.com/products/tips-links-and-forms/

FIGHTING OWL NEWS

U.B. SMART STUDENTS STUDY HOW TO STUDY

by Jason

"How you learn is as important as what you learn" says Mr. Skillsworth

Big news from Rm. 400. Mr. Skillsworth's study skills class is underway. Students are learning that good study skills take time, practice and discipline, but they're worth the effort.

"As you move up to high school and college, good study skills are very important to your success as a student." said Mr. Skillsworth. "They help you be a faster, more efficient and effective learner."

His students totally agree. Alison, a 7th grader, said "Good study skills take a lot of the frustration and _____ out of learning. The skills, techniques, and strategies I learn in this class will be part of my study routine all the way through high school and _____."

Students are using *The Middle School Student's Guide to Study Skills*. They must bring it to _____ class. It contains the _____ they need for class activities and homework.

Grades are based on in-class activities, homework completion, and consistent, everyday use of the skills learned in the class. At the end of each unit, students _____, debate

or discuss study skills and high school and college readiness topics. All students mus _____ in the discus sions, debates and blogs.

On the first day of class, students learned tha *learning* is the _____ _____, and ability t _____ knowledge.

A.J., a 7th grader said "I really need to learn thes skills. Even though I study a lot, I forget what learn. I have a hard time _____ what I studied.

Elena wants to learn good test-taking skills so sh can better demonstrate her knowledge. "Ther are so many ways my teachers ask me to sho what I know, such as: _____

_____

_____

Students compared the traits of successful stu dents with the traits of successful athletes. "Thes people have many traits in common," said M Skillsworth," (List five – your choice.) _____

_____

_____

Assisting Mr. Skillsworth are Miss Loveless, M Viejo, and everyone's favorite science teache Ms. Pell.

| stress | every | acquisition | true/false test | retention | demonstrate | oral presentation | worksheets |
| short answer test | | multiple choice test | blog | college | essay test | participate | remembering |

Name: _____

What are Study Skills?

1. The term *study* skills is misleading. Why?

    _____
    _____
    _____

2. What does being a *faster, more efficient and effective student* mean to you?

    _____
    _____
    _____

3. What are your three **worst study habits**? What problems have they caused for you?

    _____
    _____
    _____

4. What are your **most productive study habits**? How have they helped you be a more successful student?

    _____
    _____
    _____

5. *"How you learn is just as important as what you learn."* Comment:

    _____
    _____
    _____

6. What's the most **frustrating and stressful part of learning** for you? How does it make you feel about your **abilities** as a student, and your academic future in high school and college?

    _____
    _____
    _____

7. What **grade** would you give your **current study skills and habits**?

    A+   A   A-   B+   B   B-   C+   C   C-   D+   D   D-   F

Dear Parent or Caregiver,

Today I participated in my study skills class based on *The Middle School Student's Guide to Study Skills*. One of the best ways I can prepare for high school and college is to use good study skills whenever I am learning.

I learned:

1. Learning is the acquisition of _____, which can occur in many ways.

2. Some knowledge is intended to be short-term, but most of what students learn in school is intended to be remembered for a long period of time. If you forget what you learned soon after you studied it, you did not learn _____. *Learning includes the* _____ of knowledge, which is the ability to remember what you learned.

3. Good study skills make students _____, more _____, and _____ learners.

4. Study skills are not limited to _____ for tests and quizzes; They are skills, practices and strategies for all _____ of learning.

5. Learning is measurable. As part of the learning process, students must be able to successfully _____ their knowledge in a variety of assessment (measurement) formats.

Ask me about the skills I learned today! Your support at home will help me make good study skills daily habit.

Thank you for all you do for me every day.

Sincerely,

_____

_____

_____

_____

_____

_____

_____

_____

_____

_____

_____

_____

_____

_____

_____

_____

_____

_____

_____

METACOGNITION: THE SELF-AWARE STUDENT

In Chapter 1 you considered the traits of winning athletes. Successful athletes practice long hours to perfect their skills and techniques. What goes through the mind of a good athlete when they are training? Are they thinking about what they watched on TV the night before? Are they wondering what to wear to school the next day? Do they just go through the motions of practice?

Good athletes do not just "go through the motions" of practice! Successful athletes focus, laser-like, on their skills. They set goals to know what they want to achieve. They control their body movements, adjust their speed, motion, and strategy for optimal performance. They gauge their progress by timing themselves, tracking completions, and assessing their performance. A good athlete is *self-aware*.

Self-awareness is an important trait for students too. In this chapter you'll learn the importance of being a self-aware, *metacognitive* student.

Chapter 2 Learning Goals:

☐ define metacognition.
☐ list the traits of a self-aware student.
☐ identify poor metacognitive skills in a series of examples.
☐ complete a survey of their personal metacognitive skills.

What is *metacognition*?

Successful students are self-aware learners who consciously monitor and focus on their learning as they learn. In other words, they *think about their thinking!* Thinking about thinking is called *metacognition*, and it's an important study skill.

What are the traits of a metacognitive student?

✓ **FOCUSES ON A SINGLE TASK**

Multitasking means trying to pay attention to, or work on several tasks at the same time. Neuroscientists (those are scientists who study the brain) have found that humans simply cannot focus well on more than one task at a time. Trying to focus on several matters at once creates a lot of conflict within the brain. When the brain is forced to switch back and forth between tasks and activities, it constantly struggles to focus and refocus. It is an inefficient and unproductive way to learn. **Laser-like focus on a single task is a trait of a metacognitive student.**

✓ **IDENTIFIES LEARNING GOALS**

Studying is not unlike many of the other activities you engage in during the day. If you stop at the store on the way home from school, you generally know why you're there, and what you want to get. Before starting a learning task, such as homework, reading, or studying for a test or quiz, the metacognitive student takes a minute to identify the information their brain should be retrieving from the task. Identifying specific learning goals is kind of like creating a shopping list for your brain, telling it what information to pick up as you study. **Identification of specific learning goals is a trait of a metacognitive student.**

✓ **ASSESSES LEARNING ENVIRONMENT**

Physical surroundings impact a student's ability to meet their learning goals. A metacognitive student assesses their learning environment and makes adjustments to control and manage their learning. "Environment" can include where and when you study, with whom you study, and how you study. The metacognitive student is able to recognize a poor study environment and adjust it, or seek out a new environment which better facilitates learning. **Monitoring and adjusting their learning environment to optimize learning is a trait of the metacognitive student.**

✓ **ADJUSTS THINKING**

Metacognitive students are alert to changes in their thinking, such as when their mind wanders off task, or when they don't understand something. They are aware of attitudes or thoughts that distract them from their learning goals. They adjust their thinking and refocus. If a particular learning strategy isn't working very well, the metacognitive student adjusts to use a different strategy. **Actively monitoring and controlling their thought processes as they learn is a trait of a metacognitive student.**

✓ **GAUGES PROGRESS**

The metacognitive student checks their progress toward their learning goals by testing their knowledge as they learn. They pause to check their comprehension of reading material. They restate concepts in their own words. They check whether they understand the big idea of a lesson. They check their answers for accuracy. They reflect on their learning. **Metacognitive students know that it is important to test themselves before they are tested by their teacher.** When a metacognitive student doesn't understand something, they ask for help instead of ignoring it, or assuming they'll figure it out later. **The ability to gauge progress toward their learning goals is a trait of a metacognitive student.**

What is metacognition in action?

Let's observe metacognition in action. Read the profiles below. Which student is focused on the task of learning? Who has identified their learning goals, and has a clear understanding of what they are supposed to retrieve from their learning tasks? Which student is focused on the single task of learning, monitors and adjusts their thinking, and gauges their progress?

Issa, a middle school student, is in her room doing homework. She keeps her cell phone out of her workspace because she knows she gets distracted by texting. She's reading a chapter in her science textbook, learning about gravitational force—specifically Newton's Laws of Motion for a quiz on Wednesday. Issa comes across a word she doesn't understand. She pauses and thinks "Uh oh, I don't understand that word. I will need to know what it means, or the rest of this chapter probably won't make much sense." She checks the definition, then rereads the sentence, inserting the definition in place of the actual word. She asks "does that make sense? Do I understand now?" When she's sure she understands, she continues reading.

By contrast, here's Chris:

Chris, a middle school student, is on the sofa in the family room. He's doing his homework—sort of. Books and papers are spread out around him. As he reads, he keeps an eye on the sports channel, eats a burger, makes a couple of calls, texts his bros' about plans for the weekend, and throws the ball for his dog. He's working on a chapter in his science textbook—something about gravity and Newton—maybe Einstein—he's not sure. Anyway, it's boring. He's in a hurry to finish because he's meeting friends at the movies. He notices that there's this one word that keeps showing up all over the chapter. He doesn't have a clue what it means. He's gotten tripped up on that word before. He ignores it and keeps going assuming he'll figure it out eventually.

Which student are you more like? If you find yourself identifying more with Chris than with Issa, get to work on your metacognitive skills!

The Metacognitive Student

1. Focuses on a single task.
2. Identifies their learning goals.
3. Assesses and adjusts their learning environment.
4. Monitors and adjusts their thinking.
5. Gauges progress toward their learning goals.

CLASS ACTIVITY WORKSHEET

Name: _____

Metacognitive Muddle

Hey kids! **Metacognition** means *thinking about thinking*. Metacognitive students are **self-aware** students. They focus on learning as they learn. They identify their **learning goals** and **monitor progress** toward their goals. Metacognitive students **assess and adjust their learning environment** to keep it free from distractions. Read the profiles below and tell whether the student is a **metacognitive student**.

1. Is the student is **focused on learning**? Are they **multitasking?** (How can you tell?)
2. Has the student **identified their learning goals**? (How can you tell?)
3. Does the student make **adjustments to their learning environment** to overcome problems? (If so what? If not, what changes do you recommend?)
4. Does he or she **make adjustments to their thinking or learning strategies** and optimize learning? (If so, how? It not, what do you recommend?)
5. Does the student **accurately gauge their progress**? (How? If not, what do you recommend?)

"Hi! I'm Ali. I usually do my math homework on the bus on the way home from school. If I rush, I can finish all the problems before we get to my stop. The bus is crowded and noisy, but I like talking to the kids around me as I work on the problems – it makes math less boring. I have a quiz tomorrow, so on the ride home today I reviewed stuff that might be on the quiz. I hope I remember! I totally never feel like I have a good grasp of what I'm supposed to know before my teacher moves on to the next chapter, but so far this semester, I'm passing the class. Awesome!" **Is Alison a metacognitive student? Why or why not?**

_____

_____

_____

"Hey, I'm Max. OK, well life science is by far my worst class. For one thing, it's super hard. My teacher gives us way too much homework. Also, it's first period which starts at 7:45 and it's hard for me to stay awake that early in the morning and then, you know, my mind starts wandering. I especially struggle with the labs, because I don't get what's going on or what the point of it is. I usually start my science homework about 9:00 at night because I have lacrosse practice from 5:00-7:00. Then I have to eat dinner and do a little gaming because a dude's gotta have some fun, right? I study on my bed. I don't get through much of the reading before my mind starts wandering again and pretty soon I'm zzzzzzz. Gotta sleep sometime, right? **Is Max a metacognitive student? Why or why not?**

_____

_____

_____

_____

"I'm A.J. OK, overall, I'd say I'm a pretty good student. I like my teachers – they're cool. I'm pretty good about doing my homework. I follow directions. I do the assignments and reading for all of my classes. My mind wanders a lot. I lose focus but I do my homework without complaining. I don't even think about it – I just get through the reading and worksheets and that's what counts, right? I study a lot before tests and quizzes. I always think I'm prepared, but it's really weird, because my scores are low. I don't get it. It's kinda discouraging." **Is A.J. a metacognitive student? Why or why not?**

_____

_____

_____

_____

"Hello, I'm Elena. My "problem" class is literature. I totally struggle with all those long, boring "thou" and "thee" 19th century poems. I was getting low quiz scores. I decided that I needed to improve my focus and concentration to work through those difficult passages. I was doing my homework with friends, but we talked a lot. Personally, I need total quiet – no distractions. So, I started going to the library twice a week to do the reading. That really helped. The unit on literary devices was so confusing. Allegory, allusion, alliteration – OMG they all sound the same! My teacher said that we have to be able to define the device and use it in our own writing. Now I learn three devices per week, and make three examples. I show the examples to my teacher to make sure they're right. Now I ace the quizzes." **Is Elena a metacognitive student? Why or why not?**

_____

_____

_____

_____

Name: _____

Metacognitive Homework Survey

Being a self-aware, metacognitive student is about what's going on in your head while you are learning. When you learn, don't just go through the motions. Engage your brain and focus on one task at a time. Identify your learning goals, adjust your environment and thinking to optimize learning. Gauge your progress. Be a metacognitive student!

What time did you start your homework? _____ What time did you finish? _____

List the subjects you worked on for homework:

_____

_____

Select one of the above subjects. Identify your homework **learning goals**. Be specific.

_____

_____

As you worked, were you **focused on a single task**, or were you paying attention to other tasks or activities, such as the TV, loud music, texts, phone calls, or chatting with friends? Discuss:

_____

_____

_____

Describe your **learning environment** (location, noise, activity level, etc.) where you do homework.

_____

_____

_____

Do you need to **adjust or control your environment** to optimize learning? How? Be specific.

_____

_____

_____

Do you need to **adjust or control your thinking process** to optimize learning? How? Be specific.

_____

_____

_____

Do you **gauge your progress** toward learning goals by restating what you learned in your own words, testing yourself, or creating examples?

_____

_____

_____

What are your **metacognitive strengths**? Laser-like focus? Adjustable thinking? Your excellent learning environment? Discuss:

_____

_____

_____

What are your **metacognitive weaknesses**? Discuss:

_____

_____

_____

List three things you will begin doing immediately to be a **self-aware, metacognitive student**.

1. _____

2. _____

3. _____

Pledge of the Metacognitive Student

I, _____, Middle School Student, do hereby make this Pledge:

From this day forward, I will not just go through the motions of learning. When I am learning, I will:

- Focus on the single task of learning as I learn.
- Identify my specific learning goals.
- Adjust my learning environment to optimize learning.
- Monitor and adjust my thinking to optimize learning.
- Gauge progress toward my learning goals by testing myself, reflecting on my learning, restating concepts, or making examples.

From this day forward, I will be a metacognitive student!

Signed: _____

Dear Parent or Caregiver,

Today I participated in my study skills class based on *The Middle School Student's Guide to Study Skills*. One of the best ways I can prepare for high school and college is to use good study skills whenever I am learning.

I learned:

1. _____ about _____ is called *metacognition* and it's an important trait for a self-aware student.

2. The metacognitive student does not _____, which means trying to pay attention to other tasks while learning; they _____ on the single task of learning.

3. A metacognitive student identifies their specific _____ goals, so their brain knows what information to retrieve as they study.

4. A metacognitive student monitors their _____ environment and _____ processes, and makes _____ to optimize learning.

5. A metacognitive student gauges _____ toward their learning goals by checking comprehension, self-testing, and putting concepts into their own words. A metacogntive student tests themself before their _____ tests them.

Ask me about the skills I learned today! Your support at home will help me make good study skills daily habit.

Thank you for all you do for me every day.

Sincerely,

_____

A BIT ABOUT BRAINY

Most people go through their day talking, walking, learning, eating, sleeping, practicing sports or listening to music, never giving a single thought to the amazing organ that does it all for them:

Their **brain!**

Do you take your brain for granted? Have you ever wondered how all that information from the outside world works its way through your skull to become knowledge and memory?

The human brain works 24/7, non-stop, 'round the clock. It weighs only about 3 lbs. but it processes information incredibly fast. It is a very sophisticated organ.

In this chapter you'll explore how all that sensory data (that's the stuff you see, hear, smell, and feel) finds its way from the outside world into your brain to be acquired and retained as knowledge.

Knowing a bit about how your brain learns can help you understand how and *why* to study!

Chapter 3 Learning Goals:

☐ identify and label parts of the brain involved in learning.

☐ describe the basic processes by which the brain converts sensory data to knowledge.

☐ create a plan for maintaining a healthy brain.

Let's start with basic brain structure:

Hemispheres

The brain has two halves. If you place a finger between your eyes and draw an imaginary line up through your forehead, across the top of your skull, and down to the nape of your neck, you'll trace a rough division of the two halves of your brain. The halves are called *hemispheres*. Each hemisphere has four *exterior lobes* which generally function as follows:

Frontal Lobes

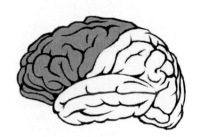

The lobes at the front of the brain are called the *frontal lobes*. They are the largest lobes. Behind those is the prefrontal cortex which is key to reasoning, problem solving, making decisions, and coordinating speech. When you're thinking about the sequence of a math formula, or resisting the impulse to grab that donut out of your friend's hand, your frontal lobe is at work. Quick! What's 21 + 8? Someone with a prefrontal cortex injury or disease would find this very difficult – maybe even impossible to do. People with prefrontal cortex injuries or diseases may also be impulsive and have problems controlling their behavior. For successful learning, it's very, very important to protect your prefrontal cortex from injury.

Temporal Lobes

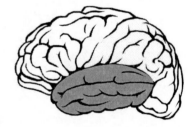

Above your ears lay the *temporal lobes*. They process what you hear, like speech and music. They are also involved in forming long term memories.

Parietal Lobes

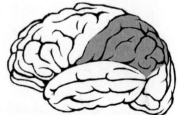

The *parietal lobes* are on the top of your exterior brain. They are involved in spatial orientation and sensory integration. The parietal lobe is constantly working to move the parts of your body where you want them to go. When you're shooting baskets, or reaching for a glass of milk, the parietal lobe is directing your body movements, telling it how hard to throw the ball, or exactly how far to reach for the glass, and how much effort it will take to lift it. It senses the distance and navigates the movements of your limbs. People who have sustained damage or disease to this area of the brain can find it very difficult to make even simple exact movements.

Occipital Lobes

The *occipital lobes* are on the back of the head. They are mostly involved with vision. Right now, your occipital lobes are actively processing the words you are reading on this page!

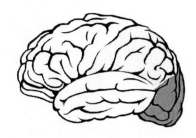

The Interior Brain

Deep in the brain, beneath the exterior lobes is the *interior brain*. The *Limbic System* is located within the interior brain and contains structures important to learning:

Hypothalamus (hy•po•thal•a•mus)

Hungry? Thirsty? Sleepy? This structure constantly monitors internal systems like body temperature, hunger and fatigue. Its function is to keep everything in balance. If your hypothalamus senses that you need to eat or sleep, or that you are too hot or too cold, it may distract you from learning, and nag you until you take care of your body.

Hippocampus (hip•po•cam•pus)

Ground zero for learning, memory and recall. Can you believe this tiny structure is responsible processing most of what you learn and converting sensory data (what you see, hear and feel) to memory? The conversion of information to memory is not an instantaneous process. It can take several exposures to information before a memory is formed well-enough to be recalled.

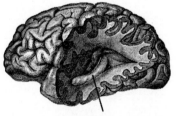

Hippocampus

Amygdala (ah•mig•dah•la)

Boo! The amygdala is responsible for emotions like fear, happiness and sadness. Ever wondered why it's easier to recall (or harder to forget) something really scary, sad or happy—even if it happened years ago? Experts believe that your amygdala may more forcefully imprint emotional memories, which enables them to store faster, longer and stronger.

Neurons, Dendrites, Axons and Synapses

Sensory information from the outside world moves into the limbic system structures along nerve cells called *neurons*. The brain is made up billions of neurons. Each neuron has thousands of branchlike extensions called *dendrites* and *axons*. These constantly receive and transmit electrical impulses to areas called *synapses*. Synapses enable neurons to communicate and process information.

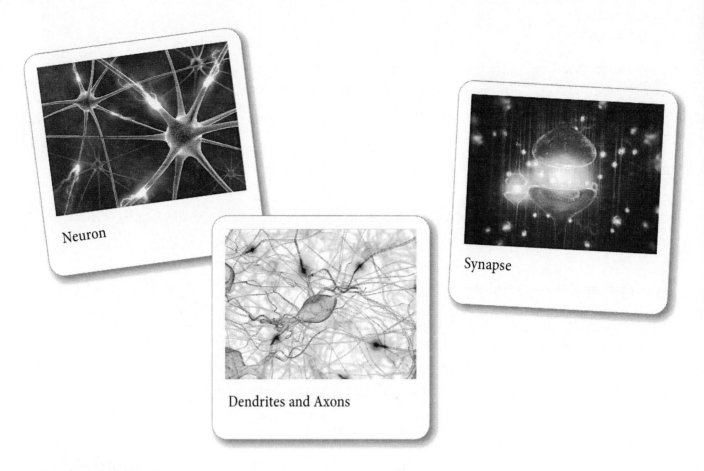

Neuron

Dendrites and Axons

Synapse

What is Memory?

The brain doesn't actually have a memory "bank" or a specific place where knowledge and memories are all neatly stored away. Memory is actually a *stored pattern of synaptic connections*. When you read, study and review, your brain forms new synapses and synapse patterns, and strengthens old ones. The first time you learn something, it is unfamiliar to your brain. Your brain has to create a synaptic pattern for the information. If you study it only once, it can be difficult to recall later, because the synaptic connections are not well established. **With more study and review, the synaptic patterns and connections strengthen, making recall easier.** Do you know there can be up to 1,000,000,000,000,000 synaptic connections in your brain? (Souza, How the Brain Learns, 2006). No excuses! You are capable of learning a lot.

Be good to your brain – you need it.

Even when doing a simple math calculation, hundreds of millions of your brain's neurons, dendrites, axons and synapses are actively transmitting impulses and chemicals enabling you to come up with the correct answer. The brain truly is an amazing organ! Treat it well. Don't take Brainy for granted.

CLASS ACTIVITY WORKSHEET

Name: ______________________

Name the part of the brain and describe its function.

Frontal Lobe LOBE

Function:
reasoning, problem solving
making decisions &
coordinating speech

Parietel lobe LOBE

Function:
Special orientation
sensory integration

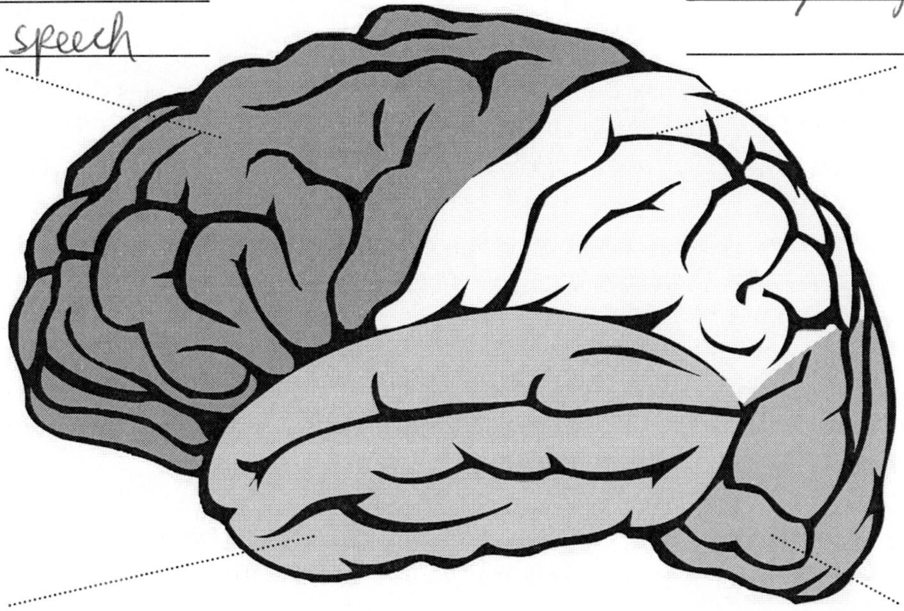

Temporal LOBE

Function:
long term memories
speech and music

Occipital LOBE

Function:
Vision

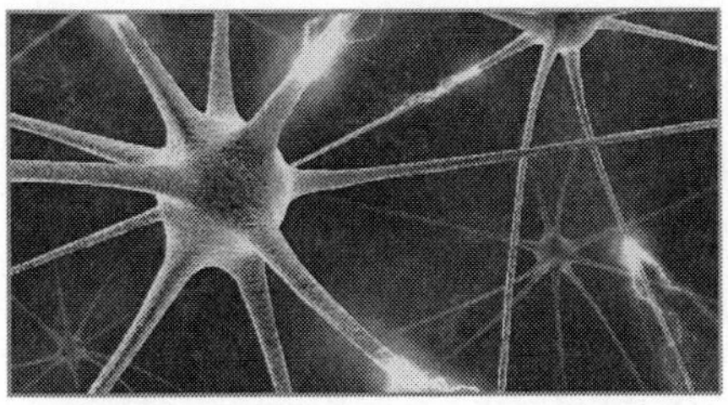

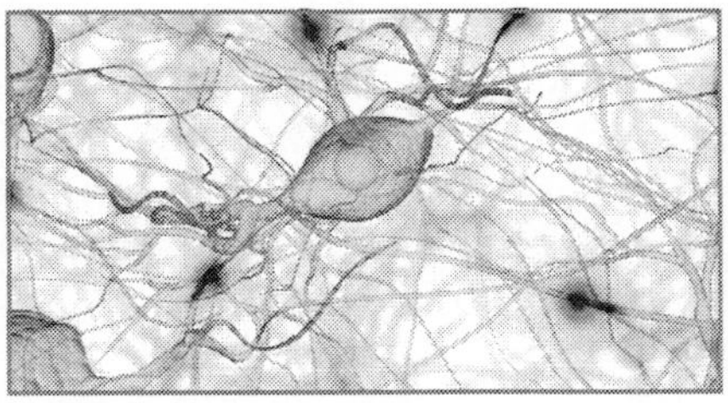

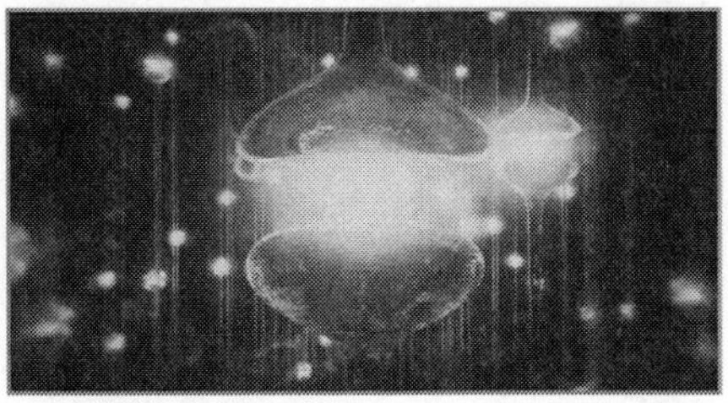

Neuron:
cells for which
sensory info
travels nerve cell

Dendrites and Axons:
Brain cells

Synapse:
electrical impulses
are transmitted to
communicate information

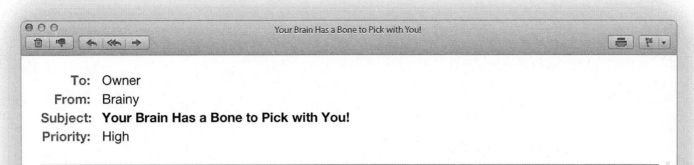

To: Owner
From: Brainy
Subject: **Your Brain Has a Bone to Pick with You!**
Priority: High

Dear Owner:

I work 24 hours a day, 7 days a week, 365 days a year for you. How do you thank me? You treat me like I mean nothing to you. Riding around on your bike and skateboard without a helmet, leaving me open to all sorts of injuries if you fall… Do you have any idea how hard it is for me to make repairs in here?

Btw, you know all that junk food and sugary stuff you eat? I'd hardly classify it as "food." Just because *you* like it doesn't mean *I* like it. I need food that's nutritious. I'd feel a lot better if you'd eat a healthy breakfast in the morning.

While I'm on the subject, do you realize how often I'm thirsty? My neurons, dendrites, axons and synapses need water to work efficiently so you can learn. What the heck! Why so stingy with the water? Six to eight glasses a day, please. Soda and caffeine drinks don't count.

Just a warning: don't even think of using alcohol, drugs, or tobacco, or I'm talking a serious s-l-o-w-d-o-w-n in the work I do for you. I promise you will not like it.

I'd also appreciate 8-9 hours of sleep every night. While you're off snoozing like a princess, I get to all of my chores, like restoring your mental and physical energy. You know how you get all cranky when you're tired? That's me (my hypothalamus to be exact) telling you to get to sleep so I can work!

By the way, to learn something new, you have to review it more than once. When you study and review, I form new synapses, and strengthen synaptic patterns and connections. That creates strong neural pathways which make it easier for you to recall the information. If you study or review something only once, I will have a hard time learning it.

One more thing. Would you mind taking a break from those video games? Too much annoys me and makes me nervous. Here's what I like: I like fresh air. I like exercise. I like reading. I like stuff like chess and puzzles. I'm no whimp. I like challenge. We're in this together.

Sincerely,
Brainy

Re: Sorry

To: Brainy
Subject: Re: Sorry
From: Owner

Dear Brainy:

I'm sorry, sometimes I'm not very good to you. I need to take care of you, so you can take care of me and I can learn. Here's my personal plan to keep you healthy:

When I'm biking, skateboarding, skiing or snowboarding I will protect you by wearing a _____; It's hard to fix a brain injury. I will always wear my seat belt in the car!

I promise to feed you better. I'll improve my diet, starting with these three changes:

a. _____

b. _____

c. _____

I didn't realize you need water to process information and learn. A dehydrated brain doesn't work efficiently. I will drink water every day and avoid soda and caffeine drinks.

I will not use alcohol, tobacco or drugs.

I will try to go to bed by _____ (time) to get 8-9 hours of sleep. You need me to sleep so you can get busy sorting and storing information, and restoring my mental and physical energy. No wonder I feel so yucky when I don't get enough sleep.

I will limit my video gaming to _____ minutes per day.

I will exercise every day. Here's are some activities I'll do for exercise:

_____

_____

_____

I understand that you need me to study and review information to strengthen synapses and create new ones so I can learn. Study and review build a strong memory, which helps me learn and recall information.

Brainy, I know you're no wimp. I know you like challenge. I promise I'll engage in at least one non-school related, mentally challenging activity every day, such as:

ME HAPPY! THANKS.

_____

_____

Sincerely,
Your Owner,

_____

Dear Parent or Caregiver,

Today I participated in my study skills class based on *The Middle School Student's Guide to Study Skills*. One of the best ways I can prepare for high school and college is to use good study skills whenever I am learning.

I learned:

1. The brain is divided into halves called _____, made up of four exterior lobes called the _____, _____, _____, and _____.

2. The Limbic System is located in the interior brain and includes the _____ (monitors internal systems), _____ (key to learning and memory) and _____ (related to emotional memory.)

3. Information from the outside world moves through the brain via nerve cells called _____ which have thousands of branchlike structures called _____ and _____.

4. Memory is actually a stored _____ of synaptic connections; Studying forms new connections and strengthens old patterns, making information easier to _____.

5. It can take several _____ of information before a memory is formed well-enough for recall.

Ask me about the skills I learned today! Your support at home will help me make good study skills daily habit.

Thank you for all you do for me every day.

Sincerely,

_____

MENTAL THROWDOWN: EFFORT VS. INTELLIGENCE

What's your personal opinion about *intelligence?* Do you think people are born with their basic level of intelligence or do you think people can actually *learn* to be smart? Think carefully! Your answer is important, because according to psychologists at Stanford and Columbia Universities[1], how you think about intelligence can affect your success in school.

In 2007, these psychologists were curious as to why middle school students with relatively equal abilities, could have such different academic outcomes. Why do some students thrive in school, but others struggle, they wondered? Why do some enjoy the challenge of learning, yet others do their best to avoid it? Their study lead to an interesting discovery about intelligence. They found that students' personal beliefs about the nature of intelligence can have a big impact on their achievement in school.

Generally, students who believe that intelligence can be developed and grown do better in school than students who believe that intelligence is fixed trait—something they are born with and can't significantly alter or improve.

[1] Blackwell, Kali, and Dweck 27

Chapter 4 Learning Goals:

☐ identify as a growth or fixed mindset learner.
☐ list the traits of growth mindset learners.
☐ compare the roles of effort, intelligence and experience in learning.

The psychologists call students who believe that intelligence is fluid and developable *growth mindset learners*. Students who believed the opposite—that intelligence is fixed and basically unalterable, are called *fixed mindset learners*.

Fixed Mindset Learners

Some students believe that intelligence is an unalterable trait—that people are born with a certain level of intellectual ability which, as a matter of genetics cannot be improved or expanded. In other words, they have a **fixed view of intelligence**. This mindset can actually inhibit a student's success. Fixed mindset learners:

➜   believe intelligence is **genetically fixed and cannot be altered**.

➜   **label themselves** (and others) as "smart" or "dumb."

➜   believe learning and accomplishment are **outside of their personal control**.

➜   **avoid challenge**.

➜   **give up** easily.

➜   blame failure on a **lack of intellect** rather than inadequate effort. ("I don't have a brain for math!" vs. "I didn't study hard enough or pay attention in class.")

Growth Mindset Learners

Growth mindset learners believe that intelligence is a fluid and controllable trait. They attribute academic success to **effort and hard work**. They believe that like a muscle, the brain becomes stronger with use and challenge. Overall, these students are more successful than their entity counterparts, and are able to overcome many obstacles to learning. Growth mindset learners:

➜   believe basic ability can be **developed through hard work, effort and experience**.

➜   **embrace challenge**.

➜   **reject labeling** themselves or anyone else as "smart" or "dumb."

➜   focus on **strategy and processes** while learning (rather than strictly on outcome or grades.)

High achievers beware!

Psychologists have made another surprising discovery about intelligence. High achieving students who receive a lot of praise for their successes, or have a reputation as "smart" kids are particularly at risk for becoming fixed mindset learners. When these students become overly concerned with maintaining their identity as high achievers, they often begin avoiding challenge in order to avoid failure and losing their smartipants reputations. Remember this: *Brainy likes challenge.* Never back off of intellectual challenge because you're worried about failure! Challenging your brain makes it even smarter.

Can your IQ actually change?

IQ, which stands for *Intelligence Quotient*, is the measurement of a person's intelligence. IQ tests are usually given at school, and are used as predictors of educational achievement in students.

Until recently, it's been believed that a person's IQ is basically unalterable. In other words, it's been the general belief that you're born with a level of intelligence which dictates your abilities for your lifetime. Researchers at the University of London recently confirmed that this is not true. IQs rise and fall, *particularly in teens*. In an experiment, they administered IQ tests and MRI/brain scans to 33 kids in 2004 when they were 12 to 16 years old. Four years later they retested the kids. Many of their IQs had changed. Some had increases of up to 20 points! Of course some IQs had also declined, further revealing the importance of protecting your intelligence by keeping the brain challenged. **If you aren't satisfied with your IQ, work hard! You can improve it.**

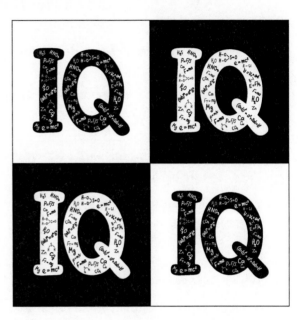

IQs can change, particularly in teenagers.

What does it all mean?

Genetics plays a roll in intelligence of course, but there's no getting around the fact that keys to achievement are effort and hard work. Students who embrace academic challenge, put in the effort and maintain a belief in their ability to increase their intelligence are more successful students. IQ is not a fixed trait. Yes, you can learn to be smart!

Name: _____

What's Your Opinion?

Read the question. Select a or b.

1. **Poor Elliot. Ever since first grade he's gotten low scores in math. He's now in the 7th grade, and his math grades haven't improved much. Elliot dreams of studying aerospace engineering and one day piloting commercial space flights. That requires excellent math skills. What advice would you give Elliot?**

   a. Don't give up! Work hard. Believe in yourself. You can improve your math skills and pursue your dream.

   b. Dude, consider a different career. By now it's pretty obvious you can't do the math.

2. **Wow! You do your homework every night. You do all of the assigned reading. You pay attention in class. You do all of this because:**

   a. You like to learn new things.

   b. If you don't, your grades will drop and you'll be in trouble with your parents.

3. **Which of these statements best sums up your opinion about intelligence:**

   a. A person can actually learn to be smart.

   b. You are who you are. You can't learn to be smart. Intelligence is a trait you're born with.

4. **Wow! Maddie is really smart! She has an IQ of 120.**

   a. Maddie's IQ is no guarantee of her success in life.

   b. Maddie's so lucky because she will succeed in life.

5. **There are a lot of problems in your science class: broken equipment, disruptive students, and ever since your teacher messed up his back slipping on a dissected frog, you've had a string of substitutes who don't teach much. You:**

   a. Do whatever it takes to make up for the lack of resources: supplement your learning with an online program, take advantage of the free tutoring offered at your school, and keep up with all of the reading and homework, hoping your teacher will return soon.

   b. Resign yourself to the fact that you won't be learning much in science this year...

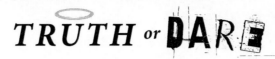

TRUTH *or* DARE

Psychologists have shown that a student's beliefs about intelligence can effect their academic success. Fixed mindset students believe that intelligence is a fixed trait – and cannot be altered. Growth mindset students consider intelligence as a fluid and controllable trait, and believe that effort, hard work and challenge account for most of a student's success. Is it possible that you believe you're a **growth mindset** student, but your **actions and attitudes are those of a fixed mindset** student? Dare to find out! Take the **Truth or Dare** survey. Total your score and find your profile below.

TRUTH	Totally always	Usually, almost always	Sometimes	Rarely	No way, are you joking?	DARE *Watch out! The scoring guide changes...*	No way, are you joking?	Rarely	Sometimes	Usually, almost always	Totally always!
I believe that effort, hard work and challenge are keys to success.	5	4	3	2	1	I worry people will think I'm dumb if I fail.	5	4	3	2	1
My school work reflects a high level of effort.	5	4	3	2	1	I blow through my homework just to get it over with!	5	4	3	2	1
I focus on and value learning strategies and processes (not just my grade in a class or on a project.)	5	4	3	2	1	When I get a bad grade, I blame the teacher, school, confusing instructions, basically anything or anyone but me.	5	4	3	2	1
I accept personal responsibility for my academic destiny.	5	4	3	2	1	Setbacks discourage me.	5	4	3	2	1
I'm ok with academic challenge because I know it will make me mentally stronger.	5	4	3	2	1	I procrastinate or just give up when faced with a difficult assignment.	5	4	3	2	1
I accept criticism or negative feedback from my teachers as guidance to help me improve my skills.	5	4	3	2	1	My self-image is tied to my success as a student.	5	4	3	2	1

Total *TRUTH* _____   Total DARE _____

Truth + Dare = _____ Check your score on the next page!

If you scored above 48:

Your actions and attitude show that you understand that effort, hard work and challenge are keys to success. You know that intelligence is not fixed, and that the harder you work, the smarter you get. You care about your grades, but also about learning. Keep up the good work! You're a mental heavy-lifter.

If you scored between 36 and 48:

You're not totally comfortable with the idea that effort, hard work and challenge are keys to achievement. You attribute your occasional failures to not being "smart enough," to something your teacher did or didn't do, or that your school isn't as good as some other school. Sometimes your focus is more on the grade you will receive than what you are learning. You are on the cusp of greatness. Embrace challenge and up your effort level!

If you scored below 36:

You may say you believe that intelligence is not a fixed trait, but your actions speak otherwise. Your beliefs and attitude may be sabotaging your achievement. You know "those other kids" who are great students? They're not smarter than you – they're just working harder! Take a look at the time you spend on homework. Is it enough? How hard do you work on projects? Do you give up when faced with an academic challenge? Get your brain to the mental gym and do some heavy lifting. Start with the subject that is of most interest to you. Challenge yourself to increase your effort level and make your brain stronger. Be a mental heavy lifter.

Dear Parent or Caregiver,

Today I participated in my study skills class based on *The Middle School Student's Guide to Study Skills*. One of the best ways I can prepare for high school and college is to use good study skills whenever I am learning.

I learned:

1. To be a successful student, _____ and _____ are more important than your intelligence level.

2. A _____ learner believes that people are born with a certain intellectual ability which cannot be improved or expanded upon.

3. A _____ learner believes that intelligence improves with use and challenge of the brain.

4. A recent study showed that IQs can rise and fall as much as _____ points, particularly in the _____ years!

5. High achieving students should be careful not to fall into the high achiever trap. Don't avoid intellectual _____ for fear of failing and losing a reputation as a smart student. Don't become a(n) _____ mindset student.

Ask me about the skills I learned today! Your support at home will help me make good study skills daily habit.

Thank you for all you do for me every day.

Sincerely,

_____

WHAT DID YOU LEARN?

Name: _____

> **WHAT DID YOU LEARN ABOUT STUDY SKILLS & THE PROCESS OF LEARNING?**

1. Your brain is not a muscle, but it is *like* a muscle because:

   _____

   _____

   _____

2. Do you believe intelligence is a fixed and unalterable trait? Why or why not?

   _____

   _____

   _____

3. What would you say to a student who claims that he or she cannot improve upon their intelligence?

   _____

   _____

   _____

4. Why does a *metacognitive* student make a point of identifying their specific learning goals?

   _____

   _____

   _____

5. Study skills are not limited to studying for tests and quizzes. Where else do they apply?

   _____

   _____

   _____

6. List three characteristics, traits or attitudes that successful students and successful athletes have in common:

   _____

   _____

   _____

7. *Learning is the acquisition, retention, and ability to successfully demonstrate knowledge.* How might you be asked to demonstrate knowledge in an academic (school) setting? How will you demonstrate what you have learned in your study skills class?

_____

_____

_____

_____

8. In the brain, is the *hippopotamus* ground zero for learning? If not, what is?

_____

True or False:

9. _____ *Neurons, axons, dendrites* and *synapses* contribute to the brain's intake and processing of sensory information into recallable memories.

10. _____ Review and study of information strengthens synapses and synaptic patterns, which makes information easier to recall.

11. List three things you can do to *montior, adjust and control* your personal learning environment and thinking process for optimal performance:

_____

_____

_____

_____

12. What is *multitasking* and why is it a poor way to learn?

_____

_____

_____

* Ever since kindergarten, Kendra has had a reputation for being one of the smartest students in school. She's won a lot of awards, and teachers often use her essays and reports as examples of excellent work. Now that she's in middle school, she seems worried about losing her "smart student" reputation. She's avoiding intellectual and academic challenge by taking classes that are way too easy for her. For book reports, she rereads books she's already read. What's your advice to Kendra?

_____

_____

_____

WHAT'S IN STYLE?

Have you ever noticed that you take in and process information better in a particular format? Do you learn better when you read words or hear them? Do you need to touch and hold an object to understand it?

For many years, cognitive psychologists (those are psychologists who explore mental processes) have conducted studies and experiments to understand how people learn, hoping to find ways to make learning easier and more efficient. In the 1970s, a theory developed that people have different styles of learning based on their senses: Visual (pictures), auditory (hearing), and kinesthetic (movement.) The Learning Style Theory is also known as VAK Learning = *Visual, Auditory, and Kinesthetic Learning.*

This theory states that everyone's brain is genetically wired to prefer one of the VAK sensory modes for taking in information. The VAK theory has been discussed and debated for years. Experts agree that our brains have a preferred or dominant sensory mode for taking in and processing information for learning. Although it is not the exclusive way we learn, our preferred sensory mode influences our ability to comprehend and retain information. Knowing your preferred learning style enables you to select resources and develop strategies which can help you learn more efficiently and effectively.

Chapter 5 Learning Goals:

☐ list and define VAK learning styles.
☐ explain the benefits of knowing your dominant learning style.
☐ discover your learning style.
☐ list a variety of style-compatible learning strategies.

What are the benefits of knowing your preferred learning style?

Metacognitive students strive for awareness of their personal learning habits and patterns. The more you know and understand about your personal learning habits and patterns, the better you are able to recognize and correct unproductive ones. Understanding VAK learning styles, and identifying their preferred VAK mode of learning enables a student to:

→ identify and incorporate into their study routine, **strategies and resources compatible with their preferred style**.

→ **compensate** for in-class instruction that favors a different style.

→ expand their **awareness and use of strategies and resources** for multiple sensory learning modes.

Visual-Spatial Learners

 Have you ever heard the expression *"A picture is worth a thousand words?"* Visual-spatial learners acquire and retain knowledge best when information is presented in a **visual format** such as a **book, article, website, photographic image**, or **video**. A visual-spatial learner approaches information *holistically*, needing to see the "big picture" before proceeding to step-by-step learning. Visual learners prefer handouts to read and study, power points, videos, and whiteboard visuals. They often take detailed notes, use highlighters or color code to mark text, create and study diagrams, charts, timelines, sketches, and other visual aids. If you are a visual learner, make an effort to incorporate visual learning strategies into your study routine.

Auditory Learners

 Auditory learners are **hearing-dominant learners**. They acquire and retain information best by hearing it. They learn through their ears. These students gain the most from **lectures, discussions, read-alouds, audio recordings** and **podcasts, taped lectures**, and by **incorporating music into their learning**. An auditory learner's comprehension improves by reading aloud, and orally summarizing or reteaching what they have read. Auditory learners benefit from group discussions and group study, because putting concepts into their own words, and verbalizing information helps them remember it. If you are an auditory learner, make an effort to incorporate auditory learning strategies into your study routine.

Kinesthetic Learners

Kinesthetic learners are also called *tactile* learners. Tactile means feeling and touching. Kinesthetic relates to physical movement. These students learn best through **hands-on activities**, or learning that **incorporates physical motion**. Traditional learning, where students sit at a desk reading a textbook or listening to a teacher, is less effective for the tactile learner. Tactile learners improve their focus and comprehension when they get up every now and then to stretch and move, or even just move their foot or chew gum while studying. Tactile learners touch and manipulate things to learn, and should participate in lab or workshop activities whenever possible.

Movement = Creativity

Do you know that many technology companies have basketball courts, ping pong and pool tables, walking paths, volleyball courts, and full-sized swimming pools at their office campus? Some companies even have an eight-person bicycle where riders face each other in a circle and peddle their way through a meeting. These facilities and toys are not just for fun. **Tech companies understand that for many of their employees, physical movement inspires creativity and learning.** If you are a kinesthetic learner, make sure to include movement in your learning routine.

Would you like to go to a meeting on an eight-seater bike? (*www.conferencebike.com*)

Name: _____

Learning Style Strategy Survey

Cognitive psychologists say that our brains have a **genetically preferred sensory mode for receiving and processing information.** Some people are **visual-spatial learners.** Others are **auditory learners. Kinesthetic learners** learn best by doing and moving. Below is a list of VAK strategies. Circle **V, A or K** if you think the strategy is Visual, Auditory or Kinesthetic (or a combination.) Check the box next to the item if you think it's a good strategy for you. Include it in your study routine!

☐ create graphs, charts and diagrams V A K	☐ make recordings V A K
☐ listen to audio or e-books V A K	☐ draw cartoons or graphic novels V A K
☐ create maps V A K	☐ create a poster for a project V A K
☐ map study V A K	☐ study graphs, charts or diagrams V A K
☐ debate V A K	☐ set up experiments V A K
☐ use graphic organizers V A K	☐ make oral reports/presentation V A K
☐ read text V A K	☐ use highlighters and color markers to designate important information V A K
☐ study pictures or other images V A K	☐ color-code notes V A K
☐ draw/sketch ideas and concepts V A K	☐ make dioramas V A K
☐ hand make/assemble models V A K	☐ write a script V A K
☐ create computer graphics V A K	☐ make or study timelines V A K
☐ play board games V A K	☐ watch an educational (tutorial) video V A K
☐ play games that involve physical movement V A K	☐ listen to an educational (tutorial) audio podcast V A K
☐ learn with a study group V A K	☐ read aloud/recitation V A K
☐ create animation V A K	☐ teach someone something you learned V A K
☐ act or role play V A K	☐ watch a play or performance V A K
☐ make a video for a class project V A K	☐ reenact an event or experiment V A K
☐ listen to low volume music when studying V A K	☐ listen to an educational (tutorial) podcast on the go V A K
☐ make/use flashcards V A K	
☐ record (themselves) reading a textbook or novel chapter for later listening V A K	

Name: _____

Visual – Auditory – Kinesthetic

The Learning Style Theory states that our brains are genetically wired to prefer a particular sensory mode for taking in and processing information. Take the **Learning Style Quiz/Assessment** assigned by your teacher, then answer the questions below and complete the charts. Be prepared to discuss your answers in class.

What is your dominant learning style? _____

Do you agree with the outcome of the Learning Style Assessment? Why or why not?

_____

_____

_____

Consider each of the VAK learning styles. Brainstorm and list all of the learning strategies you can think of that are compatible with the learning mode. (You may refer to the chart on page 48 for help.)

Dear Parent or Caregiver,

Today I participated in my study skills class based on *The Middle School Student's Guide to Study Skills*. One of the best ways I can prepare for high school and college is to use good study skills whenever I am learning.

I learned:

1. The Learning Style Theory (VAK Learning) proposes that knowledge is acquired and processed in three sensory modes: _____, _____, or _____.

2. Experts agree that the human brain has a genetically _____ sensory mode of receiving and processing information, although no one learning style is the _____ way a student learns.

3. Knowing their preferred learning style is a study skills benefit, because it enables students to include style-compatible resources and _____ in their learning, and compensate for in-class instruction which _____ a different style.

4. _____ learners take in and process information best from a visual format, such as pictures, images and words; _____ learners need to hear information, such as verbal instructions, lectures and recordings.

5. Kinesthetic learners are also called _____ learners; they need to engage in physical _____ as they learn, such as a lab activity or assembling a model. Many _____ companies recognize the relationship of physical movement to creativity and learning, and offer activities for employees to think on the _____.

Ask me about the skills I learned today! Your support at home will help me make good study skills daily habit.

Thank you for all you do for me every day.

Sincerely,

_____

LEARNING RESOURCES & MULTIMODAL LEARNING

Way back in the groovy 1970s, when cognitive psychologists first became aware of the importance of learning styles, it was very difficult for students to actually locate and use resources that were compatible with their personal learning style. A student's learning experience was pretty much limited to 1) the textbook, and 2) the teacher. Not so groovy!

Fast forward to the 21st century. You are the first generation of learners to have access to nearly unlimited educational and tutorial resources compatible with any learning style. Thanks to the internet, these resources are instantly available, 24/7, to enhance your personal learning experience.

What's *your* excuse? Do you include VAK educational resources in your learning, or are you stuck in the 1970s? As you move up into high school and college, you are expected to assume more personal responsibility for your learning. That means knowing how to reach beyond your teacher and textbook for supplemental and tutorial resources to enhance your learning, or help you overcome a learning challenge.

Chapter 6 Learning Goals:

☐ define multimodal learning.
☐ identify a variety of sensory mode resources to create a learning plan.
☐ review and rate an educational/tutorial website.

How do you find resources compatible with your learning style?

There's an abundance of awesome online VAK resources right at your fingertips: Online lectures, video tutorials, amazing websites, broadcasts, podcasts, and historical data and images provide students with immediate access to learning resources. More and more content goes online everyday. Much of it is created by some of the world's greatest thinkers and experts in their field. It's inexcusable to give up in the face of a learning challenge! Knowing where to find reliable VAK resources is an excellent study skill. Many students don't realize that tutorial help is available online, 24/7 in all subject areas, for all learning styles:

➜ Visual learners can bring history or science alive on websites like Eyewitness to History (www.eyewitnesstohistory.com), Cells Alive (www.cellsalive.com), YouTube.com/education, or learning.snagfilms.com. When you find a website that brings greater depth or clarification to the content you are learning or helps you overcome a learning challenge, bookmark it!

➜ Auditory learners can download audio books from any number of sites, including Librivox (www.librivox.com), make and replay audio recordings of their notes or textbook chapters on Vocaroo (www.vocaroo.com). When you find a recording that brings greater depth or clarification to the content you are learning or helps you overcome a learning challenge, download it!

➜ Kinesthetic learners can download lectures to their mobile devices and listen on-the-go. There are math tutorials, history videos, world language (auditory) pronunciation guides, study guides for novels, interactive maps, and geography websites. Download books from websites like audiobooksforfree.com. librivox.org and gutenberg.com for free! The choices are endless! Music is great. But when you workout or just hang out you can also listen to insanely good podcasts, audio books, and mindblowing lectures. Kinesthetic-compatible resources are unlimited.

The American Library Association is the go-to group for kids' websites. If you're looking for a good, educational, quality website check out ALA's Great Websites for Kids (gws.ala.org)

Bookmark your go-to websites

The websites listed on the chart on pages 57 through 60 represent just a fraction of the amazing resources available online for middle and high school students. Review and research these websites. Select and bookmark a few websites that appeal to your learning style. When you encounter a learning dilemma, or simply want to enhance your learning, log on to your go-to website and get the information you need.

What is multimodal learning?

Experts advise against relying too much on any one sensory mode—even if it is your preferred learning mode. Mix it up every now and then! **Multimodal learning incorporates many sensory modes into a study routine, and it's a particularly effective way to learn.** For example, visual learners always benefit from listening to an audio podcast. Audio learners can enhance their learning by constructing a model or diagramming a concept. Kinesthetic learners can benefit from studying maps, charts and images or listening to a lecture. The bottom line is: Brainy likes to have information presented to it in a variety of modes. The more and different ways you learn and review information, the stronger your synaptic patterns and connections become. That improves your ability to comprehend and remember information.

Name: _____

It's a VAK Match Up!

Hear ye! Learning is not limited to a textbook or worksheet. Thanks to this thing called "the internet," students have access to resources for all learning styles. I command you to include strategies and resources from **It's a VAK Match Up** in your personal learning routine.

Profile: Victor
- struggling in science
- teacher prefers lectures
- loses track of the sequence of steps in labs
- needs directions to be repeated
- doesn't get the "big picture"
- needs to find a helpful online resource

What is Victor's learning style? _____

Create a learning plan for Victor:

_____

_____

_____

_____

Are there any websites on the chart on pages ___-___ which might be helpful for Victor? _____

What is Ariana's learning style? _____

Create a learning plan for Ariana:

_____

_____

_____

_____

Profile: Ariana
- slow reader
- low comprehension
- likes literature
- can't remember what she reads
- enjoys role playing
- needs to find a helpful online resource

Are there any websites on the chart on pages ___-___ which might be helpful for Ariana? _____

Profile: Kevin
- athletic
- struggles in history
- gets distracted
- can't remember information
- likes to build stuff
- hates sitting and listening!
- needs to find a helpful online resource

What is Kevin's learning style? _____

Create a learning plan for Kevin:

_____

_____

_____

_____

Are there any websites on the chart on pages ___-___ which might be helpful for Kevin _____

Review these sites and award one to five ☆s!

M = Math; S= Science; H/SS = History/Social Studies; L/LA = Literature/Language Arts; GI = General Information; SA = Study Aids; WL = World Language; AV = Audio or Video content; I = Interactive; L = Links to outside resources

Website and URL	M	S	H/SS	L/LA	GI	SA	WL	AV	I	L	RATING
Smarthistory.com smarthistory.khanacademy.org											☆☆☆☆☆
Sweet Search sweetsearch.com											☆☆☆☆☆
Science Daily sciencedaily.com											☆☆☆☆☆
Open Yale Courses oyc.yale.edu											☆☆☆☆☆
Comic Master comicmaster.org.uk											☆☆☆☆☆
StudyBlue studyblue.com											☆☆☆☆☆
Nasa Kids Club www.nasa.gov/audience/forkids											☆☆☆☆☆
Internet History Sourcebooks Project www.fordham.edu/halsall											☆☆☆☆☆
Science Made Simple sciencemadesimple.com											☆☆☆☆☆
Novel Guide www.novelguide.com											☆☆☆☆☆
Math Forum mathforum.org											☆☆☆☆☆
MyVocabulary.com www.myvocabulary.com											☆☆☆☆☆
Famous Poets and Poems famouspoetsandpoems.com											☆☆☆☆☆
PinkMonkey www.pinkmonkey.com											☆☆☆☆☆

Website and URL	M	S	H/SS	L/LA	GI	SA	WL	AV	I	L	RATING
Gradesaver www.gradesaver.com/study-guides											☆☆☆☆☆
Archiving Early America www.earlyamerica.com/series.html											☆☆☆☆☆
Eyewitness to History www.eyewitnesstohistory.com											☆☆☆☆☆
World Atlas www.worldatlas.com											☆☆☆☆☆
Biography of America www.learner.org/biographyofamerica											☆☆☆☆☆
Virtual Field Trips ldshomeschoolinginca.org/vft.html											☆☆☆☆☆
Odyssey Online carlos.emory.edu/ODYSSEY											☆☆☆☆☆
Latitude and Longitude www.chemical-ecology.net/java/lat-long.htm											☆☆☆☆☆
Cultural Maps xroads.virginia.edu/%7EMAP/map_hp.html											☆☆☆☆☆
Mr Dowling's World www.mrdowling.com/602-darwin.html											☆☆☆☆☆
National Geographic for Kids kids.nationalgeographic.com/kids											☆☆☆☆☆
Nation Master www.nationmaster.com/index.php											☆☆☆☆☆
Online Atlas go.hrw.com/atlas/norm_htm/world.html											☆☆☆☆☆
Kids Web Japan web-japan.org/kidsweb											☆☆☆☆☆
Animated Atlas www.animatedatlas.com											☆☆☆☆☆
Hyperhistory Online www.hyperhistory.com/online_n2/History_n2/a.html											☆☆☆☆☆

Website and URL	M	S	H/SS	L/LA	GI	SA	WL	AV	I	L	RATING
BBC History www.bbc.co.uk/history/ancient/egyptians/launch_gms_pyramid_builder.shtml											☆☆☆☆☆
Quick Maps of the World www.theodora.com/maps											☆☆☆☆☆
Interactive Geography Quiz www.ilike2learn.com/ilike2learn											☆☆☆☆☆
Biographies www.biography.com											☆☆☆☆☆
Algebra Help www.algebrahelp.com											☆☆☆☆☆
Algebra www.aplusmath.com											☆☆☆☆☆
Brightstorm www.brightstorm.com											☆☆☆☆☆
Utah Education Network www.uen.org/k12student											☆☆☆☆☆
Folger Shakespearean Library www.folger.edu/template.cfm?cid=2594&CFID=3736 9972&CFTOKEN=29822245											☆☆☆☆☆
Math for the Left and Right Brain www.ixl.com											☆☆☆☆☆
National Science Foundation www.nsf.gov/news/overviews/astronomy/index.jsp											☆☆☆☆☆
Brain Pop www.brainpop.com											☆☆☆☆☆
Cells Alive www.cellsalive.com											☆☆☆☆☆
Inner Body www.innerbody.com											☆☆☆☆☆
Blobz Guide to Electric Circuits www.andythelwell.com/blobz											☆☆☆☆☆

Website and URL	M	S	H/SS	L/LA	GI	SA	WL	AV	I	L	RATING
NASA Solar System Exploration solarsystem.nasa.gov/index.cfm											☆☆☆☆☆
Fun Brain www.funbrain.com											☆☆☆☆☆
ThinkQuest library.thinkquest.org											☆☆☆☆☆
Books Should Be Free www.booksshouldbefree.com											☆☆☆☆☆
Librivox librivox.org											☆☆☆☆☆
Audio Books for Free www.audiobooksforfree.com/screen_main.asp											☆☆☆☆☆
Story Nory storynory.com											☆☆☆☆☆
Wild Animal Chronicles www.nationalgeographic.com											☆☆☆☆☆
National Geographic www.nationalgeographic.com											☆☆☆☆☆
Sixty Second Science www.scientificamerican.com											☆☆☆☆☆
Apple iTunes Educational Podcasts itunes.apple.com/us/genre/podcasts-education-k-12/id1415?mt=2											☆☆☆☆☆
Historical News Journals www.historicalnewsjournals.com											☆☆☆☆☆
Khan Academy www.khanacademy.org											☆☆☆☆☆
Mathtrain TV mathtrain.tv											☆☆☆☆☆
MathTV.com www.mathtv.com/videos_by_topic											☆☆☆☆☆

Name: _____

☆ ☆ ☆ ☆ ☆
Review and Rate an Educational Website

There's a huge amount of information online to enhance your learning experience. Your teacher will assign one or more educational tutorial websites from pages 57-60 for you to review and rate. Award the website one to five ☆s. Share your review with your classmates. If you have a go-to educational app, share it too.

Website **Title:**

_____

Circle the website's subject area(s):

M = Math   S = Science   H/SS = History/Social Studies   LA = Language Arts

GI = General Information   SA = Study Arts   WL = World Language

Describe the **purpose** of the website (ie. math tutorial website). What skills does it address?

_____

_____

_____

What grade level(s) does the website apply to? _____

Do you like/dislike the design or look of the website? (Is it colorful? Attractive? Bland? Boring?)

_____

_____

_____

Does this website draw your interest and make you want to use it?

_____

Is this website interactive? (Can you play games or take quizzes?) Describe:

_____

_____

_____

Describe the activities the website provides for learning a skill. _____

_____

_____

Does the website have an **affiliation**? Is it related to or sponsored by a college or university, publisher, government department or school?   Yes   No

If yes, what is the affilation? _____

Does the site ask for **personal information** about you or your family, or ask you to register or create an account?   Yes   No   (Don't register or provide information without parental permission!)

Rate the **quality of the text, images and graphics**:   Excellent   Very Good   Good   Poor

Does the website have **video content**?   Yes   No

If yes, rate the quality of the video: Excellent   Very Good   Good   Poor

How's the site **organized**? Is it **easy to navigate**? Can you **find the information** you're looking for?
     Excellent   Very Good   Good   Poor

Does the site try to **sell** you something, or require a **subscription**?   Yes   No
(Never buy or subscribe without parental permission.)

Is this website free?   Yes   No   Can't Tell

Would you recommend this site to a **visual**, **auditory** or **kinesthetic learner** (or combination)?   V   A   K

Do you think this website is a **helpful** tutorial/educational resource?   Yes   No

Additional comments, such as useful information about the site, cool or unusual features.

_____

_____

_____

Overall, how many stars do you give this website?   ☆   ☆   ☆   ☆   ☆

Do you have a go-to website you use for homework help or tutoring not listed on the chart on pages 57-60, which you can recommend to classmates? Write the name, URL and a brief summary of the website.

_____

_____

_____

Reviewed by: _____   Date: _____

Dear Parent or Caregiver,

Today I participated in my study skills class based on *The Middle School Student's Guide to Study Skills*. One of the best ways I can prepare for high school and college is to use good study skills whenever I am learning.

I learned:

1. Thanks to the internet, excellent learning style-compatible resources are instantly available to _____ or _____ learning. Most online resources are _____! (Cost nothing.)

2. Audio learners can find excellent educational audio podcasts on _____, and can even read aloud and record their class notes or textbook chapters, and _____ to study.

3. As you move up into high school and college, you will assume more personal _____ for your learning; knowing how to locate and use educational and tutorial websites is a good _____ skill.

4. Experts believe that students should not rely exclusively on one learning style. Go _____! Incorporate many sensory _____ into your study routine.

5. Even though the 1970's were _____, a student's learning was pretty much limited to their _____ and _____. Now, because of the _____, students have instant access to excellent tutorial resources to supplement their learning in all subjects.

Ask me about the skills I learned today! Your support at home will help me make good study skills daily habit.

Thank you for all you do for me every day.

Sincerely,

_____

NOTES

THERE'S MORE THAN ONE WAY TO BE SMART!

Have you ever noticed that a student who's really good at one subject may struggle in another? For example, a student who takes on the most heinous algebra equation with complete ease, may struggle with an oral presentation in history, or a student who expresses a complex concept through art, can't explain it in an essay. Why?

In Chapter 6 you learned about VAK learning styles. Learning styles relate to informational *input*—how a person most efficiently takes in and processes information. What about the other side of the coin? Do people have a dominant informational *output* mode?

In the 1980s, a professor of education at Harvard University named Dr. Howard Gardner thought a lot about how people show their intelligence. He believed that the traditional measure of intelligence—based on an IQ test measuring only math and verbal abilities, was too limited. Intelligence, he argued, is more than a score on a test! Intelligence has many forms, and can be displayed in many ways. In fact, Dr. Gardner identified eight types of intelligence. These are now referred to as Gardner's Multiple Intelligences. Just like learning styles, everyone has a dominant intelligence.

Chapter 7 Learning Goals:

☐ summarize Gardner's Theory of Multiple Intelligences.
☐ list Gardner's eight intelligences.
☐ design a variety of responses to a project based on intelligence types.

ELENA DEMONSTRATES *EIGHT* DOMINANT INTELLIGENCES!

How can knowing your intelligence type help you be a better learner?

Knowing your dominant intelligence type helps you better manage your learning by enabling you to:

➜ make the most of your **innate abilities**.

➜ **compensate** for your weaknesses.

➜ utilize your dominant intelligence when **selecting or designing a project**.

➜ select a **college study or career path** compatible with your intelligence type.

What are the multiple intelligences?

Linguistic intelligence. A linguistically intelligent person is sensitive to words, the meaning of words, speaking and writing. They often excel at things like story and poetry writing, speech and debate, oral reports, reading, writing, and spelling. Can you think of a friend, classmate, or family member who displays linguistic intelligence?

Musical intelligence. A musically intelligent person has a heightened ability to hear tones, rhythm, musical patterns, and pitch and timbre. They often excel at or easily handle musical activities, sound mimicry, playing an instrument, music composition, writing lyrics, rhythms, sound patterns, singing, participating in choir, rap and rap lyric composition, sound editing and sound production. Can you think of a friend, classmate, or family member who displays musical intelligence?

What's your intelligence type?
- ☐ linguistic
- ☐ musical
- ☐ logical/mathematical
- ☐ visual/spatial
- ☐ bodily/kinesthetic
- ☐ intrapersonal
- ☐ interpersonal
- ☐ naturalistic

Logical/Mathematical intelligence. A person who is logically or mathematically intelligent is able to see relationships between objects, create and interpret data. They excel at creating and recognizing number patterns, sequence data, solving puzzles, making and using spreadsheets, creating computer programs, solving geometric problems, and making scientific predictions. Can you think of a friend, classmate, or family member who displays logical/mathematical intelligence?

Visual/Spatial intelligence. Visually/spatially intelligent people are able to perceive and visualize objects. They often excel at art, in creating and using graphs, charts and patterns, painting, sketching, drawing. They excel at making visual representations of concepts, such as a map or a timeline of an historical event, video game graphics, CGI, building architecture and engineering. Can you think of a friend, classmate, or family member who displays visual/spatial intelligence?

Bodily/Kinesthetic intelligence. People who are bodily/kinesthetically intelligent, excel at activities requiring body movement, physical action and control. They have excellent hand-eye coordination and dexterity. They excel at physical activities like athletics and dance, and also at constructing models, labs, sculpture, surgery, and other activities requiring good hand-eye coordination. Can you think of a friend, classmate, or family member who displays bodily/kinesthetic intelligence?

Intrapersonal intelligence. Intrapersonally intelligent people connect with their inner feelings. They're introspective, self-reflective and intuitive. They are perceptive. They are good at controlling their destiny because they are aware of their personal strengths and weaknesses. They make self-aware decisions. They do well on individual projects. Can you think of a friend, classmate, or family member who displays intrapersonal intelligence?

Interpersonal intelligence. Interpersonally intelligent people are adept at understanding the actions, emotions, moods, intentions and feelings of others. They interact well with their peers and are good at seeing or presenting problems from many perspectives. They are good mediators, can facilitate conflict resolution, and lead group meetings or projects. They excel at debate, team sports, clubs and group projects. Can you think of a friend, classmate, or family member who displays interpersonal intelligence?

Naturalistic Intelligence. A naturalistically intelligent person is in tune with nature. These people excel at nurturing and exploring the environment through subjects connected to the study of nature, like biology, zoology, geology, meteorology, environmental science, and oceanography. They are sensitive to nature and changes to the environment. They excel at activities like gardening, agriculture, caring for animals, oceanography and environmental science. Can you think of a friend, classmate, or family member who displays naturalistic intelligence?

You probably have a sense of your personal strengths and weaknesses. Consider each of the above intelligences. Which do you think is your dominant intelligence? Which intelligence do you believe is your weakest? Go online and search "multiple intelligence assessments." You can take a short test that will confirm your beliefs—or maybe surprise you!

Are intelligences the same as learning styles?

Intelligences are not the same as learning styles. Learning styles relate to informational *input*—how information is received and processed. Intelligences relate informational *output*—how people express their knowledge and abilities. For example, it's likely that the great environmentalist Rachel Carson was naturalistically intelligent, but she could have been a visual, kinesthetic or auditory learner.

Name: _____

Multiple Intelligences: Work'n It Out in Different Ways

Intelligence is more than a score on a test. Intelligence can be displayed in lots of ways. According to the Theory of Multiple Intelligences, there are many different types of intelligences. Everyone has a **dominant** (but not exclusive) **intelligence**. Use your dominant intelligence to make the most of your innate abilities!

Project time! Your history teacher wants his class to learn all about the Boston Tea Party. He knows what a diverse and clever group of students he has, so he's given you freedom to design your own projects. Suggest ways the eight intelligence types can approach this project showcasing their diverse intelligences.

Linguistic Intelligence. (Traits: sensitive to words, the meaning of words, speaking and writing; excels at story and poetry writing, speech and debate, oral reports, reading, writing, spelling.)

_____

_____

_____

_____

Musical intelligence. (Traits: ability to hear tones, rhythm, musical patterns, and pitch and timbre; excels musical activities, sound mimicry, playing an instrument, music composition, writing lyrics, rhythms, sound patterns, singing, choir, rap and rap lyric composition, sound editing and production.)

_____

_____

_____

_____

Logical/Mathematical intelligence. (Traits: recognizes relationships between objects; excels at creating and recognizing number patterns, interpreting and sequencing data, solving puzzles, making and using spreadsheets, creating computer programs, solving geometric problems, game code-writing and making scientific predictions.)

_____

_____

_____

_____

Visual/Spatial intelligence. (Traits: perceives and visualizes objects; excels at art, in creating and using graphs, charts and patterns, painting, sketching, drawing, visual representations of concepts.)

_____

_____

_____

_____

Bodily/Kinesthetic intelligence. (Traits: excels at activities requiring body movement, physical action and control; excellent hand-eye coordination and dexterity, athletics, dance, model building.)

_____

_____

_____

_____

Intrapersonal intelligence. (Traits: understands inner feelings; introspective and self-reflective, perceptive, and able to identify and correct personal weaknesses; works well on individual projects.)

_____

_____

_____

_____

Interpersonal intelligence. (Traits: understands actions, emotions, moods, intentions and feelings of others; interacts well with peers; see problems from many perspectives; excels at mediation and conflict resolution, leading group activities, meetings or projects debate, team sports, and clubs.)

_____

_____

_____

_____

Naturalistic Intelligence. (Traits: in tune with nature and the environment; excels at subjects connected to the study of nature such as biology, zoology, geology, meteorology, environmental science, and oceanography; sensitive to changes to the environment.)

_____

_____

_____

_____

Name: _____

Making the Most of Your Intelligence

Take the Multiple Intelligence Assessment assigned by your teacher, then answer the questions below.

What is your dominant intelligence type? _____

Do you agree with the outcome of the assessment? Why or why not?

_____

_____

_____

In your opinion, which of the eight intelligences do you definitely *not* display? How can you tell?

_____

_____

_____

School and community clubs, activities and after school progams provide excellent opportunities to explore and develop your intelligence type. For example, a visually/spatially intelligent student would enjoy an art competition or club; a linguistically intelligent student can develop skills in the debate club; the Environmental Club is a good choice for a naturalistically intelligent student. Go to your middle school's website. List clubs, activities, and after school programs available to students:

(   ) _____   (   ) _____

(   ) _____   (   ) _____

(   ) _____   (   ) _____

(   ) _____   (   ) _____

(   ) _____   (   ) _____

(   ) _____   (   ) _____

(   ) _____   (   ) _____

Review the above list. What intelligence types are represented in the clubs and activities? Mark (LI) if the club or activity would appeal to a linguistically intelligent student, (MI) if the club or activity appeals to a musically intelligent person, etc. (See abbreviations below). Circle programs, clubs and activities that appeal to your intelligence type and make a plan to participate. If you don't see a club or activity for your intelligence type, talk to your teacher or counselor about starting one at your school. Developing your your unique intelligence is a good study skill.

VSI = Visually/Spatial Intelligence   BKI = Bodily/Kinetic Intelligence
LI   = Linguistic Intelligence   Intra = Intrapersonal Inteligence
MI   = Musical Intelligence   Inter = Interpersonal Intelligence
LMI = Logical/Mathematical Intelligence   NI   = Naturalistic Intelligence

Dear Parent or Caregiver,

Today I participated in my study skills class based on *The Middle School Student's Guide to Study Skills*. One of the best ways I can prepare for high school and college is to use good study skills whenever I am learning.

I learned:

1. Learning styles and _____ are not the same. Learning styles relate to informational _____. "Intelligences" refer to informational _____.

2. Gardner identified _____ intelligences: _____,
    _____, _____,
    _____, _____,
    _____, _____ and
    _____.

3. Everyone has a _____ , but not exclusive, intelligence; knowing yours can help you make the most of your innate abilities, recognize and compensate for your _____ .

4. An _____ intelligent person is self-reflective, self-aware intuitive and perceptive.

5. A/An _____ intelligent person is adept at understanding the feelings, emotions and motives of others.

Ask me about the skills I learned today! Your support at home will help me make good study skills daily habit.

Thank you for all you do for me every day.

Sincerely,

_____

Name: _____

WHAT DID YOU LEARN ABOUT LEARNING STYLES & MUTIPLE INTELLIGENCES?

1. Bailey is a *kinesthetic learner*. Gia is an *auditory learner*. They are in the same conversational French class and plan to study for the midterm together. The midterm will focus on vocabulary and pronunciation. Locate at least two online French tutorial or educational resources. Provide the website name and URLs. Find a tutorial website for the language you are studying in school, and write the name of the site and URL.

   _____

   _____

   _____

   _____

2. Ryan exhibits *visual/spatial intelligence*. He's good at all kinds of drawing and design. His bros Pedro and Steven play in the school jazz band. They exhibit *auditory intelligence*. The three of them have been assigned to a group project for U.S. History. The teacher wants students to collaborate, using their unique intelligences to design a presentation commemorating Pearl Harbor and America's entry into WWII. Ideas?

   _____

   _____

   _____

   _____

3. List two adjectives that describe an *intrapersonally* intelligent person:

   _____   _____

4. Your teacher has assigned Shakespeare's *As You Like It* as required reading for the entire class. OMG! You haven't a clue what the characters are saying. Knowing that you are an *auditory learner*, you decide to read along in the book as you listen to a theatrical production of the play. Find an audio recording of the play online. Write the URL here:

   _____

   _____

True or False:

5. _____ Caroline is president of the middle school student activities committee. Several students have quit the committee because she doesn't get along well with others. She tends to see things only from her own perspective. She disregards the actions, moods, and feelings of other students. Caroline has poor *intrapersonal intelligence*.

6. _____ A *naturalistically intelligent* person would probably enjoy an assignment about the effects of climate change on bird migration.

7. _____ You cannot be intelligent in more than one way.

8. _____ A *visual-spatially intelligent* person is adept at poetry writing, speech and debate, but don't ask them to create a graph or design a poster!

9. _____ A good learning program is multimodal, incorporating strategies and resources from all learning style modes, with an emphasis on the student's preferred or dominant style.

10. _____ Knowing your dominant intelligence can help you compensate for your weaknesses and capitalize on your strengths.

11. In your opinion, what makes an educational/tutorial website or app worth 5 ☆s?

_____

_____

_____

_____

12. How can joining a school club or after school activity help students develop their unique talents and intelligence?

_____

_____

_____

_____

NOTES

THAT'S MY ROUTINE AND I'M STICK'N TO IT!

rou•tine noun \rü-'tēn\

a: a regular course of procedure

b: habitual or mechanical performance of an established procedure

Have you ever done the wrong assignment for homework? Have you ever lost a book or paper you needed for homework somewhere in your house? Isn't it frustrating?

Homework isn't much fun to begin with, but doing the wrong assignment and searching for books and papers takes homework frustration to another level.

In the next few chapters, you will investigate *pre-learning strategies.* Those are things students can do before starting homework to make learning faster, more efficient, and less frustrating. The first of these strategies is to develop (and stick to) a *homework routine.* A simple, brief homework routine makes your time more productive, and can save you hours of annoyance.

Chapter 8 Learning Goals:

- ☐ state the benefits of a consistent homework routine.
- ☐ describe five pre-learning strategies for improving homework efficiency.
- ☐ design a to-do list.

What's a homework routine?

The word *routine* has gotten a bad reputation. It's become synonymous with dull and predictable, even boring. So unfair! Routine can be a beautiful thing, especially where homework is concerned. As you move up into high school and college, the volume and difficulty of your homework will increase. It will also comprise a significant portion of your grade. It's important to set the stage for working efficiently and productively. Developing and sticking to a *homework routine* is an excellent pre-learning strategy for middle school, high school and college. A simple five minute homework routine can save you hours of work and significantly reduce stress.

What are the benefits of a homework routine?

A homework routine:

➔   establishes a more **successful and productive learning environment**

➔   helps students **avoid organizational disasters**

➔   **reduces stress and frustration** over homework (for students and their parents!)

➔   helps students **overcome procrastination**

➔   **saves time**

What's a homework routine?

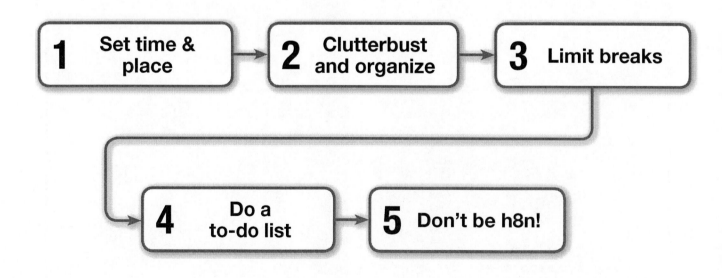

Set time & place

DON'T DO! Don't be a homework nomad, wandering from place to place to do your homework – one night in your room, one night at the kitchen counter, one night on the sofa… All that wandering can cause **organizational disasters** like misplaced papers or lost or forgotten books or homework.

DO! Stake your claim! **Set up a personal and permanent study zone at home.** Make sure it's well-lit, comfortable, and free from distractions. Keep your school stuff there – and *only* there. When you get home from school, put your backpack and books at your workspace, not in the entry hall, or on the kitchen table. **As much as possible, do your homework at the same time and in the same place every day.** Routine is key for avoiding organizational disasters.

Clutterbust and organize

DON'T DO! A messy, cluttered desk is distracting and can cause you to **lose worksheets, homework, books and handouts**. Searching through clutter for papers, pens and other stuff is just one big, frustrating, yucky waste of your valuable time. Say **no** to a messy desk! If your desk is cluttered, your mind will be too.

DO! Before starting homework, take a couple of minutes to **clutterbust and organize** your workspace. Toss out trash. File or toss old papers. Stack books and papers neatly. Clear a space large enough to hold an open textbook and open binder. **An organized, uncluttered workspace improves homework productivity and efficiency.** It also reduces stress. Keep your computer desktop organized and uncluttered too! Create and label folders. Place documents and downloads in the correct folder. Make it easy to sort and find things. Hint: There are a lot of free desktop organization wallpapers online.

Limit breaks

DON'T DO! Don't take long breaks. Breaking too frequently or for too long **disrupts your concentration** and drags out homework time for longer than necessary.

DO! Work steadily without a break for a set period of time or until you've fully completed an assignment and it's **filed in your binder.** Breaks include checking Facebook or texts every other minute. Do not multitask. **Focus on one task at a time.** Limit breaks to **5 minutes per half hour** of homework. As your concentration and attention span improve, increase your break-free study time to one full hour.

Do a to-do list

DON'T DO! Don't assume you know what your assignments are and start working without confirming details. Teachers make changes or additions to assignments all the time.

DO! Check your planner, check the class webpage, and review your notes before you start working. **Confirm assignment details** like page numbers, chapters and problem numbers. If you're confused, call or text a classmate (someone less confused than you, obviously.) **Make a to-do list** including all assignments and non-assignment related tasks, such as getting a permission slip signed, or making sure you have that note you need to get out of class for your orthodontist appointment. Seriously – it takes about two minutes to make a to-do list, but it can save you hours of trouble.

Don't be h8n!

DON'T DO! Don't be h8n on your homework! Resentment, annoyance, impatience and all those **negative emotions are big downers**. A bad attitude makes it harder to get the job done and shows up in the quality of your work.

DO! Remember the traits of the growth mindset learner? That student understands the benefit of effort and challenge. Even if you think homework's boring, or that you've already mastered a skill or concept, Brainy's neurons and synapses may need a bit more practice to form strong connections and memory patterns. You don't have to love homework (that might be weird), but H8n on it distracts your brain from working efficiently. **Adjust your attitude. Engage your mind in the homework process.** You can't avoid it, so make it work for you and *learn* from it.

Just do it!

Establishing and sticking to a homework routine can actually be a liberating experience. It frees you from the worry of organizational disasters, ensures that you have completed all of your work, and helps you overcome procrastination. A homework routine is a beautiful thing for middle school right through high school and college!

Name: _____

Just a Routine Survey!

The word *routine* has gotten a bad reputation. It's become synonymous with dull and predictable – even boring! But *routine* is a beautiful thing, especially where homework is concerned. A homework routine makes your time more productive, reduces stress, and helps you avoid organizational disasters. A homework routine can be a kind of pre-learning ritual to help you focus, and prepare your mind to learn.

From 1-10 (**10 = "Awesome & Totally True"; 1 = "Not in a Million Years"**) how efficient and productive is your homework routine? Read the statements below and select the number that best describes your routine.

1. **I do my homework at about the same time every night (give or take an hour.)**

   10   9   8   7   6   5   4   3   2   1

2. **I do my homework in the same place every night.**

   10   9   8   7   6   5   4   3   2   1

3. **My desktop is clean and clutter-free!**

   10   9   8   7   6   5   4   3   2   1

4. **I have a trash can at my workspace and I use it.**

   10   9   8   7   6   5   4   3   2   1

5. **My home workspace is private enough for me to leave books and papers on the desktop without worrying they'll be messed with or lost.**

   10   9   8   7   6   5   4   3   2   1

6. **When I do homework, I focus on one task at a time, and do not multitask.**

   10   9   8   7   6   5   4   3   2   1

7. **My homework breaks are short (no more than 5 minutes.)**

   10   9   8   7   6   5   4   3   2   1

8. **When I start homework, I check my planner to confirm assignment details.**

   10   9   8   7   6   5   4   3   2   1

9. **When I start homework, I review the class webpage to confirm assignment details.**

   10   9   8   7   6   5   4   3   2   1

10. **When I start homework I review class notes.**

    10   9   8   7   6   5   4   3   2   1

11. **I make a to-do list before I start my homework, which lists all of my homework assignments.**

    10   9   8   7   6   5   4   3   2   1

12. **My to-do list includes non-assignment tasks (like getting a permission slip signed or putting a book in my back pack.)**

    10   9   8   7   6   5   4   3   2   1

13. **I am able to work steadily for at least 30 minutes before I take a break.**

    10   9   8   7   6   5   4   3   2   1

14. **As I do my homework, I reject downer feelings about it (like resentment, annoyance or boredom.)**

    10   9   8   7   6   5   4   3   2   1

15. **As soon as I complete an assignment, I file it in my binder.**

    10   9   8   7   6   5   4   3   2   1

Total: _____

120-150	Ritual status. You understand and appreciate the value of a pre-learning *routine*. You have a consistent and productive homework routine. Your good pre-learning skills will serve you well through high school and college. Great job!
105-119	Your homework routine is pretty good, but needs attention in a few places. Review your answers to the survey. Hone in on your weakness. Is it a messy workspace? Too many breaks? Poor attitude? Over the next few weeks make an extra effort to improve your routine and shore up weaknesses.
75-104	Review your answers to the survey. Circle any questions you answered with a 7 or less. If you're feeling stressed about homework, there's a good chance that the deficiencies in your homework routine are major factors. Correct your habits and practices now so they don't follow you to high school and college.
Below 75	Review the habits and strategies in the survey questions. Select two per week to incorporate into your homework routine. You will see your grades go up and your stress level fall. By the time you get to high school, your homework routine may reach ritual status.

Name: _____

Do a To-Do

Making a **To-Do List** is an excellent homework routine. It takes only about a minute to make, but can have a big impact on your success as a student. A **To-Do List** helps you focus on homework goals, and assures that you complete *all of* your assignments *every day*. A **To-Do List** also gives your busy brain a break, because once you write an item on your list, Brainy can relax and stop worrying about remembering it!

THANKS! ME LIKE.

Your assignment (select one):

1. There are many good, free To-Do List design templates online. Some are simple *("Write down your tasks and cross them off as you finish.")* Others are more elaborate, allowing you to prioritize tasks, make notes and track status. Go online and search "to-do list templates." Review the designs. Select one that's right for you. Print a copy and bring it to class. Compare your selection with your classmates'. Stock your workspace with a 30-day supply. **Make your to-do list a daily study habit.**

2. Design your personal To-Do List. Use period prompts, such as "1st period homework", "2nd period homework"... etc., or subject prompts like "science homework", "language arts homework"... or any other prompt that works for you. Include a prompt for non-assignment/related tasks, like bringing a form to the attendance office or returning a library book. Customize your design with graphics, photos of friends, your team's logo, a holiday motif, whatever! Bring your to-do list to class to share with other students. Stock your workspace with a 30-day supply. **Make your to-do list a daily study habit.**

To do on _____(DATE)_____

FIGHTING OWLS
PELLET POWER!

1. _____   5. _____
2. _____   6. _____
3. _____   7. _____
4. _____   8. _____
Non-assignment tasks: _____

_____

_____

Dear Parent or Caregiver,

Today I participated in my study skills class based on *The Middle School Student's Guide to Study Skills*. One of the best ways I can prepare for high school and college is to use good study skills whenever I am learning.

I learned:

1. Establish a homework _____. As much as possible, do your homework at the _____ time and in the _____ place every day.

2. Before starting homework, take a couple of minutes to _____-bust and _____ your workspace.

3. Work for at least _____ minutes without a break, or until you've _____ an assignment and _____ it in your binder. "Breaks" include checking _____ or _____.

4. Check your planner before you start your homework. Check the class webpage and notes. Know exactly what your _____(s) is/are; Make a _____ - _____ list including all of your assignments and non-assignment tasks.

5. Bad _____ like resentment, annoyance, and impatience distract Brainy from working efficiently; Homework has its benefits: it helps build strong synaptic connections and patterns, so it's easier to _____ the learned information.

Ask me about the skills I learned today! Your support at home will help me make good study skills daily habit.

Thank you for all you do for me every day.

Sincerely,

_____

THE ORGANIZED WORKSPACE

Why do business people work in office spaces or cubicles reserved just for them? Why don't they wander around the office and work wherever they want?

Ergonomics is the study of human ability and productivity in relationship to their work surroundings. The goal of an *ergonomist* (ergonomic scientist) is to determine what physical conditions increase or decrease worker productivity.

Ergonomists tell us that productivity is closely related to a worker's physical surroundings. People are happier and work more efficiently when they have a comfortable space of their own to work in. Productivity also increases when workspaces are organized and stocked with the supplies workers need to get the job done.

It's no different for students. The space where you study and do your homework affects the quality of your work and your ability to manage your time. As you move up into high school and college, the increased volume and difficulty of your homework will require you to spend a lot of time at your workspace. Your work environment is very important to your success as a student.

Chapter 9 Learning Goals:

☐ state the elements of a productive home workspace.

☐ list the supplies students need at their workspace to maximize productivity and efficiency.

☐ critique his or her home workspace for productivity and efficiency.

What makes a workspace work?

Location

A good workspace is a **private, quiet and comfortable area, free from distractions**, like television, people talking, stereos, phones, or video games. It doesn't have to be a big area, but it should be a place you have relatively to yourself, so you can leave items like books, papers and projects on your desktop, without fear of them being messed with or thrown out. It could be located in your bedroom, attic, basement, den—anywhere in your home, as long as it's private and comfortable. If you can't find a space at home, talk to your mom or dad about going to the public library several times a week to do your work. You won't be allowed to leave your stuff on the desktop, but the library does provide a comfortable, distraction-free workspace. If you're distracted by noise, consider getting a set of noise canceling headphones, a white noise machine, or a small tabletop fountain, which are inexpensive and can be found at most office supply stores.

Your workspace can be located anywhere in your house, as long as it's private and comfortable.

Desktop

Give yourself enough space to work comfortably. A desktop surface should be large enough to hold an open textbook and binder, or laptop computer—so at least 18" deep and 30" wide. A straight-backed and comfortable chair is a must.

Lighting

Lighting is so important to human productivity that there is even a special field of ergonomics devoted to it. It's called *light ergonomics* and it's the study of the relationship between the light source and the individual. Poor lighting has been found to cause all sorts of problems including **low productivity, high error rates, headache, lack of mental alertness and general yuckiness**. Poor lighting has even been found to **slow neuron function**, which has a direct effect on learning. Even if you have a good overhead ceiling light, consider adding task lighting, like a desktop lamp. Position the lamp so that the light falls directly on the page or computer keyboard, without creating a glare or a shadow. Try out different bulb wattages or even light filters to find what works best for you. If you're feeling drowsy when you study, low lighting could be the culprit.

Light ergonomics is the study of how people react to light.

Supplies

Have you ever sat down to do your homework, all ready to be productive, only to discover that, in order for you to complete your work, you'd have to go to the office supply store for something you're missing? Delaying a project until you have the right supplies is a frustrating, inefficient way to work. Stock your workspace with the supplies you need for homework and projects. You don't need top-of-the-line supplies. Inexpensive ones work fine. Access to a computer with a printer, and a strong, reliable internet connection is important for middle school. But if the computer with its many temptations (YouTube, Facebook, Instagram, etc.) is a distraction for you, keep it out of your workspace.

✓ Binder paper/graph paper
✓ #2 pencils
✓ pens
✓ markers
✓ colored pencils
✓ ruler with metric and standard measurements
✓ glue sticks
✓ yellow highlighter
✓ scissors
✓ scotch tape
✓ stapler and staples
✓ three hole punch
✓ index cards (blank and lined)
✓ erasers
✓ pencil sharpener
✓ white out
✓ paper clips
✓ calculator/scientific calulator
✓ compass, protractor
✓ dictionary and thesaurus
✓ foreign language dictionary
✓ graph paper and math supplies
✓ trash can
✓ bulletin board - post notes, class schedules, memos and important papers right where you can see them! (Don't forget tacks or magnets.)

✓ double sided tape
✓ poster board
✓ Accordion files or several large manila envelopes (to store graded papers, class notes, and handouts you may need later.)
✓ In-box or low-profile basket (keeps papers from piling up, provides a place for your mom or dad to put papers or books you leave around the house.)
✓ Access to a computer with a printer.
✓ flash drive 2-4 GB
✓ yellow stickies
✓ printer paper
✓ extra printer cartridges
✓ Photos of your BFFs, team photos, cool posters, stickers, decals, notes, etc.

Notes:

Name: _____

You are an *ergonomist*. You study the effect of a worker's surroundings on their efficiency and productivity. You know that a student's workspace affects the quality of their work and their ability to manage their time. You are interviewing a middle school student about their home workspace. Pair up with a classmate. Take turns playing the role of an ergonomist. Make recommendations to improve the student's home workspace.

Does Your Workspace Work for You?

Ergonomist: _____   Student: _____

Q. **Do you have a location at your home where you do homework?**   yes   no   several

Q. **Within your home, where is your workspace located? (If the student works in more than one space, list all.)**

_____

_____

Q. **Consider each of the locations and select one as your primary and permanent workspace.**

_____

Q. **Is this location quiet?**   yes   no   sometimes

Q. **Is this location distraction-free? _____ Is it away from people talking? _____**

Is it away from t.v. sights and sounds? _____ Is it away from other noise or commotion? _____

Q. **As you do your homework, are any of these devices at your workspace:**

cellphone   iPod   computer/laptop   tablet   T.V.   gaming equipment

Q. **As you do homework, are you distracted from your learning goals by any of the above devices? Explain:**

_____

_____

_____

Q. **Do you have a strong, reliable internet connection at your workspace?**   yes   no

Q. **Do you have access to a printer?**   yes   no

Q. **Is your workspace reserved primarily for your personal use?**   yes   no   I share with others.

Q. **Is your workspace comfortable?**   yes   no   somewhat   Too comfortable!

Q. **Do you have a straight-back, comfortable chair?**   yes   no

Q. **Is your desktop surface area size adequate?**   yes   no

Q. **Estimate size of the desktop surface area:** _____ x _____

Q. **Do books, papers or other items clutter your desktop?** yes   no

Q. **Describe the lighting:** overhead   desktop/task   both

Lighting is important. Low lighting slows neuron function.

Q. **Does your workspace lighting need improvement?**
    Is it too dull? _____   **Too bright?** _____

Q. **Does the lighting cast a glare or shadow your working area or computer screen? Explain:**

_____

_____

Q. **How is the temperature and ventilation in your workspace?**
    Hot and stuffy? _____   Chilly? _____   Just right? _____

Q. **Is your workspace personalized with class schedules and calendars, photos of friends, posters, art work, awards, or other decorations of your choice? Describe your workspace design and any changes you would like to make so your workspace expresses who you are.**

_____

_____

_____

Q. **Overall, is your workspace environment a pleasant and productive place to work? Why or why not?**

_____

_____

_____

Interviewer's three recommendations for making this student's workspace work better:

_____

_____

_____

Signed: **Recommendations accepted:**

_____   _____
Ergonomist   Student

Name: _____

Workspace Inventory

It's frustrating when you don't have the supplies you need to get your homework or project done! For maximum productivity and efficiency, your workspace(s) should be stocked with the supplies you need to get the job done. Use this form to take an inventory of your home workspace. Then head to the office supply store to get what you need.

Shopping List

Got it! ☐ binder paper	Got it! ☐ compass, protractor
Got it! ☐ #2 pencils	Got it! ☐ dictionary and thesaurus
Got it! ☐ blue, black and red pens	Got it! ☐ foreign language dictionary
Got it! ☐ markers	Got it! ☐ graph paper
Got it! ☐ colored pencils	Got it! ☐ trash can
Got it! ☐ ruler with metric and standard	Got it! ☐ posterboard
measurements	Got it! ☐ bulletin board + tacks or magnets
Got it! ☐ glue sticks	Got it! ☐ accordion file or several large
Got it! ☐ yellow highlighter	manila envelopes.
Got it! ☐ scissors	Got it! ☐ in-box or low-profile basket
Got it! ☐ scotch tape	Got it! ☐ computer with a printer (or access
Got it! ☐ stapler and staples	to one.)
Got it! ☐ three hole punch	Got it! ☐ flash drive 2-4 GB
Got it! ☐ index cards (blank and lined)	Got it! ☐ extra printer cartridges
Got it! ☐ erasers	Got it! ☐ yellow "stickies"
Got it! ☐ pencil sharpener	Got it! ☐ printer paper
Got it! ☐ white out	Got it! ☐ double-sided tape
Got it! ☐ extra printer cartidges	Got it! ☐ white noise machine, headphones
Got it! ☐ paper clips	or small fountain (optional)
Got it! ☐ calculator	

Dear Parent or Caregiver,

Today I participated in my study skills class based on *The Middle School Student's Guide to Study Skills*. One of the best ways I can prepare for high school and college is to use good study skills whenever I am learning.

I learned:

1. Elements of a productive workspace include a distraction-free _____, well-stocked _____, and good overhead and task _____. A workspace should also be relatively private and free from _____!

2. Stock your workspace with the _____ you need to get the job done.

3. _____ *ergonomists* tell us that poor _____ can make you feel tired and sleepy and can even slow neuron function! Consider using a _____ light to illuminate the page or keyboard.

4. Access to a computer with a _____ and a reliable internet connection is important for middle and high school, but if the computer distracts you from getting your work done, keep it out of your workspace.

5. Your workspace is a great place for _____-expression. _____ your workspace with photos of your friends, teammates, cool posters, stickers, awards, decals, notes, college logos, etc. You'll be spending a lot of time there, so make it a place where you won't mind _____.

Ask me about the skills I learned today! Your support at home will help me make good study skills daily habit.

Thank you for all you do for me every day.

Sincerely,

_____

SYLLABUSTED!

Wouldn't you love to be able to predict the final grade you'll get in a class? Don't you wish you could read your teacher's mind, to know exactly how they'll grade you, and what it takes to get an "A" in their class? You can—sort of. Just read the *syllabus!*

A syllabus is a document a teacher writes to provide students with an overview of their course. It's usually distributed the first day of class. Unfortunately, many students merely glance at it and toss it in their backpacks. Do not do this! The syllabus is one of the most important documents you'll receive from your teacher all year. It provides valuable insight into how your teacher will run the class, how the content is organized, what your teacher expects you to do, and how you are to do it. In short, the syllabus is your teacher's game plan, and students are players responsible for knowing what's in it.

Get into the pre-learning habit of carefully and thoroughly reading your teacher's syllabus. It's an important study skill for middle school, high school, and college.

Look out, you've been *syllabusted!*

Chapter 10 Learning Goals:

- ☐ explain the purpose of a syllabus.
- ☐ tell how to use a syllabus to align time & workload to a teacher's priorities and expectations.
- ☐ draft a mock syllabus.

LIFE LESSONS WITH MR.SKILLSWORTH!

Why is the syllabus important?

A middle school syllabus is usually a fairly simple document and middle school teachers often have similar policies and plans for their classes. But as you move up into high school and college, syllabuses are more complex, detailed, and increasingly important to your success in a class. In high school and college a syllabus can be several pages long!

What do you do with a syllabus?

The syllabus is such an important document, it deserves a place of honor. **Put it in a sheet protector and store it in the front section of your course binder.** You'll be referring to it frequently. If your teacher doesn't provide you with a copy of the syllabus, but posts it on the class webpage, print two copies. Put one on the bulletin board or wall at your workspace, and one in your binder. Download a copy of the syllabus to your mobile so you have access to it at all times.

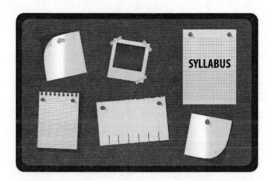

Post a copy of the class syllabus on the bulletin board at your workspace.

What's in a syllabus?

A typical syllabus addresses several topics relevant to the course:

Course title and description. The syllabus includes the name and level of the course, such as Honors or Advanced. It includes the course term (e.g. one year or a semester) and a brief description of the course.

Objectives. The syllabus includes a list of course objectives. Those are the skills the teacher wants students to learn in the class.

Teacher's contact information. Teachers can be kind of picky about how, when, and where students may contact them. No surprise—they have many students to care for and a lot of work to do. If your teacher sets office hours or restricts modes of contact, they'll tell you about it in the syllabus. Respect their rules.

Expectations and attendance policies. Sometimes this section is just a repeat of the usual stuff, like "all students are expected to be seated by first bell," but it also holds information about the consequences of tardies and what constitutes an excused absence. It may set out whether and under what conditions, students are allowed to make up an assignment, homework or test, as well as rules regarding submission of late work and extra credit. Since even one zero can have a major impact on your overall grade in a class, know how to make up missed assignments, tests or quizzes. Whenever you are absent, mark the deadline for making up missed work in your planner.

Course calendar. The course calendar is more than just a list of dates and deadlines. It reveals the progression and pace of the class, and gives you a sense of the difficulty of the course. Compare the workload and pace of your various classes so you can anticipate periods of increased demand on your time and energy. In your planner, highlight days and weeks that you can expect to be very busy. Balance your workload and manage your time accordingly.

Tests and important dates. Write all assignments, exams, quizzes, and other dates and deadlines in your planner (or enter them into your electronic calendar if you use one.) Include recurring events too, like your English teacher's infamous Friday morning quizzes. For assignments or projects that will take extra time and effort, note the date you should begin working, as well as the date the project is due.

Note the date you should begin working, as well as the date the project is due.

Grading plan and policy. Heads up! This is probably the most important part of a syllabus. The teacher's grading plan reveals key details about grades and score calculations. In the grading plan your teacher tells you, straight up, what their learning and assignment priorities are, and how to get a good final grade in the class.

➜ **Method** - The grading plan identifies the method for grading assignments, quizzes and tests (numerical scores vs. letter grades.)

➜ **Formula** - The grading plan tells you the formula for converting numerical scores to letter grades, such as 87% = B+.

➜ **Categories** - Homework, papers, projects, tests, quizzes, class participation—basically anything that gets graded or scored, is categorized in the grading plan.

➜ **Weights** - For purposes of calculating a student's final grade in the class, weights are assigned to categories. For example, a teacher who places a high priority on homework will assign a heavier weight to homework completion scores. That tells you a good homework completion score is important to your final grade in a class.

Here's a tip: Use your teacher's grading plan as a workload and time management guide. If a teacher weights a test as 40% of a student's final grade in a class, and homework as 20% of the final grade, is it more productive to spend your time studying for a test, or making up a missing homework assignment for which you will receive 50% credit? Do the math! That doesn't mean you can skip your homework, but in a time crunch, put your effort into the categories your teacher values most. **Synching your time and effort to your teacher's priorities helps you successfully balance your workload and manage your time.**

Here's another tip: Using your teacher's grading plan, you can actually calculate the exact score you will need to achieve on any remaining tests and quizzes in order to earn your desired final grade in a class. Give it a try: Go to www.conquercollege.com (Amazing Grade Calculator) and plug in your teacher's categories and weights. Plug in your current scores, and calculate the score you must achieve on any upcoming graded assignment or quiz in order to earn your desire final grade in a class. **Knowing how to calculate your grade is a good study skill because it helps you gauge your progress in a class, and tells you how much time and effort you need to apply to an upcoming assignment or test to achieve or maintain a desired final grade.**

Using a grade calculator, you can target the exact score you need on a test or quiz to get your desired grade in a class.

Texts and supplies. School budgets are tight, so students are increasingly asked to provide their own supplemental resources and supplies, such as books for their literature class. The syllabus identifies the resources and supplies students need, and when they're due. You might even earn points by getting resources in on time, so pay attention to the due date.

Academic Honesty Policy. Don't assume that because you're such an angel you needn't be concerned with academic honesty. Your teacher may have a much broader definition than you of what constitutes cheating or plagiarism. Know your teacher's rules, definitions and consequences. As you move up into high school and college, academic honesty policies get more more complex, and students can inadvertently violate rules. The consequences of academic rules violations in high school and college are very serious indeed. Get into the habit of reading the syllabus to understand what's ok, and what may land you in hot water.

Name: _____

You Be the Teacher!

Do you have a hobby or skill? Do you play a sport? Can you play a musical instrument, train a dog, cook or ski? Imagine you are teaching a course in your hobby, sport, skill or talent. Draft a syllabus for your course.

Course title and description. *(What will you call your course? Is it a beginner course? Advanced? Honors? How long is it? One semester? Two or three weeks? In 40 words or less, write a description of your course.)*

_____

_____

_____

Objectives. *(What skills do you want your students to learn?)*

_____

_____

_____

Contact information and office hours. *(Do you use email? Is it OK for students to call you? Where's your office? Be specific about how, when and where students may contact you.)*

_____

_____

_____

Textbooks and supplies. *(List resources by title. You may invent a textbook title for this exercise; List supplies and materials. For example, if you're teaching a course on skateboarding, will students be required to bring a skateboard to class or will one be provided? What about helmets and elbow pads?)*

_____

_____

_____

Course calendar. *(Schedule two weeks of your course. List topics students will study and when the topics will be covered e.g. Week one: pp 22-41 – Skateboarding History. Will you schedule a field trip? Quiz and tests?)*

M	T	W	Th	F
M	T	W	Th	F

Tests and quizzes *(List 2 quizzes and 1 test. What will be tested? Will tests be essay, multiple choice, short answer, or T/F?)*

_____

_____

_____

Expectations and attendance policies. *(Be clear about your expectations and attendance policies. Define "excused" and "unexcused absences" and their consequences. State your rules for making up missed work.)*

_____

_____

_____

Grading plan *(How you will grade your students? Will you use letter grades? Numerical scores? If you use numerical scores what formula will apply? e.g. 85% = B. State your numerical score formula.)*

_____

_____

_____

Categories and weights *(What skills do you want your students to learn? List your grading categories and assign a weight to each based on its importance. Percentages should add up to 100.)*

Grading Plan: Skateboarding 101	
Skateboard maintenance	10%
Skating safety tips and rules	20%
Skating Terminology	10%
Half Pipe execution	15%
Class Participation	10%
Balance and Maneuvering	20%
History of Skateboarding	10%
Skate Park Design	5%

Category	Weight/Percentage of Grade
_____	_____
_____	_____
_____	_____
_____	_____
_____	_____
_____	_____
_____	_____
_____	_____
	100%

Academic honesty policy *(What constitutes plagiarism? What is cheating? What resources are students not allowed to use? Write the rules and consequences for violating academic honesty policies in your class.)*

_____

_____

_____

Name: _____

GAME PLAN

A **syllabus** is your teacher's **game plan** and you are responsible for knowing what's in it. Reading and understanding the syllabus is an important **pre-learning strategy** for middle school, high school, and college.

SYLLABUSTED!

1. It's the first day of school. Your algebra teacher just handed out the course syllabus. He "suggested" that students read it. If you know what's good for you (and you should, because you just finished a lesson about it) what will you do with the syllabus?

   a. Glance at it and toss it into your backpack until spring.
   b. Take a look at it sometime around finals to make sure you've done all the assigned reading.
   c. Read it carefully, put it in a sheet protector in your binder and use it as a guide for the course.
   d. Turn it over and use it as scratch paper.

2. You need to talk to your teacher about a grade you received on your English essay. Because of the short passing period, she prefers not to to talk to students immediately after class. She holds regular office hours. Where can you find her office hours, office location and contact information?

   _____

3. It's Sunday night. You were out of town all weekend at a soccer tournament. You're stressed because you have a biology quiz in the morning that's worth 15% of your grade in the class, and you haven't studied. You also have 10 vocab cards due tomorrow as part of your teacher's weekly vocab card assignment. The weekly vocabulary cards are worth 10% of your final grade and will take you about two hours to finish. In a time crunch, to which of these activities should you assign the highest priority? How can you tell?

   _____

   _____

4. Budget cuts have hit your school. Students have been asked to purchase their own books for their reading class. Your mother has asked you for the names of all of the books you will need so she can save money by buying them on the used book website. In what section of the syllabus can you find the list of books and the dates they are due?

   _____

5. You have six periods not including P.E. Each teacher has provided their students with a syllabus. You've put them into sheet protectors in your binders. You've downloaded copies. You've reviewed them and entered all test, quiz, project and other dates for each class into your planner for the entire semester. How can listing all of the dates and deadlines for all of your classes in a single place (your planner) help you be a better student? Once you list due dates and deadlines, what should you do?

_____

_____

_____

_____

True or False:

6. _____ You are an honest and good person, so you do not need to concern yourself with understanding academic honesty policies.

7. _____ The syllabus will tell you how many days you have to make up work after an excused absence.

8. _____ As you move up into high school and college, syllabuses become easier to understand and less relevant to your academic success in a class.

9. _____ The course calendar is a useful tool because it enables you to anticipate heavy work periods, which helps you balance your workload and manage your time.

10. _____ If you know your teacher's grading plan, you can actually calculate the score(s) you will need to get on remaining tests, quizzes and assignments in order to get a desired grade in a class.

✳ **Bonus:** You have an important math test next week. It's worth 20% of your grade. Here are your grades in the class so far:

	Score	Percent of final grade
(Quiz)	78	10
(Homework)	92	30
(Project)	88	20
(Test)	90	20
Upcoming Test	?	20

Go to www.conquercollege.com. Find your current average: _____

What score do you need to get on your upcoming test to bring your overall grade in the class up to an A? _____

Dear Parent or Caregiver,

Today I participated in my study skills class based on *The Middle School Student's Guide to Study Skills*. One of the best ways I can prepare for high school and college is to use good study skills whenever I am learning.

I learned:

1. A syllabus is like your teacher's _____. Students are like players on their team, responsible for _____ what's in it. Reading and understanding the syllabus is an excellent _____ strategy for all subjects.

2. The syllabus belongs in a sheet protector in your _____, and on the wall or bulletin board at your _____.

3. When you get a syllabus, review it for assignment, test, quiz and other important due _____ and _____. Write them in your _____. For long term assignments, note the date you should _____ working as well as the date the project is _____.

4. Any assignment or activity which receives a grade or score is categorized and given a _____ for purposes of calculating your final _____ in the class; Grade calculator programs, such as *www.conquercollege.com* allow students to plug in categories, weights and scores to predict their _____ grade in a class.

5. The weight your teacher assigns to a grading category indicates the _____ he or she has given that skill. Knowing your teacher's grading plan can help you manage your _____ and balance your _____.

Ask me about the skills I learned today! Your support at home will help me make good study skills daily habit.

Thank you for all you do for me every day.

Sincerely,

_____

GETTIN' YOUR SCHEMA ON!

*Bonus! Translate from Klingon:

Chapter 11 Learning Goals:

☐ define schema.
☐ state the benefits of activating schema as a pre-learning strategy.
☐ describe nine schema activation techniques.

Imagine you're an alien. You just crashed-landed your spaceship on earth. You weren't planning on coming here. You've had no prior contact with earthlings. You know zilch, zero, nada about life on earth.

OK, *that* might be an acceptable excuse for having no preexisting knowledge relevant to the human experience, but that's about the only excuse! Everyone else, even middle school students, have some prior knowledge about almost everything. It may be a little, it may be a lot – but it's there, inside their head.

Prior knowledge is called *schema* and it's uber-important, because schema provides links and context for new, incoming information. Schema is acquired as facts and ideas learned in a formal school setting and by life experience. By now you've had quite a bit of both. The fact is, students rarely learn something completely new. Textbooks, lessons and curriculum are designed to progressively build skills and knowledge. What you studied today in science has a connection to something you learned or studied before—maybe a week ago, maybe last year. You have a developed a schema in all subjects. In this chapter you'll learn how and why to activate your schema as a pre-learning strategy.

UNDER WHICH CONDITION IS IT PERMISSABLE TO CLAIM ZERO PRIOR KNOWLEDGE?

Are schemas related?

Schema does not confine itself to a subject or content area. It flows (or should flow) freely between subjects. A concept you learned in science can provide prior knowledge (schema) for a story in your literature class. A book you read in literature, a movie you saw over the summer, or a conversation you had with your grandpa, can provide a schema for a history topic. Let your schema flow between subjects!

What can your schema do for you?

When you're faced with the task of learning something new, don't assume you know nothing about it. *Get your schema on!* Activating your schema fires up Brainy's dendrites, axons and synapses to prepare them to link to new information. That improves comprehension, makes learning more meaningful, and information easier to recall.

What are schema activation techniques?

Teachers often start a lesson by reviewing a prior lesson, or by engaging students in a discussion or brainstorming session about the lesson topic. Those are schema activation techniques. It's like stretching before a workout. Those activities help your brain summon prior knowledge so it can more easily link to the new information. Here are some techniques you can use to activate your schema when you are learning on your own:

Class Notes

Class notes are like a "do-over" of important parts of a lesson, and are an excellent way to activate your schema. Review class notes prior to doing the homework for that class. Don't rush through your notes and toss them aside. Read them, asking *What was the objective of this lesson? What information did my teacher want me to take away from this class?* Circle unclear or incomplete information to identify potential weak links or gaps in your prior knowledge. **Reviewing your notes brings relevant information from your memory into your conscious thought.**

Brainstorm

Before reading new material, brainstorm what you already know about the topic. Don't jump in and start reading without a warm up. **Scribble down words, notes, names, ideas or events.** Don't worry about being neat. It's just a free-form technique to call up information from deep in your brain.

Old Worksheets and Quizzes

Don't toss out old worksheets and quizzes. **File them in your binder or study folder** at your workspace and review them to activate your schema whenever you are building on a skill you previously learned in a class.

K-W-L Chart

The K-W-L chart can be quite effective for activating prior knowledge. When you're reading something new or are assigned a difficult project, create a simple K-W-L chart on a piece of binder paper or index card. Under K, write a few short statements about what you already know—it's like a quick review. Under W, write what you want to know. Write a short summary of what you learned under L when you finish reading. **A series of K-W-L charts completed over several weeks makes an excellent study guide.**

KWL – *The Odyssey*

K	W	L
After leaving Calypso, Odysseus' ships are blown off course by Poseidon.	Does Odysseus survive?	Yes, he is rescued by the intervention of Athena and lands at Scheria.

KWL Charts completed over several weeks make a great study guide.

Preview Chapter Headings

Whether you're reading a textbook or handout from a teacher, **always preview the materials before reading**. Scan the text. Preview the headings. Read the chapter questions. That will help you get your schema on and prepare your brain to accept the information. (You'll learn more about pre-reading strategies in Chapter 13.)

Quiz Yourself

Self-questioning is like brainstorming, but at a deeper level. Instead of pulling up bits and pieces of factual information, self-questioning **recalls concepts and significant information**. Before starting an assignment, quiz yourself: *What do I already know about this? Can I summarize my knowledge or restate important concepts? Can I put information into chronological order? Can I make up a short story about what I know, such as summarizing a historical event, or biological process?*

Concept Mapping

You've probably used a concept map in class. Concepts are written in circles or boxes. Relationships between concepts are indicated by connecting lines. General concepts are at the top or center of the map. Details or specific concepts are placed below or around the general concept:

Concept maps are useful for stimulating the recall, organization and sequence of prior

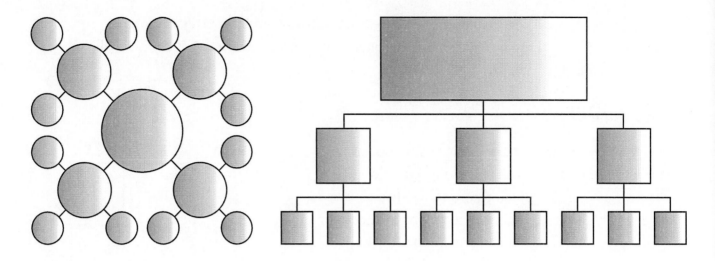

knowledge. They are particularly useful tools for visual learners. A timeline is a concept map that can help you recall the order or context of historical events. Go online and research "concept map templates." You'll find dozens of designs. Select a few that appeal to you and store copies in your binder and at your workspace. Use them for sorting out relationships, concepts or events, and review them to activate your schema.

Predict

Before starting an assignment or reading, ask yourself: *Based on what I already know, what do I predict will happen?* Make it a game: *What three things do I expect to happen and why?* Reward yourself when you're right.

Wikipedia/Google Searches

Wikipedia is not a citable source, but Wikipedia and online factual searches can help build schema. For example, build prior knowledge about a novel by researching facts about the author. What was the author like? What time period did they write in? Did their life experiences influence the writing of this novel? Explore the novel's setting. For example, if the novel is set in 1850 California, spend a few minutes on Wikipedia or a good history website, learning what was going on in California at that time. Look at old photos. Study a map of 1850 California. Pull up old newspaper articles. Create a mental vision of the novel's setting, so that the story runs like a movie in your head as you read. **Simple research takes only a few minutes, but goes a long way to build your schema and make new information meaningful and memorable.**

It takes only a few moments to use any one of these schema activation techniques, but it's worth the time. Activating your schema makes learning easier, and improves comprehension and recall. It's an excellent pre-learning study skill.

Name: _____

Activate Your Schema!

Earthling teachers often start a lesson by brainstorming about the lesson topic, or reviewing a prior lesson. Those are **schema activation techniques** to help students summon prior knowledge so they can more easily link to the new incoming information.

1. You now have a schema for *schema*. **Brainstorm** what you know about **schema** and **pre-learning schema activation techniques**. Scribble your notes and thoughts here. Don't worry about spelling or grammar.

2. Create a **K-W-L** Chart for Chapter 11: Gettin' Your Schema On. (Example:)

K	W	L

3. **Self-quiz.** If you quizzed yourself about schema and schema activation techniques, what three questions would you ask? Write your questions and answers.

Q. _____

A. _____

Q. _____

A. _____

Q. _____

A. _____

4. Review Chapter 11. Complete the **concept map** of schema activation strategies.

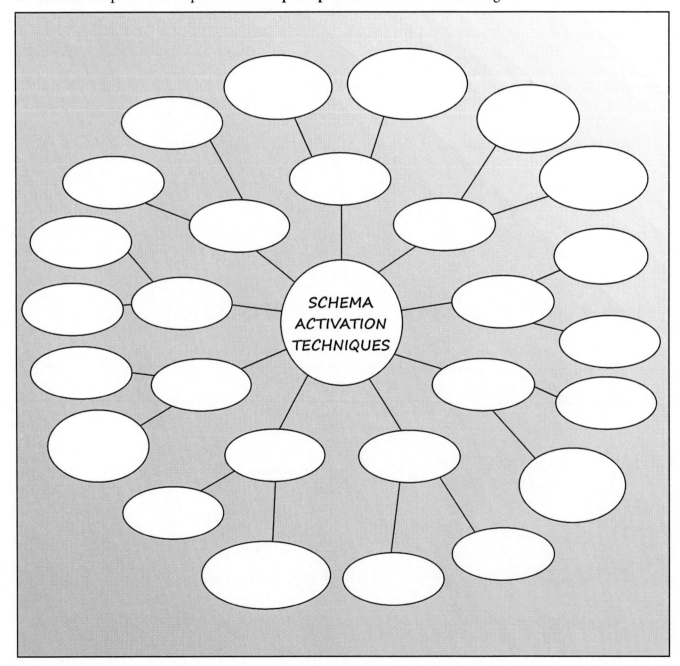

Name: _____

Gettin' Your Schema On

Prior knowledge of something is called **schema**. Schema provides links for newer, incoming information, making it easier to remember. Activating schema is a good pre-learning strategy because it improves comprehension, makes learning more meaningful, and fires up your brain's dendrites, axons and synapses to link to new information.

1. Your teacher just assigned a book called *The Pearl*. Other than the fact it was written by a guy named John Steinbeck, you know nothing about it. How can you build a schema for *The Pearl*?

    _____

    _____

    _____

2. Your teacher wants you to read one chapter of *The Pearl* each night. What techniques can you use to activate your schema of the characters and prior events in the book?

    _____

    _____

    _____

3. Kelly's algebra class just started a new chapter. Her teacher said this chapter builds on the concepts and formulas students learned in the prior chapter. What techniques can Kelly use to test her prior knowledge of concepts and ideas before moving on to the new chapter?

    _____

    _____

    _____

4. By the time Katie gets home from softball practice and starts her science homework, she can't remember much of what she learned in class that day. What techniques can she use to activate his schema of the day's science lesson?

    _____

    _____

    _____

5. Emilio's science teacher is totally into innovation and invention. She wants students to write an essay comparing the twentieth century tech revolution with the Industrial Revolution. Emilio studied the Industrial Revolution in history. How can his prior knowledge of history help him with his science

essay? What techniques can he use to summon his schema of names, dates, events and inventions of the Industrial Revolution?

_____

_____

_____

_____

6. What schema activation techniques are effective for organizing data or sequencing information?

_____

_____

7. Britta's literature class will soon read *One Thousand Paper Cranes,* by Ishii Takayuki. It is a story about a young victim of the atomic bombing of Hiroshima. In history last year, Britta studied about WWII. In science, she learned about radiation and nuclear energy. What prior knowledge might Britta have which can make the story more meaningful to her? Suggest some schema activation techniques for Britta.

_____

_____

_____

8. Have you ever taken a road trip through the west and actually looked up from your video game long enough to observe your surroundings? Have you ever hiked through a forest or camped by a river? How might these activities add to a student's schema of American history?

_____

_____

_____

_____

9. Have you ever watched a lightning storm or experienced a hurricane? How might that add to your schema for science and math?

_____

_____

_____

10. How is knowledge like water?

_____

_____

_____

Dear Parent or Caregiver,

Today I participated in my study skills class based on *The Middle School Student's Guide to Study Skills*. One of the best ways I can prepare for high school and college is to use good study skills whenever I am learning.

I learned:

1. Knowledge links to _____; Prior knowledge can be in the form of facts and ideas acquired in a formal _____ setting. It can also be the result of _____ experience.

2. A student rarely learns something completely new. Textbooks, lessons and curriculum are designed to _____ build skills and knowledge.

3. Activating your _____ before learning new stuff is an excellent pre-_____ strategy.

4. Activating schema helps students identify _____ in knowledge which, if not addressed can weaken learning links.

5. Techniques for activating and building schema are:

    _____

    _____

    _____

    _____

Ask me about the skills I learned today! Your support at home will help me make good study skills daily habit.

Thank you for all you do for me every day.

Sincerely,

_____

Name: _____

WHAT DID YOU LEARN ABOUT PRE-LEARNING STRATEGIES?

1. What are the benefits of a *homework routine?*

   _____

   _____

   _____

   _____

2. Many students don't like doing homework, but it's important to set aside negative feelings about it, like anger, impatience, and resentment because these feelings:

   a. prevent you from working efficiently
   b. make it difficult to focus
   c. affect the quality of your work.
   d. all of the above

3. Good lighting at your workspace is important because it:

   a. improves productivity and mental alertness
   b. illuminates the correct answers
   c. makes you look fabulous while you study
   d. None of the above

4. State two advantages of a workspace that is adequately stocked with supplies.

   _____

   _____

5. Quinn loves technology. She keeps in all of her devices within reach as she does homework. She has a laptop, iPod, cell phone and Xbox. She plays games on her cell phone, texts friends, surfs YouTube and updates his Facebook status as she works. Now her grades are falling and her parents are threatening to take away ALL of her tech toys until winter break if she doesn't get a handle on it. What's your advice to Quinn about her workspace?

   _____

   _____

   _____

   _____

6. What information would you not find in a syllabus?

   a. School dress code
   b. Teacher's office hours and contact information
   c. Expectations, classroom rules and honesty policy
   d. Grading plan and score calculation summaries

7. List the steps you should take when you receive a syllabus from your teacher:

   _____

   _____

   _____

   _____

8. How can you can use a syllabus to your advantage?

   a. align your time and workload management
      with your teacher's priorities and expectations
   b. compare your workload with other classes to
      anticipate periods of heavy demand
   c. know how to make up for absences and missing
      assignments
   d. all of the above

9. What are the benefits of activating your schema before learning new material?

   _____

   _____

   _____

10. Activating your schema is an excellent *pre-learning strategy* because it can make you a faster, more efficient and effective student. Which of these are *schema activation techniques*?

    a. brainstorming, KWL chart, self-questioning
    b. reviewing notes, predicting, reviewing old quizzes and worksheets
    c. prior chapter review, concept mapping
    d. all of the above

NOTES

NOTES

ACTIVE LEARNING IN A PASSIVE LEARNING WORLD

Learning seems like the ultimate passive activity doesn't it? After all, it involves little to zero physical activity. More often than not, students sit at their workspace or in a classroom, verbally or visually receiving information from a textbook or a teacher. That's not very active. Can learning be active?

In the early 20th century, learning was all about sitting quietly at a desk, passively accepting information from a teacher or textbook. Then a psychologist named Jean Piaget (pi-yah-zhey) came along and proposed something pretty radical. He proposed that a mind that actively questions, explores, and assesses information as it learns, learns more deeply and more meaningfully. Piaget believed that the student who searches for, and actively constructs an answer, rather than simply accepting the answer handed to them, is a better learner. Piaget called this active learning theory *constructivism*: Active learners take in information and experiences, compare them to previous ideas and experiences, add to or alter beliefs, and *construct a personal base of knowledge.*

In the next few chapters, you'll explore *active learning.* It's not about running around your classroom—it's about opening your mind and heart to learning.

Chapter 12 Learning Goals:

- ☐ define constructivism.
- ☐ compare the traits of active vs. passive learners.
- ☐ determine whether you are an active learner.

What are the benefits of active learning?

Active learners:

→ build a large **schema**

→ **remember more** of what they learn because it has personal meaning to them

→ are **self-confident** students

→ are **motivated** to learn

→ use their knowledge to **find creative solutions** to problems

→ seek not just the right answer, **but *why* an answer is right or wrong**.

What are the traits of a passive vs. active learner?

Read the chart on page 127. Compare the traits of an active learner with the traits of a passive learner. Then think about your own learning. Are you an active or passive learner? If you find yourself identifying more with the traits of a passive learner, make a plan to activate your learning! Here are some suggestions:

1. Join a school club or activity that brings learning alive, such as your school's environmental club, or world cultures association.

2. Read more!

3. Read more non-fiction.

4. Watch a documentary.

5. Be curious! Investigate random topics for fun.

6. Study maps.

7. Read or watch travelogs.

8. Talk to your counselor about planning for college.

Take advantage of the many opportunities available to you which enable you to construct your personal base of knowledge. It's a good study skill for middle school, high school, and college.

THE ACTIVE LEARNER... ☺	THE PASSIVE LEARNER... ☹
Connects. An active learner knows that what they learn in the classroom has actual **connections to the real world**. It's true! Learning comes alive in plays and rallies, at political meetings and rallies, at tide pools, community museums, on hiking trails, at science exhibits, and academic competitions. Learning plays out every day in real life in the news. Active learners **construct** their personal knowledge by connecting it to their schemas and to the real world around them.	**Isolates.** A passive learner **isolates** their learning from the real world and learns only in the classroom. A passive learner would reject a weekend visit to a museum, ignore a plea from a local charity for volunteers, turn down an invitation to see a play, and consider attending a community council meeting a waste of time. Don't isolate your learning. Seek out opportunities to connect to the world outside the classroom.
Takes it personally. What you learn now and how well you learn it will impact your later life. The active learner makes learning their **personal responsibility.** They pursue strategies for better learning, including adopting good study and organizational skills. They set education goals, and work around obstacles to achieve them. Active learners take college preparation seriously. Active learners understand that they control their learning.	**Avoids responsibility.** A passive learner expects their teacher or school to be 100% responsible for their learning. Many students are in less-than-ideal academic settings. A passive learner assumes that the poor learning environment is **out of their control.** *Own your learning and you can overcome almost any obstacle.* Read books. Watch the news. Join an academic club. Talk to your counselor about college. Take an honors class. What you learn and how far you go in life is up to *you.*
Rejects passivity. Active learners question, analyze, dissect ideas, reflect on, debate, wonder, disagree, compare...Yes, they actually **think** about what they've learned. They reach beyond just knowing the right answer to fully understanding why the answer is right.	**Learns like a zombie.** Learning by **rote and memorization** with little real understanding of a topic is a classic passive learner trait. Passive learners are more concerned about their grades than about actually learning something.
Looks inward. The active learner looks within for motivation. **Intrinsic motivation** can come from something as simple as the enjoyment of learning, or pride in accomplishment. It may also come from knowing that learning and actively using your education are the keys to meeting your life goals.	**Depends on rewards.** A passive learner depends on **extrinsic motivators** like rewards or gifts of money to learn. In high school and college, extrinsic rewards are few and far between. A passive learner may suffer a motivational crisis when the rewards run dry. Developing your personal intrinsic reward system builds mental toughness.
Engages. The active learner knows that intellectual conversation won't kill them. The active learner has the **confidence** to engage in intellectual discussion and debate.	**Hides out.** A passive learner keeps their intelligence **in the closet.** Let it out!
Prepares. Everyone's busy, and it can be hard to keep up with responsibilities. The active learner knows that their job is to be a good student. They prepare for class by **doing their job:** reading, studying and doing their homework.	**Slacks.** A passive learner comes to class **unprepared,** not knowing what's going on and not caring. They don't do the reading. They don't study much. What they don't realize is that even a boring class is a lot less boring when you're prepared.
Is open-minded. An active learner has an **open mind.** That doesn't mean they adopt every new idea that comes their way, or change their core values. Active learners are open to new ideas, even if it's just for the purpose of expanding their schemas.	**Grows mental mold.** A passive learner has a **closed mind.** Like an old gym bag, it's dark in there and starts to stink.

Name: _____

What Would the Active Learner Do?

An active learner questions and explores as they learn. They build large schemas and remember more of what they learn because it has personal meaning to them. They are self-reliant and motivated students. Read the questions below and select the answer that best describes how an active learner would react to the situation. Be prepared to discuss the active learning principles and opportunities, and how <u>you</u> would react in a similar situation.

1. At a wedding reception, Alison is seated next to her second cousin's adorable Great Auntie Crizelda. In the course of conversation, Auntie C mentions that she grew up in Alabama in the 1930's. What a coincidence! Ali's literature class is reading *To Kill a Mockingbird* which takes place in Alabama in the very same era. Auntie C clearly likes to gab, and still has all her marbles. If Ali is an active learner, what will she do?

   a. Realize that Auntie C may have some interesting and relevant knowledge, mention the book she's reading, and politely engage her in a conversation about life in 1930s Alabama.

   b. Excuse herself and head for the buffet.

   c. Assume Auntie C doesn't know anything and wouldn't want to talk to her about it anyway.

   d. Fail to see a connection.

Will Ali miss a great opportunity to connect her learning to the real world?

2. Elena's friend Katie is in hot water with her parents. After seeing her mid-term grades they are convinced she is a slacker. As a last resort to motivate her to learn, they've offered her $20 for every B and $25.00 for every A on her report card. Unlike Katie, Elena is an active learner. Her advice to Katie includes <u>each</u> of the following EXCEPT:

   a. "Since the best long term motivation is intrinsic, find something within yourself that inspires you to learn. It can be a love of learning, or a personal challenge to do better, or wanting a bright future including college and a good career."

   b. "Money and gifts are temporary fixes for a serious motivational problem."

   c. "Girl, hold out for more money!"

   d. "This will do little to correct your slacker tendencies."

What's Elena's advice to Katie?

3. Jason is uncomfortable in his social studies class. Once a week the class discusses a current social issue. Some kids come from different backgrounds, and Jason thinks they have the weirdest opinions. They say stuff that neither he, nor any member of his family would ever agree with. As an active learner, he should:

    a. Tell them to keep their opinions to themselves.

    b. Just keep tellin' himself that his opinions are right and to not get caught up in all their weirdness.

    c. Say nothing. Try not to listen or let it bother him.

    d. Keep his mind open! Jason doesn't have to buy into their opinions, or change his core values, but knowing how others think and understanding why they think it (right or wrong) is a tasty morsel of knowledge to add to his schema, and an opportunity to practice articulating his own ideas.

Jason is uncomfortable with other people's opinions.

4. The teachers at U.B. Smart Middle School are emphasizing high school and college readiness, so they're challenging students to s-t-r-e-t-c-h their brains and become active learners. They want students to question, analyze, dissect ideas, reflect, debate, wonder, disagree, and compare! This makes Max unhappy. He's prefers rote and recite learning. He reviews the materials and memorizes for tests. He worries his test scores will fall if he changes how he learns. Explain to Max why it's worth embracing his teachers' active learning challenge.

Max isn't sure he likes this new "active" approach to learning.

_____

_____

_____

_____

5. Design a word wall with active learning terms from the chart on page 127.

Name: _____

Action Hero or Purely Passive?

Students who actively question, explore and assess information as they learn are better learners. They build larger schemas, and are self-confident, motivated students. How about you? On a scale of 1 to 10 (1 = "No, not at all" and 10 = "Totally and absolutely!") how active a learner are you?

Do you connect?

Do you connect your learning in school to the real world all around you? Whether it's by going to a museum, analyzing a current event, volunteering, or getting involved in a community project, do you involve yourself in projects or activities offering real world experience?

| 10 | 9 | 8 | 7 | 6 | 5 | 4 | 3 | 2 | 1 |

Are you responsible for you?

How likely are you to search for resources to supplement, clarify or expand on what you learn in class? A student who accepts personal responsibility for his or her own learning, works to overcome obstacles to learning, and puts serious thought and planning into their academic future, like preparing for college. Do you feel *and act* responsible for your own learning and academic future?

| 10 | 9 | 8 | 7 | 6 | 5 | 4 | 3 | 2 | 1 |

Is your brain engaged?

Is your mind actively engaged as you learn? Do you question and analyze? Do you reflect on your studies? Do you consider learning as more than just short term memorization for a test?

| 10 | 9 | 8 | 7 | 6 | 5 | 4 | 3 | 2 | 1 |

Does your motivation come from within?

If you rely too much on external motivators like gifts, praise, money or even threats of punishment to learn or study, you could face a motivational crisis when the motivation well runs dry. The most reliable source of motivation comes from *within*. How intrinsically motivated are you to learn and achieve?

| 10 | 9 | 8 | 7 | 6 | 5 | 4 | 3 | 2 | 1 |

Is your intellect out of the closet?

When was the last time you discussed a political issue or read about a current global event just because you wanted to know about it? How likely are you to engage in intellectual discussion, debate, or analysis outside of the classroom?

10   9   8   7   6   5   4   3   2   1

Are you the King or Queen of Slackerdom?

Preparing for class means keeping up with the assigned reading, doing your homework and whatever else your teacher assigns, and bringing required materials and attitude to class. When you get to class, how prepared are you to learn?

10   9   8   7   6   5   4   3   2   1

Is your mind open?

Do you enjoy experiencing other people's opinions and hearing about their beliefs even if you don't agree with them? Do you appreciate the value of new information, even if it's just for the purpose of expanding your schema?

10   9   8   7   6   5   4   3   2   1

TOTAL _____

ACTION HERO! **58-70**

SEMI-SLACKER **42-57**

PURELY PASSIVE **21-41**

CHECK YOUR PULSE. YOU'RE FLATLINING! **Below 20**

Dear Parent or Caregiver,

Today I participated in my study skills class based on *The Middle School Student's Guide to Study Skills*. One of the best ways I can prepare for high school and college is to use good study skills whenever I am learning.

I learned:

1. Piaget's Theory of _____ holds that students learn best when they take in information, compare it to previous information and experiences, form beliefs, and construct their own personal _____ of the world.

2. A good strategy for constructing personal knowledge is to seek out ways to _____ what you learn in school to the real world all around you. Learning comes alive in: _____

   _____

3. Don't expect your teacher to be _____% responsible for your learning. You have a great deal of personal _____ over it, even in a less than ideal academic or home setting. Take responsibility for your learning and your personal academic future. Own your learning and you can overcome almost any _____.

4. Active learners take in information and ideas then _____, _____, _____, _____, _____, _____...!

5. Engaging in an intellectual discussion debate or analysis will not _____ you! It might even be fun.

Ask me about the skills I learned today! Your support at home will help me make good study skills daily habit.

Thank you for all you do for me every day.

Sincerely,

_____

NOTES

BATTLE PLAN SQ3R

As WWII raged in the 1940's, the United States military was responsible for training millions of soldiers for battle. Upon enlistment, soldiers were sent to basic training and assigned manuals, guidelines, and training materials to read. Soldiers had to quickly master volumes of information, then head overseas into battle. Knowing that their men's survival depended on how well they comprehended and remembered the information in the training materials, the military began using **SQ3R**.

Was SQ3R a secret weapon? No. Brainwashing? No. A battle plan? Sort of. SQ3R is a battle plan for...*reading!* The military began using an active reading technique developed by Francis Robinson, a professor of psychology at Ohio State University. SQ3R (also known as SQRRR) enabled WWII soldiers to read training manuals quickly, with improved comprehension and retention of content. It was so successful that after the war, it began to be taught in American schools.

In this chapter you'll learn how to be an active reader using SQ3R reading strategies. If it was good enough to beat the Nazi's, it's good enough for you!

Chapter 13 Learning Goals:

☐ explain the benefits of active reading.

☐ describe SQ3R active reading techniques.

☐ apply SQ3R active reading techniques to an expository passage.

When do you use SQ3R?

Have you ever noticed that it's easier to read a novel, like a Harry Potter book, than a textbook? Why? Isn't reading just *reading*? Why is reading nonfiction more difficult than reading fiction?

Reading for information, like reading a textbook, is called *expository reading*. Reading for pleasure, like reading a good story, or a gossip or sports magazine is called *ludic* (loo-dik) *reading*. Reading for pleasure is relaxing and usually doesn't take much mental effort, especially when you get caught up in a story. **Expository reading is more difficult because you are on a mission to obtain information and achieve certain learning goals.** That requires effort and a special set of reading skills.

When you read expository text, you are on a mission to obtain information and achieve certain goals.

As you move up into high school and college, your academic success will depend on your ability to read, comprehend, and recall a great deal of nonfiction, expository text. **Studies show that if you open up your textbook and begin reading without preparation, you'll remember less than 30% of what you read by the next week.** Good study skills include using special reading strategies to improve your comprehension and memory of nonfiction text. Guess what? SQ3R provides these very skills!

What is SQ3R?

SQ3R stands for:

SURVEY ➜ QUESTION ➜ READ ➜ RECITE ➜ REFLECT!

SURVEY

Expository reading requires a patient approach. Don't plunge right in and start reading. Begin with a **survey of the chapter**. The survey gives you the big picture of what you will read. Note the title. Turn the pages and preview headings and subheadings. Consider what they reveal about the text's purpose. Check out illustrations, charts, and photos. Flip through the pages and survey bolded words. Turn to the end of the chapter and read the summary. Finally, observe how the information is organized. It is organized that way for a reason. Organize your thoughts about the content the same way.

QUESTION

Based on information acquired from the survey, ask yourself questions to activate your schema: *What do I know about this topic? What's the big picture? What context does this information fit into?* Textbooks often provide questions or state learning objectives at the beginning or end of a chapter. **Read the questions or objectives.** They identify the important ideas and topics you will read for.

READ

Expository reading is an active process requiring concentration and energy. Be attentive. Be focused. Don't let words just slip past your eyeballs. **Read for ideas, and with the intent to understand.** Identify the point of each section. Write out answers to the chapter questions as you read. Review pictures, charts, maps, and illustrations to help you create a visual image of the content in your mind.

RECITE

It may feel weird at first, but reciting answers aloud is one of the best ways to activate and strengthen neural pathways for memory. Read and answer the chapter questions aloud. **Explain the main concept(s) in your own words.** Do it again, trying not to look at the book. Tell yourself a short story about what you read, with a beginning, middle and end. If you can't explain an idea or concept, go back, reread that section and try again.

REFLECT

Close the book. Reflect on what you read. This gives Brainy a chance to sort and organize the information. Ask yourself: *What do I now know about this subject? How does this information fit in with what I already knew? What might my teacher ask me in class or on a test? What do I need to reread for clarification? Are there any gaps in what I can recall?*

Whenever you're assigned expository reading, remember your battle plan for comprehension and retention of content: *SQ3R!*

Name: _____

I ♥ SQ3R

In high school and college, your academic success will depend on your ability to read, comprehend, and recall nonfiction text. Active reading strategies help students understand more of what they read, and retain it in memory longer. Whenever you're assigned reading from your textbook, follow these strategies: **Survey, Question, Read, Recite and Reflect!**

Survey

What is the **title** of the chapter? _____

List one **heading**: _____

List one **subheading**: _____

Did you review **charts and diagrams?** _____ Illustrations/photos? _____ **Bolded words?** _____

Does the chapter have a **summary?** _____ Read it and list the **main ideas**:

_____

_____

_____

Return to the beginning of the chapter. Turn the pages. Observe how the chapter is **organized**. Describe how you will organize the information in your mind: _____

_____

_____

Question

Ask yourself: *Based on the survey, what do I know about what I am about to read? What do the title, headings and subheadings tell me? Can I fit this information into my schema? Can I see a "big picture"? Write your answers here:*

_____

_____

Review chapter questions or learning objectives. Identify the **ideas** you will read for:

_____

_____

Read

Did you read **actively**, with **concentration and energy?**	yes	no
Did you read with the **intent to understand?**	yes	no
Did you **identify the point** of each section?	yes	no
Did you read for **ideas?**	yes	no

Read for ideas with the intent to understand.

Students who use highlighters: Did you **read all the way through a paragraph** before highlighting a passage or text?	yes	no
Did you **write down the answers** to the chapter questions as you read?	yes	no

Recite

Did you read the chapter questions and **recite the answers aloud?**	yes	no
Did you put **important concepts into your own words?**	yes	no
Can you **summarize the information** with a beginning, middle and end?	yes	no

Reflect

How does this new information **fit into your schema?**

_____

_____

Do you need to **reread** any part(s) of the chapter for **clarification** or to **fill gaps in knowledge?**

_____

_____

Write three questions about important **ideas or concepts** from the chapter (including charts and diagrams) that you might be asked on a **test:**

1. _____

_____

2. _____

_____

3. _____

_____

BATTLE PLAN: SQ3R

ATTENTION! During WWII, the United States military trained millions of soldiers for battle. Before going overseas, soldiers went to basic training where they were given manuals and training materials. Their survival depended on their ability to learn the content quickly and thoroughly. The military used SQ3R to improve soldiers' reading comprehension and retention. SQ3R is a battle plan for active reading! Your mission: Decode the SQ3R steps and describe your battle plan.

UVSREY = _____

_____

_____

_____

_____

TNUISQEO = _____

_____

_____

_____

_____

DERA = _____

_____

_____

_____

_____

_____

CTERIE = _____

_____

_____

_____

_____

_____

TRFLCEE = _____

_____

_____

_____

_____

_____

Dear Parent or Caregiver,

Today I participated in my study skills class based on *The Middle School Student's Guide to Study Skills*. One of the best ways I can prepare for high school and college is to use good study skills whenever I am learning.

I learned:

1. As students move up into high school and college, their academic success increasingly depends on their ability to read, comprehend, and recall _____ text.

2. SQ3R or stands for: _____ _____
   _____ _____ and
   _____

3. For SQ3R, *survey* means: Look at the chapter _____,
   _____ and _____. Get the _____
   picture! Note how the content is _____.

4. For SQ3R, *recite* means to answer questions _____ and put important ideas and concepts into _____,
   without looking at the book.

5. _____ is an essential SQ3R strategy which gives the brain an opportunity to sort and organize information. Students should consider how the information fits into their _____, what they might be asked on a _____, and whether there are _____ in information (indicating the need to reread.)

Ask me about the skills I learned today! Your support at home will help me make good study skills daily habit.

Thank you for all you do for me every day.

Sincerely,

_____

NOTES

HEY, ARE YOU LISTENING?

Is there a difference between *hearing* and *listening?* We use the words interchangeably, but do they mean the same thing? Is "Do you hear me?" the same as "Are you listening to me?"

Hearing and listening are **not** the same:

> To *hear* means: to *perceive or apprehend by the ear.*

> To *listen* means: to hear something *with thoughtful attention and give it consideration.*

Hearing is a passive activity; listening is not.

As a student, much of what you are responsible for learning is delivered through lecture or spoken instructions. In high school and college, lectures will be longer and more complex. Spoken instructions will be quick and concise. When your teacher speaks, you should always hear "with thoughtful attention and consideration." That's right – you should *listen.*

Do you know that good listening skills are not automatic? Developing good listening skills requires practice, effort, and discipline. It's important to your success as a student that you develop active listening skills in the classroom.

Chapter 14 Learning Goals:

☐ state the benefits of active listening.

☐ describe active listening strategies.

☐ identify personal behaviors and attitudes which prevent active listening in the classroom.

What is active listening?

Active listening is a method of listening in which the listener:

→ focuses **all of their attention** on what the speaker is saying.

→ listens for **concepts and ideas.**

→ checks for understanding by **interpreting concepts in their own words.**

→ actively **avoids distraction.**

→ **monitors the quality** of their listening.

What are the benefits of active listening?

As as student, much of what you must learn and remember is delivered verbally through lecture or oral instruction. Active listening strategies improve comprehension and increase the retention of verbal information. Active listening also prevents students from misunderstanding content, or missing important instructions.

What are active listening strategies?

Decide to listen.

Yes, it's that simple. Make a conscious decision to listen to your teacher. Clear your mind of your own thoughts. Control your mind from wandering. Don't zone out. Focus, and actively try to absorb what your teacher says.

ACTIVE LISTENING

1. Decide to listen.

2. Listen for ideas.

3. Make eye contact.

4. Value visuals.

5. Make connections.

Listen for ideas.

Don't just hear words—listen for ideas. Teachers speak in ideas. They may have different lecture styles, but they are usually clear about the main points they want to get across to students, and don't drop information bombs without warning. Main points or ideas are often preceded by phrases emphasizing the importance of the information such as:

"The most important thing is…" or
"The main characteristics are…" or
"This is what I want you to know…" or
"This will be on the test…"

Make eye contact.

Eye contact tells your teacher that you're awake and listening. It also helps to keep your mind from wandering. Facial expressions and gestures convey thoughts too, so keep your eyes on your teacher to improve your understanding of the subtleties of verbal information.

Value visuals.

Senses work together: *Eyes support ears; ears support eyes.* When your teacher uses power points, videos, overheads or other visuals, look at them! Copy important visuals in your notes (unless your teacher posts the image on the class webpage.) Visual images make verbal content more meaningful and illustrate principles of the lecture.

Make connections.

As you listen, make connections between what your teacher says and what you already know. Get your schema on! Search your mental data base for connections to prior knowledge. Interpret concepts as they are presented. If you can't make a connection or interpret a concept, raise your hand and ask. Odds are other students aren't getting it either. Don't sit and let information you don't understand wash over you. Get involved and ask!

What prevents students from actively listening in the classroom?

Certain behaviors, habits, and attitudes can interfere with a student's ability to actively listen. Usually, students are completely unaware of the problem. For example, a lack of self-control can cause a loss of focus. Boredom is an attitude, and it distracts students from learning. Students can also get side-tracked by something a teacher says that they don't understand. Others lose focus on the message when there is something about the messenger that bothers them. The poor acoustical quality of the classroom, or noise from outside can interfere with listening. **Active listeners monitor the quality of their listening.** They self-correct behaviors that prevent active listening, and seek assistance when they are prevented from listening because of noise or other interferences outside of their personal control.

Boredom is an attitude that distracts students from listening.

While hearing is a passive activity, listening is not. Active listening requires effort and concentration, but it can greatly improve your comprehension, and ability to recall verbally delivered content. Get into the habit of using active listening skills in class. It's a great study skill for middle school, high school and college.

Name: _____

What's Holding YOU Back from Being an Active Listener in the Classroom?

The concept of active listening is simple: Decide to listen, listen for ideas, make eye contact, pay attention to visuals aids, and make schema connections! So why are so many students poor listeners? What behaviors, habits and attitudes **prevent** students from actively listening? What's holding you back from being an active listener in the classroom? (Check all that apply.)

1. **When I'm in class listening to my teacher I often:**

    ☐ play with a pencil or pen.
    ☐ look around at friends.
    ☐ text.
    ☐ get lost in my own thoughts (it's so beautiful in there!)
    ☐ flirt with the hot guy/gal next to me.
    ☐ finish (or start) homework for that (or another) class.
    ☐ study the insides of my eyelids.
    ☐ zone out.

    If you checked any of these boxes, poor **self-control** is holding you back from being an active listener. Do you know that the human mind processes information much faster than the normal rate of speech? In the lag time between the listener's processing and the speaker's speaking, listeners can get distracted and lose focus. **Make a conscious decision to listen.** Resist the urge to talk to a friend, flirt, text, or lose your concentration. Active listening takes practice and self-control. In high school and college you will need a great deal of self-control to succeed. Practice developing **zen-like control** over your thought processes and impulses. Start by actively listening in class.

2. **When I'm in class listening to my teacher, my usual attitude is:**

    ☐ disagreement.
    ☐ disinterest.
    ☐ boredom (I've heard it before…)
    ☐ natural resistance to whatever they say.

    If you checked any of these boxes, your **attitude** is getting the better of your listening skills. **Never assume** you already know what your teacher is going to say. Studies show that when people do this, they often hear what is expected, rather than what is actually said. If you disagree with something your teacher says, make a mental note but **keep listening!** Don't stop to form a rebuttal in your head. Stay focused. **Don't let boredom distract you from listening.** Boredom is an attitude. Active listening requires a positive attitude, and a conscious effort to generate an interest in the topic even when it's not all that interesting to you.

3. **I can't concentrate if my teacher:**

- ☐ has a weird outfit on.
- ☐ is having another bad hair day.
- ☐ has an annoying voice.
- ☐ is a substitute I don't know.

If you checked any of these boxes, **bias** holds you back from being an active listener. Remember, **it's the message, not the messenger!** Don't be distracted by physical appearance or other traits of a speaker. Active listening skills require a listener to be **objective**, not judgemental. Focus on the information.

4. **When my teacher says something I don't understand, I:**

- ☐ do not raise my hand to ask for clarification
- ☐ forget about it and move on
- ☐ obsess over it, stop listening and panic because I may have missed something important!
- ☐ would be too embarrassed to ask about it.

If you checked any of these boxes, poor **self-advocacy** skills are holding you back from being an active listener. If your teacher permits students to ask questions during instruction, or periodically stops to check for understanding, don't hesitate to **ask for clarification** if you need it. If your teacher prefers that you wait, don't panic or get distracted by your need to know. Jot the question down on your notes and **keep listening**. If you're too shy to ask, get tongue-tied or struggle with your English skills under pressure, **write the question on a piece of paper**, raise your hand and read it.

5. **When my teacher provides a visual aid like a power point, outline or document on the whiteboard or overhead projector, I:**

- ☐ continue to look at my teacher, at the floor, at the ceiling…basically anywhere but at the visual aid.
- ☐ use that time to do any of the activities listed in Question 1 above.
- ☐ fail to realize how important the visual aid is for illustrating the point my teacher is making.
- ☐ usually can't see it because something is in the way.
- ☐ struggle to copy down every word or image.

If you checked any of these boxes, poor **sensory support** holds you back from being an active listener. Part of listening is looking. Sensory data interacts: *your eyes support your ears; your ears support your eyes.* The result is improved comprehension and memory. If your view is blocked and you can't clearly see the image, politely ask your teacher if you can **move to a better vantage point**. If the image is blurry (but no one else seems to notice) you may need an **eye exam**. If you're too busy copying every detail on the slide, stop! Ask your teacher to **post the visual aids** on the class web page so you can review them again later.

Name: _____

Hey, Are You Actively Listening?

> Good listening skills are not automatic. Being an active listener requires practice and self-control. The benefits of active listening include better comprehension and improved retention.

1. What's the difference between *hearing* and *listening*?

   _____

   _____

   _____

2. Omar's teacher created a power point presentation demonstrating how to solve a difficult algebra equation. Omar can't see it because his teacher's head is in the way of the whiteboard. What should he do and why?

   _____

   _____

   _____

3. In class, don't just hear your teacher's words. Active listening means listening for _____.

   a. the bell to ring
   b. the correct answer
   c. ideas
   d. P.A. announcements

4. Active listeners make _____ between what their teacher says and what they already know.

   a. notes
   b. eye contact
   c. arrangements
   d. connections

5. In high school and college, much of what students are responsible for learning is delivered (verbally) by lecture or verbal instruction. That means active listening is an essential skill. Benefits of active listening include all of the following, except:

   a. better comprehension
   b. increased retention
   c. avoidance of misunderstandings
   d. automatic "A" on the test

6. *Refer to the worksheet on pages 148-149. Review your answers.* What's holding you back from being an active listener in the classroom? (Circle all that apply)

   a. poor self-control
   b. attitude
   c. bias
   d. poor self-advocacy
   e. poor sensory support

7. *"Active listeners monitor the quality of their listening."* Write a plan for addressing your active listening weaknesses and monitoring the quality of your listening in the classroom.

   _____

   _____

   _____

   _____

   _____

   _____

8. Teachers have different lecture styles, but generally don't drop main ideas or information bombs without a warning. What are some phrases *your* teachers use to draw their students' attention to important information?

Dear Parent or Caregiver,

Today I participated in my study skills class based on *The Middle School Student's Guide to Study Skills*. One of the best ways I can prepare for high school and college is to use good study skills whenever I am learning.

I learned:

1. *"To hear"* and *"to listen"* are not _____! To hear is *to perceive or apprehend by the ear*; To listen is *to hear with thoughtful* _____ *and give it* _____. When your teacher talks, you should always _____!

2. An active listener _____ better and _____ more of their teacher's verbally delivered content.

3. An active listener makes a conscious _____ to listen to their teacher. An active listener doesn't just hear _____; they listen for _____.

4. An active listener makes _____ contact with the teacher to keep their mind from _____, and values visuals, such as slides, overheads or examples that _____ the principles of the verbal content.

5. An active listener makes an effort to _____ behaviors or attitudes that prevent them from actively listening, such as being _____ by their own thoughts, or losing focus when they _____ information.

Ask me about the skills I learned today! Your support at home will help me make good study skills daily habit.

Thank you for all you do for me every day.

Sincerely,

_____

WHAT DID YOU LEARN?

Name: _____

Piaget was right! A mind that questions, explores, and assesses information as it learns, learns more deeply and more meaningfully. Active learners build larger schemas and remember more of what they learn because the learning has personal meaning to them. Active learners are self-confident and self-reliant students.

WHAT DID YOU LEARN, ACTION HEROES?

1. **Connect:** Discuss a project or activity you've engaged in within the past six months which connected your classroom learning with the real world. If you have none, imagine a project or activity you would like to do, and how it would connect your learning to the real world.

    _____

    _____

    _____

    _____

2. **Engage:** When's the last time you engaged in an intellectual discussion or debate outside of the classroom? What was it about? Politics? The environment? Science? A social issue? Who was involved? What was the outcome? What did you learn?

    _____

    _____

    _____

    _____

3. **Motivate:** Active learners develop **intrinsic** motivation. Are you intrinsically motivated? What are your motivators and why do they motivate you? What does <u>not</u> motivate you?

    _____

    _____

    _____

    _____

4. **Prepare:** It's your job to be a good student. Do you do your job by reading, doing homework and adequately preparing for class? Compare: *How you feel in class when you are prepared vs. how you feel in class when you are not prepared.*

    _____

    _____

    _____

5. High school and college students do a lot of expository reading, which is non-fiction reading for information. Active reading strategies are good study skills for expository reading because they improve _____.

   a. comprehension
   b. retention
   c. a and b
   d. none of the above

6. You've just finished reading a chapter in your health textbook. Using SQ3R active reading strategies, how will you *reflect* on what you have read?

   _____

   _____

   _____

   _____

7. When your teacher says something you don't understand in a lecture or lesson, what should you <u>not</u> do?

   a. Raise your hand to ask for clarification, if your teacher permits questions.
   b. Forget about it. Move on! Figure it out later.
   c. Stay calm. Don't let your confusion distract you from listening.
   d. Ask for clarification when your teacher checks for understanding.

8. One of the best (and easiest) active listening strategies is to make a conscious decision to _____!

   a. decide
   b. listen
   c. hear
   d. look

9. What does it mean to *read with the intent to understand?*

   _____

   _____

10. Is highlighting a *pre* or *post* reading strategy? _____

✱ **Bonus:** *"Active learners don't just care about knowing the right answer, they care about knowing why the answer is right."* Comment:

   _____

   _____

   _____

NAVIGATING NOTES

Have you ever:

☐ forgotten what you learned in class on the very same day you learned it?

☐ misunderstood your teacher's directions?

☐ wished you could have a *do-over* of your teacher's lectures?

You've heard it before, but it's worth repeating: In high school and college, content (that's the stuff you are supposed to learn) gets more difficult. Classes move faster and teachers' expectations increase. Lectures are longer, and packed with information you must remember. To succeed in high school and college, you'll need to take notes in class.

Middle school students are not too young to start taking notes in class. In this and the next chapter, you'll learn how to efficiently and effectively take notes. You'll also learn why it's a really good idea to get into the habit of taking notes in every class.

Let's start navigating notes!

Chapter 15 Learning Goals:

☐ explain the benefits of taking class notes.
☐ compare "to know" and "to do" information.
☐ use abbreviations for efficient note-taking.
☐ restate eight rules for navigating notes.

What are the benefits of taking notes in class?

There are many benefits to taking class notes:

➜ Notes help you **stay focused** and attentive.

➜ Notes create a **kind of journal** of what your teacher wants you to know and do.

➜ Notes make a reliable, **personalized study guide** for any subject.

➜ The **act of writing something down improves your ability to remember it**, especially for visual and kinesthetic learners.

➜ Notes can be used to **activate your schema**.

> **The Benefits of Class Notes**
> 1. Notes improve focus.
> 2. Notes provide a journal of directions.
> 3. Notes make a good study guide.
> 4. Writing improves retention.
> 5. Notes activate schema.

8 simple rules for navigating notes:

Rule #1: Note-taking is a skill developed over time.

Taking notes in class is a struggle for many students. They can't decide what to write down, or they write too much or too little. Some students can't decipher their handwriting later, and many don't know how to use their notes to study. Be patient and keep at it. Even the world's best note-taker was once a note-taking noob. You can become a good note-taker. It's not that hard.

Rule #2: Note-taking skills begin with active listening skills.

When you get to class, have a pen or pencil in hand. Open your notebook or binder to the note section. Use your active listening skills. Focus, and make a conscious decision to listen. Make eye contact, make connections, and control your own distracting behaviors and attitudes. Listen for two different, but equally important kinds of information: What your teacher wants you *to do* and what your teacher wants you *to know*.

Rule #3: Always include *To Do* Information in your notes.

To Do information is direction about what a teacher wants students to do, and how, when and where they are supposed to do it. (Think due dates, deadlines, and directions.) Sometimes students don't as listen carefully to "to do" information because there's no test on it. But if you've ever been marked down on an assignment because you handed it in late, or lost points on a project because you failed to follow your teacher's instructions, you know that "to do" information is important. It usually comes at the beginning or at the end of a class. Your teacher may verbally tell you the information, or write it on the board. It includes:

- **changes or additions** to homework assignments
- **due date** reminders
- **permission slip** or field trip information
- assignment **turn-in directions**
- **test/quiz details** (dates, type of test, supplies.)
- **lab book or journal** instructions
- **deadlines** for anything in a class

Rule #4: It's OK to be judgemental (of information, that is.)

Write down the topic or title of the lesson, then listen for main and supporting points, and important details. This is where students often get sidetracked: "Isn't everything my teacher says important?" Yes and no. Note-taking requires you to make judgements about what's important and what is not quite as important. Don't scribble down everything your teacher says or you'll end up with a disorganized mess. Deciding what to write is not hard. Here are some tips:

Tip: Teachers are usually obvious about what they think is important—after all, they want you to learn! They may repeat a point or say something like "The most important points are..." or "You will be responsible for knowing this..."

Tip: Your teacher may write words or phrases on the board or on a power point, or create examples. Copy them into your notes.

Tip: Look for patterns to emerge in how information is conveyed by your teacher. An observant student can learn to pick up on verbal cues such as changes in the volume of their teacher's voice, transitional pauses, or use of words signifying the introduction of a main point.

Tip: Do the assigned reading before class! Generally, a lecture or lesson will key off of reading material. If you have actively read the textbook, you should be able to identify the main ideas.

If you are confused about something said in a lecture, don't get distracted. Put a "?" in your notes and leave a little extra space. Ask your teacher to clarify after class. If you miss something entirely, leave a blank line and fill it in later. Skip a line between ideas and concepts to make your notes easier to comprehend.

Rule #5: B short.

When taking notes, use key words, phrases or very short sentences. Eliminate *the, a* and *an.* Don't stress about spelling or grammar. Use abbreviations, which are shortened forms of a word or phrase, much like expressions and symbols you use to text. Abbreviations help you take notes quickly, without sacrificing accuracy. Be consistent in their use so the abbreviations become part of your personal note-taking vocabulary. Abbreviate countries, states, cities, dates, measurements, chemicals, and commonly used words. Use symbols such as # for number or pound, @ for "at", $ for money, & or + for "and."

Rule #6: It's not a beauty contest.

Don't be put off of note-taking because your notes don't look as neat or pretty as the ones taken by the overachieving student next to you. Your notes need to work for you and no one else. (We'll explore note-taking forms and strategies in the next chapter.)

Rule #7: Channel your inner artist.

Not all concepts must be expressed in words. Some are better expressed and remembered as visual representations, such as parts of a cell or geologic layers. You're not limited to words when you take notes. Draw and label pictures. Create graphs for math. Diagrams, charts, flow charts, and timelines can help you understand a concept, relationship or chronology.

You are not limited to words when you take notes.

Rule #8: Use your notes!

A plain spiral notebook (one for each subject) is good for notes. Spiral notebooks keep notes in one place and in chronological order. A note section in your binder works well too, especially if you use pre-printed note forms. (You'll learn about those in the next chapter.) If you take notes in loose-leaf form, be careful to keep them in order. Mark the date and page number on the pages and file them in your binder right away.

Review your notes every night as part of your normal homework routine. Studies show that reviewing class notes within 24 hours hugely improves the amount of content you remember from the class. Add missing information, rewrite or fix unclear or illegible items. When you are waiting for class to begin, take a minute to review notes from the prior class. Reviewing notes activates your schema. Notes also make an excellent study guide.

A note about math notes: Math notes should be exact. If your teacher writes a formula or problem on the board as an example, write it down accurately. Similar problems often show up later on a quiz!

There are many benefits to taking notes in class. Learning to be a good note-taker is not hard. Start taking notes in class today. It's an excellent study skill for middle school, high school, and college.

Name: _____

B Short

Abbreviations are **shortened forms of a word or phrase**, sort of like the expressions and symbols you use to text. Abbreviations help you to take notes quickly, but accurately. **Develop a large vocabulary bank of abbreviations.** Be consistent in their use. Below are common abbreviations and symbols. Write their meanings and use them when you take notes. (Helpful websites listed below.)

kg. = _____

pop. = _____

pl. = _____

cu. = _____

c. = _____

m. = _____

oz. = _____

rqd = _____

" " = _____

poss.= _____

div. = _____

St. = _____

yd = _____

& = _____

@ = _____

¶ = _____

¬ = _____

e.g. = _____

* = _____

i.e. = _____

b. = _____

E = _____

N = _____

W = _____

S = _____

d. = _____

Mar. = _____

vol. = _____

mt. = _____

§ = _____

sq = _____

mts. = _____

~ = _____

= _____

w/ = _____

w/o = _____

b/c = _____

b/4 = _____

aka = _____

® = _____

2 = _____

wd = _____

w/i = _____

s/t = _____

re = _____

Æ = _____

Q = _____

A = _____

ch = _____

ASAP = _____

Jan. = _____

Ø = _____

∴ = _____

≠ = _____

© = _____

+ = _____

→ = _____

Need help? Want to learn more about abbreviations? Here are some good resources:

www.factmonster.com

www.english-zone.com/study/symbols.html

www.ilile.org/events/past/seminar

www.abbreviations.com

www.enchantedlearning.com

www.scribed.com

Name: _____

8 Simple Rules for Navigating Notes

In high school and college, classes move faster and the difficulty of verbal content increases. You'll need to take notes in class. Below are eight rules to help you develop good note-taking skills. Read the rules on pages 158-160, and write a short summary of each. Use abbreviations!

Rule #1: Developing note-taking skills takes time.

_____
_____
_____
_____

Rule #2: Good note-taking begins with active listening skills.

_____
_____
_____
_____

Rule #3: Include "To Do" information.

_____
_____
_____
_____

Rule #4: Be judgemental (of information.)

_____
_____
_____
_____

Rule #5: B short!

_____
_____
_____
_____

Rule #6: It's no beauty contest.

_____
_____
_____
_____

Rule #7: Channel your inner artist.

_____
_____
_____
_____

Rule #8: Store – Organize – Use!

_____
_____
_____
_____

Spiral notebooks keep notes in one place and in chronological order.

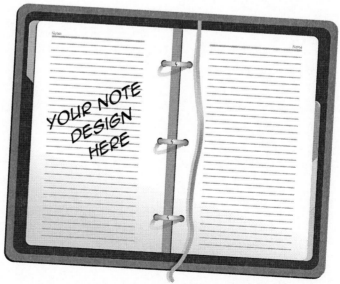

Loose leaf notes enable students to design and print their own note forms. (see chapter 16)

Dear Parent or Caregiver,

Today I participated in my study skills class based on *The Middle School Student's Guide to Study Skills*. One of the best ways I can prepare for high school and college is to use good study skills whenever I am learning.

I learned:

1. Good note-taking skills develop over _____, and begin with active _____ skills.

2. When taking notes in class, listen for two different, but equally important types of information: ***To do*** information, which is about: _____, _____ and _____ and ***to know*** information which is about _____.

3. Don't write down everything your teacher says! First write down the _____ of the lesson. Then listen for the _____ and _____ ideas. Copy your teacher's _____ into your notes.

4. If you miss something your teacher said, put a _____ on your note paper and leave a little extra _____. After class, ask your teacher to _____.

5. Review your notes within _____ hours to enhance what you remember from class. Review notes every night as part of your normal homework _____, and in class to activate your _____.

Ask me about the skills I learned today! Your support at home will help me make good study skills daily habit.

Thank you for all you do for me every day.

Sincerely,

_____

NOTES

CORNIES & INDIES & HYBRIDS, OH MY!

What's your method for taking notes in class? Do you whip out a blank sheet of binder paper and start writing?

Blank binder paper does little to inspire efficient and effective note-taking. Have you ever considered using a preprinted note form that is designed to prompt you to take good notes and guide you to listen for, and write down key information?

In this chapter you'll learn about the Cornell note-taking system. The Cornell system is a popular method for taking notes in class. It was developed by a Cornell University professor named Walter Pauk. It's been around for about 60 years, and millions of students have used this format. Why? Because it's simple and it works!

Cornell notes can be used with all learning styles, and in any subject. Cornell notes make note-taking easy, and create excellent personalized study guides. Learning to take Cornell notes is a good study skill for middle school, high school, and college.

Chapter 16 Learning Goals:

☐ describe the Cornell note-taking system.
☐ take notes using the Cornell note-taking system.
☐ design a note form to support personal note-taking needs.

What is the Cornell note format? *(see page 169)*

Date. The Cornell form provides an area for writing down the **date**. Make sure to write the date on your notes so they will be in chronological order.

Topic. This is not for writing the subject such as "math" or "history". This area is for writing the **topic of the lesson**, such as *Samurai Values & Traditions in 12th Century Japan*.

To Do. The traditional Cornell note format doesn't include a box for to-do information, but students often need a prompt to remember to listen for, and write down important tasks. **Use the To Do box to record due date, deadline and direction reminders from your teacher.** Transfer the information to your planner or ecalendar when you do your homework.

Notes Column. The large column on the right is the area for taking **notes**. Listen for **main points, and supporting ideas and concepts**, and write them here. Don't worry about structure, spelling or grammar. Use abbreviations. Skip a line between (or number) concepts or ideas. If you miss something, write ?, leave space, and fill in the information later. You can also use this area for diagrams, charts, or other visual aids that help illustrate the concepts your teacher discusses.

Cue Column. The narrow column on the left is the **cue column**. It remains empty while you are taking notes. **Review your notes within 24 hours, and reduce the content in the large right column to short descriptions, or key words and phrases.** Write them in the cue column. You can also use the cue column to formulate questions that are answered by the information in the notes column—sort of like Jeopardy! To improve your retention of the information, try using a different colored ink for each column. For example, take notes in blue ink; write cues in red.

Summary/Reflection. The summary box on the bottom is for condensing the information on the page into **manageable ideas**. Read the notes, then paraphrase or summarize the information in 3-5 sentences. Use your own words, because personalizing information improves your memory of it.

How do you use Cornell notes to study?

Cornell notes make excellent personalized study guides. When studying from your Cornell notes, cover the large note column with a piece of binder paper, or fold the note column vertically in half so only the cues are visible. Read aloud the questions or cues from the cue column, and try to recall the information in the note column from memory.

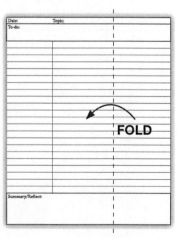

To study, fold the note column in half; Read the cues aloud, and try to recall the notes from memory.

Date: 3/22	Topic: This is for the lesson title

To-do: Listen and check the board for information about due dates, deadlines and directions.

CUE COLUMN	NOTE COLUMN
This area is completed after class, when you review your notes. Condense the information from the note column into key words, phrases or questions.	Take notes in this column. Use abbreviations. Don't try to organize an indented outline format. Just listen for and write down main points and supporting ideas.
	When you study, fold the note column in half and test your memory of the information in the notes.

Summary/Reflect:

Summarize the information in the notes here—use your own words!

Are there other ways to take notes in class?

The Matrix format is a popular note-taking system that lays out information in a table format. **This format reduces clutter, and is useful for comparing two or more topics or evaluating sets of information.** Topics (in this case DNA and RNA) are placed as headings in the top (horizontal) row of the table. In the vertical column, write the items you will compare (the Matrix on the right compares chemical structure and replication.) There can be any number of rows and columns allowing for the comparison of lots and lots of data! Use the blank square at the top left for the date and topic.

DNA & RNA Structures Nov.12	DNA	RNA
CHEM STRUCT.	INFO	INFO
REPLICA-TION	INFO	INFO

The Matrix Note format is useful for comparing information.

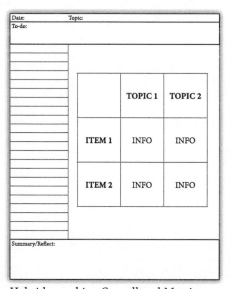

Hybrids combine Cornell and Matrix.

Indies are personalized note forms.

What's a hybrid note form?

Hybrids: Why not mix it up a little? If you like the traditional structure of the Cornell Note format, but need the practicality of the Matrix, try a Cornell- Matrix hybrid. Insert a Matrix table format into the note column of the Cornell form. For taking notes in math, print a Cornell form on graph paper.

What's an indie note form?

Indies: By now you should have a sense of your personal learning style, academic strengths and weaknesses. **Consider designing a customized note form to support your personal needs and preferences.** If you're a strong visual learner, create a note form with a large area for drawing and labeling images. Experiment with formats to find one that works for you. Customize note form styles for different subjects. For example, note forms for your history class might include a blank timeline for sequencing important dates, or a flow chart or concept map for tracking events or relationships. Color-code sections, change fonts, border styles, and sizes to help improve retention. Personalize your note forms with photos or logos.

Stock Your Binder. Make it easy to develop a note-taking habit. Stock your binder with 30-40 blank Cornell, hybrid or indie note forms. Use them in every class! You may go through several note forms in a single class, so replenish your supply each week.

CLASS ACTIVITY WORKSHEET

Date:	Topic:

To-do:

Summary/Reflect:

Name: _____

Indies Rock!

By now, you have a sense of your personal learning style, strengths and weaknesses. Design a note form to support your note-taking needs and preferences. If you're a visual learner, consider including an area for images. Color-code or change font styles to improve retention. Decorate your forms with photos or logos. **Design your note form below, then recreate it in word processing.** (If you use a note taking app, like Notability, you can create a Cornell form using the drawing tools.) Put several copies in your binder. Share your design with your class.

Dear Parent or Caregiver,

Today I participated in my study skills class based on *The Middle School Student's Guide to Study Skills*. One of the best ways I can prepare for high school and college is to use good study skills whenever I am learning.

I learned:

1. The _____ note-taking system has been used by millions of students to take notes in class. The Matrix system is a note form used to compare information or data in a _____ format.

2. Students should keep class notes in _____ order in their _____, and use them as _____ guides for tests and quizzes.

3. The Cornell note-taking form can be modified to include a *To do* box to prompt students to listen for information about _____, _____ and _____; transfer important dates into your _____.

4. On a Cornell form, notes go in the large column on the _____ side; The _____ column is on the left side, and is used for questions or condensed statements about the content in the note column. In the bottom box, reflect on and _____ the information on the page in your own _____.

5. Make it easy to develop a note-taking habit. _____ your binder with 30-40 blank note forms; you may go through _____ forms in a single class. Replenish your supply every week.

Ask me about the skills I learned today! Your support at home will help me make good study skills daily habit.

Thank you for all you do for me every day.

Sincerely,

_____

NOTES

THE HIDDEN BENEFITS OF OUTLINING YOUR TEXTBOOK

Does the thought of having to outline a chapter in your textbook bring on a fit of sighs and eye-rolling? It shouldn't, because outlining your textbook chapters is actually an easy and very effective way to learn.

The beauty of outlining is that it enables students to condense large amounts of expository information into manageable, bite-sized, and logically organized chunks that are easy for Brainy to digest. But do you know that there is another, hidden benefit to outlining your textbook? The *process* of outlining—selecting important information, shrinking it into outline format, and writing it out by hand, improves a student's comprehension and retention of the information. Outlines also make great study guides.

You may get through middle school without having to outline a textbook chapter, but outlining is a skill you'll definitely need for success high school and college. Why not start using this skill now? It's great way to learn.

Chapter 17 Learning Goals:

☐ explain the benefits of outlining a textbook chapter.
☐ create a basic Roman Numeral formatted chapter outline.
☐ outline a sample textbook chapter.

How do you outline a textbook chapter?

READ ➜ ASSEMBLE ➜ SEARCH & RECOVER

The **Read-Assemble-Search & Recover** approach to chapter outlining is simple, effective, and easy to learn. It works for e-textbooks too.

Step 1: Read

Sorry, but outlining is not a substitute for reading. It is a **post-reading (after reading) strategy** because it requires familiarity with the text. First read the chapter using active reading SQ3R strategies. Then return to outline the information.

Step 2: Assemble the Framework

When you finish reading a chapter, turn back to the beginning. Turn the pages and survey chapter **headings and subheadings**. These provide the framework for building your outline. Textbook authors organize information under chapter headings and subheadings because they want you to think about the information in that order. Assemble the framework for your outline by copying headings and subheadings. (Formatting is discussed below.)

Step 3: Search & Recover

When the framework of headings and subheadings is in place, you're good to go! Your mission? Return to the text to **search the sections and recover key points**. A section can have one or several key points. Pick out information that is important to the main concepts, such as information that was identified in the summary, bulleted or bolded words, or graphics. Number the key points and restate them in short phrases or brief sentences. Use abbreviations. Note important details or vocabulary relating to the key points.

How do you format a chapter outline? RCNi!

Students are often confused about formatting an outline, but it's actually very easy. Just remember **RCNi**. (**R**oman numeral, **C**apital letter, **N**umber, and lower case **r**oman.) The simple RCNi format **indents** at each step:

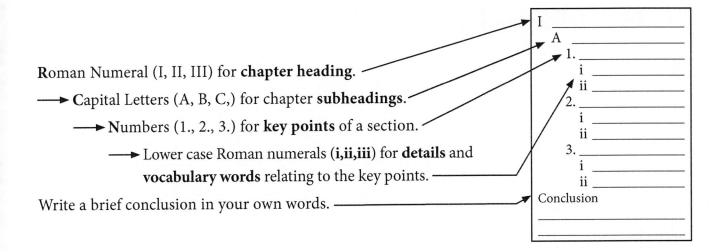

Roman Numeral (I, II, III) for **chapter heading**.

→ Capital Letters (A, B, C,) for chapter **subheadings**.

→ Numbers (1., 2., 3.) for **key points** of a section.

→ Lower case Roman numerals (**i,ii,iii**) for **details** and **vocabulary words** relating to the key points.

Write a brief conclusion in your own words.

How do you use a chapter outline?

An outline is not a substitute for reading and reviewing the textbook, but it does make a good **study guide**. A series of outlines filed chronologically in your binder provides a **progressive review of the key points** of your textbook. An outline can also be used as a **schema activation tool**. If you're early to class, or have a minute before your teacher begins instruction, review your outline to activate your schema. That will improve your ability to link to the new information you'll be learning in class.

Keep in mind that when you're outlining, you're not just creating a study guide and schema activation tool. **Much of the benefit of outlining is actually in the process of making it.** By selecting, condensing, organizing and writing information out by hand, you are strengthening those synaptic patterns and connections, which greatly improves comprehension and retention of the information.

The Benefits of Outlining Your Textbook

1. Outlines make great study guides.
2. Outlining improves comprehension and retention.
3. An outline activates your schema.

Tip: Create and store plenty of **pre-printed outline forms** at your workspace to encourage you to make chapter outlining a regular part of your normal homework routine.

Resist the urge to sigh and eye-roll when your teacher requires you to outline your textbook. Outlining is a great way to help Brainy quickly digest a large amount of information. In fact, don't wait for your teacher to tell you to outline. Do it on your own! It's an excellent study skill for middle school, high school and college.

Name: _____

Outlining a Textbook Chapter

Chapter Heading → **I** _____

_____

_____

Chapter Subheading → **A.** _____

Keypoint → **1.** _____

_____

_____

Details → **i.** _____

_____

_____

ii. _____

_____

_____

Keypoint → **2.** _____

_____

_____

Details → **i.** _____

_____

_____

ii. _____

_____

_____

Conclusion/Summary → **II** _____

_____

_____

_____

Name: _____

The Hidden Benefits of Outlining Your Textbook

The ability to outline a textbook chapter is an important study skill for high school and college. There's a hidden benefit to outlining: The **process** of searching for and recovering key information, "shrinking" it into outline format, and writing it out by hand improves comprehension and retention! Use this form to practice outlining a chapter from your textbook.

I _____
_____
_____

   A. _____
      1. _____
_____
_____

         i. _____
_____
_____

         ii. _____
_____

      2. _____
_____
_____

         i. _____
_____
_____

         ii. _____
_____

Conclusion/Summary _____
_____
_____

Dear Parent or Caregiver,

Today I participated in my study skills class based on *The Middle School Student's Guide to Study Skills*. One of the best ways I can prepare for high school and college is to use good study skills whenever I am learning.

I learned:

1. Textbook/chapter outlining is an excellent study skill that students need for success in high school and _____.

2. Outlining _____ a large amount of information into manageable, bite-sized, and logically organized chunks. The hidden benefit of outlining is that the _____ of selecting, condensing, and writing the information improves a student's _____ and _____ of the chapter content. Outlines also make good _____ guides.

3. Outlining is not a substitute for (SQRRR) active _____ of the textbook; it is a _____ (after) -*reading* skill.

4. The basic Roman Numeral outline format is popular with students. **RCNi =**

    I. Roman Numerals designate chapter _____.

      A. Capital letters designate chapter _____.

        1. Numbers designate _____.

          i. Lower case Roman Numerals designate _____.

5. For proper formatting, _____ at each step. The conclusion/summary should be in the student's _____ words.

Ask me about the skills I learned today! Your support at home will help me make good study skills daily habit.

Thank you for all you do for me every day.

Sincerely,

_____

Name: _____

WHAT DID YOU LEARN ABOUT NOTE-TAKING AND OUTLINING SKILLS?

1. List five benefits of taking notes in class.

   _____

   _____

   _____

   _____

   _____

2. Your English teacher always starts class with reminder of upcoming quizzes and project due dates. You take notes in class, but wait for her to begin instruction before you start writing. What important information are you missing in your notes?

   _____

3. If you take notes in loose leaf form, what 3 things should you do to prevent them from getting out of order?

   _____

   _____

   _____

4. Reviewing notes within _____ greatly enhances the amount of content you remember from class.

   a. 36 hours   c. 24 hours

   b. 2 weeks   d. one year

5. On a Cornell note form, what is the large column on the right used for?

   _____

   _____

6. On a Cornell note form, what is the *cue* column for, and where is it found?

   _____

   _____

7. On which part of the standard Cornell note form do you condense the information on the page into manageable ideas in 3-5 sentences in your own words?

   _____

8. The Matrix Note form is a table format and is useful for:

    a. reducing clutter
    b. comparing two or more topics
    c. evaluating sets of information or data.
    d. all of the above

9. Place the following topics and items in the correct matrix note form boxes, then create notes from chapter 16.

    Date and Lesson Title

    Topic 1   Cornell Note Form

    Topic 2   Matrix Table

    Item 1   Comparing data/concepts

    Item 2   Depicting info visually

True or False:

10. _____ Outlining condenses a large amount of information from a textbook into manageable, bite-sized, and logically organized chunks.

11. _____ Outlining a textbook chapter is an excellent substitute for reading.

12. _____ Downloading, printing and storing blank Cornell note forms and blank textbook chapter outlines in your binder and at your workspace encourages you to use them, and promotes good study skills.

13. What does R-C-N-i stand for?

    _____

    _____

14. How can students use Cornell notes to study?

    _____

    _____

    _____

    _____

15. When you take notes in class, should you try to write them in an RCNi indented outline format?

    _____

    _____

M.N.E.M.O.N.I.C.S.

Let's start this chapter with a lesson about the First Amendment:

Rabid skunks prefer green apples.

Wait a minute! What do rabid skunks and green apples have to do with the Constitution? Besides, isn't this a study skills book? You'll find the answer in this chapter!

The best way to learn something is to develop a comprehensive understanding of it. Once you understand something, it's much easier to remember details about it. But sometimes learning requires plain old memorization, especially in the case of lists of things, orders of steps, or stages of a process.

A *mnemonic device* is a technique that consolidates a lot of information into a kind of code that stimulates recall of the information. There are many types of mnemonic devices, and they can be used for any subject. A mnemonic can take some effort to create, but once you've made it and memorized it, you have a nearly foolproof and long term means of recalling the information, such as the information above about the First Amendment.

Knowing how to make and use a mnemonic is a good study skill for middle school, high school, and college.

Chapter 18 Learning Goals:

☐ explain the purpose of a mnemonic device.
☐ describe five mnemonic devices to help students recall learned information.
☐ create mnemonic representations using a variety of devices, including acronym, acrostic, name/ trait, spelling and rhyme/ song.

The Acronym

An acronym is a popular mnemonic device using a **combination of letters**. Each letter is a cue to an idea you need to remember. For example, you recently learned how to use SQ3R to be an active reader. SQ3R is also known as SQRRR, which is an acronym for Survey, Question, Read, Recite, Reflect. Whenever you see or think SQRRR it's easy to recall the steps of active reading, and recall them in order.

Acronyms are useful for all subjects—history, science, math, english etc. For example, FAMS helps you remember the names of the leaders of the women's suffrage movement: Margaret <u>F</u>uller, Susan B. <u>A</u>nthony, Lucretia <u>M</u>ott and Elizabeth Cady <u>S</u>tanton. CHONPHS will remind you that living organisms are made of molecules consisting largely of <u>c</u>arbon, <u>h</u>ydrogen, <u>o</u>xygen, <u>n</u>itrogen, <u>ph</u>osphorus, and <u>s</u>ulfur.

The Acrostic

An *acrostic* is a sentence where the first letter of each word is a cue to an idea. Can you guess the message in "*Rabid skunks prefer green apples?*" It's an acrostic representing the rights guaranteed by the First Amendment: <u>r</u>eligion, <u>s</u>peech, <u>p</u>ress, <u>g</u>rievance redress, and <u>a</u>ssembly.

Acrostics can be used for large chunks of information. Acrostics can be easier to create than acronyms, and are particularly helpful when you must recall information in chronological or other order. For example, *"Normal angels pass long years talking sweet heavenly words"* is an acrostic for the royal families of England in order of their rule: (Norman, Angevin, Plantagenet, Lancaster, York, Tudor, Stuart, Hanover, Windsor.) If you're struggling to remember the names of the four slave states that remained in the Union during the American Civil War (Delaware, Maryland, Kentucky, and Missouri) and can't come up with a memorable acronym with DMMK, how about *Dancing Makes Kids Merry or Dela and Mary took Ken to Missouri?*

Here's how to make an acrostic:

1. List the meaningful phrases, words or process steps. (If it involves ordered steps or a chronology, make sure to list them in order.)
2. Circle or underline the first letter of each key word or phrase.
3. Write the first letter of each keyword on a line.
4. Using the first letter of each keyword, create a sentence.

Here's an acrostic for the Scientific Method using the first letter of each *phrase*:

(S)tate the problem

(G)ather information on the problem

(F)orm a hypothesis

(E)xperiment to test test hypothesis

(R)ecord data

(A)nalyze data

(D)raw conclusions

s g f e r a d =

Sam gets fat energy running at ducks.

Here's an acrostic for the Scientific Method using the first letter of each *key word*:

State the (p)roblem

Gather (i)nformation on the problem

Form (h)ypothesis

Experiment to (t)est hypothesis

(R)ecord data

(A)nalyze data

Draw (c)onclusions

p i h t r a c =

Pirates in Hawaii take rare alligators captive.

Don't worry if the sentence is silly. It's only purpose is to help you correctly recall information. In fact, sometimes silly sentences are easier to recall!

Silly sentences are not a problem. *Pirates in Hawaii take rare alligator captive = The Scientific Method!*

Name/Trait Mnemonic

A name/trait mnemonic helps you recall facts about a person, place, thing or concept by inventing an **association between the name and a characteristic**. For example: Archimedes discovered formulas for the area and volume of geometric figures. (Think: arch = geometric figure = Archimedes.) *Alliteration* is a literary device that refers to the repetition of a particular sound in the first syllables of a series of words or phrases. (Think: a-a-a-literation!) Alexander HAMilton, was the first Secretary of the U.S. Treasury (Think: You can buy a lot of HAM with the Treasury.)

Again, don't worry if the association is silly. It's only purpose is to help you correctly recall information.

Rhyme it/Sing it Mnemonic

Remember this?

> *In the year 1492, Columbus sailed the ocean blue.*

It's easy to remember lyrics to songs or words to a rhyme. Harness the power of music and rhyme to improve your recall skills. Rhyme and song mnemonics put information in the form of a rhyme/poem, rap or to a familiar tune. A couple of rhyme examples are:

History: *Slavery caused the civil war to start but economics played a part.*

Literature: *When the action starts to fall, the denouement ends it all.*

Try setting information to a familiar song or rap. For example, if you can remember the tune to "Pop Goes the Weasel" you'll forever be able to recall the quadratic formula!

♪   x equals negative B

Plus or minus square root

of B squared minus four A C

♩   All over two A   ♫

Spelling and Word Usage Mnemonics

Students tend to make the same spelling or word usage errors over and over. Spelling and word usage mnemonics help. When you come across a word that gives you trouble, focus on the letter or combination of letters causing the confusion then **create an association** to remember the correct spelling. Example:

Common Misspell or Misusage	Correct Spelling or Usage	Spelling Mnemonic
seperate	separate	For an "**A**", spell sep**a**rate right
permenent	permanent	There's a "**man**" in the middle!
principle vs.	principal	The princi**pal** is your **pal**
attendence	attendance	Will you attend the **dance**?
capital vs.	capitol	The **o** in capit**o**l represents the dome of the capitol building
legable	legible	I have leg**ible** handwriting
counsel vs.	council	I am on the student council

Think m.n.e.m.o.n.i.c.s.

Whenever you have a list of items, steps or order of processes, or a chronology of events that you must remember, consider creating a mnemonic to help you recall the information. Keep a list of your mnemonics in your subject binders or on your bulletin board at your workspace. Share them with your friends and study group. Using mnemonic devices is a good study skill for success in middle school, high school and college.

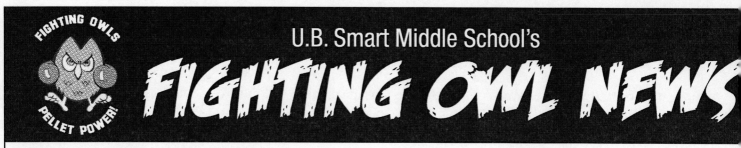

Dumb Kids Pitching Cows Over Fences Get Smashed

Don't worry, no cows or kids got hurt! Mr. Skillsworth's study skills students are learning a kind-of secret code to help them remember information, like lists of things or names, orders of steps, stages of a process, or correct spelling and word usage. The secret code is called a *mnemonic device*.

"An *acronym* is a popular mnemonic device using a combination of letters. An *acrostic* is a sentence where the first letter of each word is a cue to an idea you need to remember. Mnemonic devices can help you recall information in any subject." explained Mr. Skillsworth.

Today's headline, ***"Dumb Kids Pitching Cow Over Fences Get Smashed,"*** contains a hidden message in an acrostic for the students o Ms. Pell's science class. Can you decipher it (The answer is at the bottom of this page.)

"Mnemonic devices may take some effor to make," Mr. Skillsworth says, "but a good mnemonic is a foolproof and long term way to recall a list of words, steps or stages of process. I highly recommend adding acrostics acronyms, name/trait, spelling, and rhyme, sing mnemonics to your list of study skill and strategies."

Mr. Skillsworth Challenges Students to a Mnemonic Throw Down!

Mr. Skillsworth has challenged students to create an **acrostic**, **acronym**, **name/trait** or **spelling mnemonic** for the information below:

1. **Create an acrostic for the first six American presidents (as listed, in order of their presidency):** Washington, Adams, Jefferson, Madison, Monroe, Adams

_____

_____

_____

2. **Create an acrostic for the planets in order o their position in the solar system:** Mercury Venus, Earth, Mars, Jupiter, Saturn, Uranus Neptune

_____

_____

_____

3. **Create an acronym for the four ocean zones:** intertidal, near-shore, edge of continental shelf, perpetual darkness

_____

_____

4. **Create an acronym for the confederate states:** South Carolina, Mississippi, Florida, Alabama, Georgia Louisiana, Texas, Virginia, Arkansas, North Carolina, Tennessee

_____

_____

5. **Create an acrostic for general properties of matter:** mass, weight, volume, density

_____

_____

6. **Create an acronym for types of triangles:** Right, Acute, Obtuse, Equilateral, Equiangular, Isosceles, Scalene, Oblique

_____

_____

7. **Create an acronym for the properties of light:** reflection, refraction, transmission, absorption by matter

_____

_____

8. **Create an acronym or an acrostic for inventors of the industrial Revolution:** Awkright, Bessemer, Watt, Singer, Telford, Stephenson, Edison

_____

_____

9. **Using the letters of your first name, create an acrostic that describes your personality.**

_____

_____

10. **Create name/trait mnemonics for:**

Mitochondria:_____

OlduvaiGorge:_____

* Create a spelling mnemonic to remember the correct usage of affect vs. effect.

_____

_____

Name: _____

Spelling and Word Usage Mnemonics to the Rescue!

Some words are hard to remember how to spell or use correctly. Below is a list of commonly misspelled or misused words. Read the word, and **focus on the particular letter or combination of letters that cause the problem**. Identify the correct spelling or usage, and create a mnemonic to prompt recall of the correct spelling or usage. Then select three words you frequently misuse or misspell and create mnemonics to help you recall the correct spelling or usage.

Common Misspell or Misusage	Correct Spelling or Usage	Spelling (or usage) Mnemonic
relevent		
knowlege		
wierd		
embarass		
arguement		
definate		
dependant		
seige		
weather vs. whether	→	
good vs. well	→	

Dear Parent or Caregiver,

Today I participated in my study skills class based on *The Middle School Student's Guide to Study Skills*. One of the best ways I can prepare for high school and college is to use good study skills whenever I am learning.

I learned:

1. _____ devices are techniques to prompt the recall of lists of things or names, orders of steps, stages of a process, traits, concepts, or correct spelling and word usage.

2. A(n) _____ is a mnemonic device using a combination of _____ as cues to words or ideas.

3. An _____ is a _____ where the first letter of each word is a cue to an idea you need to remember; it's especially useful for recalling lists, steps, orders of a _____, or chronology.

4. A _____/_____ mnemonic helps recall facts about a _____, _____, _____ or concept by inventing a relationship between the name and a characteristic of the person, place, thing, or concept.

5. _____/_____ mnemonics put information in the form of a poem, rap or song.

Ask me about the skills I learned today! Your support at home will help me make good study skills daily habit.

Thank you for all you do for me every day.

Sincerely,

_____

NOTES

MEET THE ANTI-CRAM: TIME-SPACED LEARNING

In Shakespeare's play *Hamlet*, the character of Hamlet has about 1500 lines. Wow, that's a lot to remember! Have you ever been in a play and had to memorize dialogue? How did you do it? How are actors able to remember so many lines?

To memorize dialogue, actors instinctively use the kind of study techniques you will learn in this lesson. Actors know it's impossible to learn all of their lines in one study session, so they space their learning over time. They review at intervals, recite, and self-test to learn lines. This is *time-spaced learning*.

As you move up into high school and college, content will be more difficult and there will be a lot more of it. Time-spaced learning is an excellent method for improving retention of learned information. Knowing why and how to create a time-spaced learning plan is an excellent study skill for middle school, high school, and college.

Chapter 19 Learning Goals:

☐ describe how learned information is forgotten over time, as illustrated by The Forgetting Curve.

☐ explain how time-spaced learning improves retention of content.

☐ create a time-spaced learning plan using repetition at intervals, recitation, and self-testing.

Forgetting happens!

In 1885, a German psychologist named Hermann Ebbinghaus was one of the first scientists to study the process of memory. Actually, he studied *forgetting*. Ebbinghaus had been a grade school teacher in England, and later worked with a group of scientists to study how quickly students forget what they learned during the school day. Through a series of experiments, Ebbinghaus created *The Forgetting Curve* illustrating how quickly learned information is forgotten.

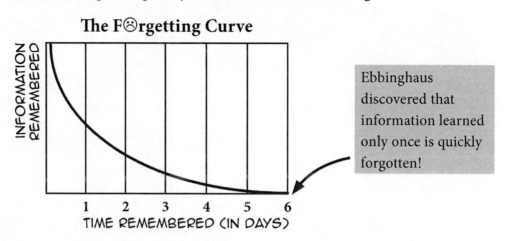

The sharpest decline in memory of learned content happens in the first twenty minutes after learning it. This memory free-fall continues for about an hour and levels off over the next few days, where little of the original learning can be recalled. Additional factors, such as fatigue, stress, and distraction can make matters worse!

Forgetting is a very slippery slope indeed! **The sharpest decline in memory of learned content happens in the first twenty minutes after learning it.** This memory free-fall continues for about an hour and levels off over the next few days, where little of the original learning can be recalled. Additional factors, such as fatigue, stress, and distraction can make matters worse!

How can students improve their retention of content?

Ebbinghaus studied how quickly information is forgotten because he wanted to develop study techniques to improve memory and recall. He experimented with all sorts of study and learning techniques. **He concluded that repetition and review of material over time results in the highest rate of retention.**

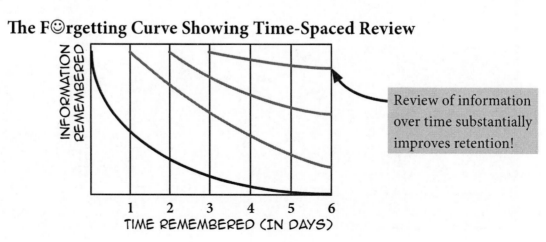

Ebbinghaus called spaced-review and repetition *spaced-repetition learning*. It is now referred to as *time-spaced learning*. Experts agree that people learn and retain information better when they study it a few times over a period of time, rather than intensely, once or twice, in a short period. If you want to improve your retention and take a lot of stress out of learning, it's worth a try!

Time-spaced learning is the "anti-cram."

To *cram* means to study very hard, with urgency, often for long hours just before a test or quiz. In spite of the fact that learning experts have repeatedly shown that cramming is stressful and doesn't work well, students continue to do it. Time-spaced learning is *anti*-cramming. Instead of learning the material once in class or as homework, then returning for an intense and often painful marathon review session before a test or quiz, time-spaced learning takes place in several short reviews at intervals spread over time.

Overall, time-spaced learners and crammers spend about the same amount of time studying, but time-spaced learning is a far more productive use of time. (Just check out the Forgetting Curve diagrams!) For students in the habit of cramming, time-spaced learning requires a change of study habits, but it's worth doing and not hard to learn.

Time-spaced learning fits easily with a busy schedule. Yes, ten (focused) minutes on the bus is enough time to review an algebra formula. Got just twenty minutes before practice? Fifteen minutes at breakfast? No problem! Whip out your notes or flash cards and review. **With time-spaced learning you do not need a large chunk of time to study effectively, but you must review at frequent, spaced intervals.**

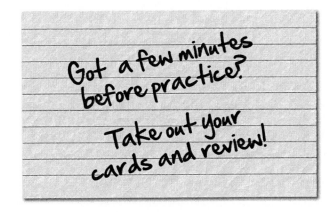

Why does time-spaced learning work so well?

Quantity: Memory studies have shown that the human brain can only handle so many ideas at one time. (Duh!) Time-spaced learning limits focus to less information, reviewed more frequently. Rather than trying to master an entire month's worth of information two nights before a quiz, time-spaced learners **progressively master small, bite-sized amounts of content**, adding to it over time, until Brainy has digested it all.

Repetition at Intervals: At the heart of time-spaced learning is *repetition at intervals*. To begin, information must be reviewed as soon as possible after learning it. For example, if you learned a difficult skill in algebra, **review it immediately in your head**, or with a friend as you walk to your next class. Recall and reflect on the main points of what you learned. Review the information again that day, and the following two days as part of your normal homework routine. Create a *mnemonic* if it's the kind of information that works with a mnemonic prompt. Then start to space reviews farther and farther apart. **The goal is to space reviews as far apart as possible, yet still be able to recall the information.** Cognitive psychologist believe that spacing the review and recall makes Brainy work really hard to retrieve information. That builds stronger synaptic patterns and connections to the learned information.

Recitation & Self-Testing: Recitation and self-testing are particularly effective study techniques because they force your brain to pull information from memory, generate an answer, and recite it aloud so you can hear it. Recite information to yourself, or reteach it to a brother, sister, parent—even your dog or stuffed animal. If you are uncomfortable reciting, try writing out your answers, and reading them aloud. **Self-testing by quizzing yourself aloud or writing out answers builds retention skills and is an important aspect of time-spaced learning.** Flashcards are simple and effective self-testing tools, and can be stored in your backpack or binder for review on-the-go. When you can say it from memory, you know it!

Time-spaced Flashcards

1. Write the information you need to learn on one side of the flashcard in short, simple sentences.

2. Write a prompt (cue word, mnemonic or question) on the other side.

3. For three days in a row, when you do homework, lay the flashcards out on your desk, prompt side up. Select a card at random; read the cue aloud.

4. DO NOT TURN THE CARD OVER. Try to recite aloud, or write out from memory, the information on the other side. Check your answer. Repeat 2x for all cards.

5. Space flashcard review intervals to every other day, then every three days. When you can recall the information after a significant interval you've learned it!

6. As your learn, add more information to your flashcard review until you have mastered all you need to learn.

Create a time-spaced plan and study schedule

Don't try to master difficult content in one or two short, painful study sessions just before a test. Break the cramming habit with time-spaced learning. Start now: create a time-spaced learning plan for at least one or two of your classes. Set your review plan intervals. Write your schedule in your planner. Make flashcards with cues and information. Stick to your review schedule. Ask your mom, dad, brother, sister or study bud to help you review. You'll notice your grades go up, and your stress level fall!

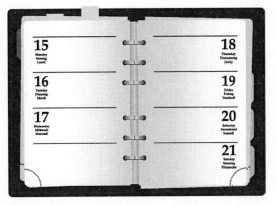

Write your time-spaced study plan in your planner.

Name: _____

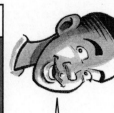

Max's Time-Spaced Learning Plan

Help! It's almost finals week at U.B. Smart Middle School. My American Government final is in two weeks. I have to be able to summarize the first ten amendments to the U.S. Constitution. That's a lot of information! Please create a **time-spaced study plan** for me so I can ace my final without cramming. Include **review at intervals, flashcards, mnemonics, recitation,** and **self-testing**. Enter the time-spaced plan in my planner below.

	MONDAY	TUESDAY	WEDNESDAY	THURSDAY	FRIDAY
W E E K 1					
W E E K 2					

Q. Max has a 20 minute break between his last period and lacrosse practice. For *time-space learning,* is this enough time to review?

Q. Max feels self-conscious reciting information aloud. Convince him that it's a good study habit.

Name: _____

My Personal Time-Spaced Learning Plan

Time-spaced learning is the *anti-cram*. Instead of learning content once or twice in class, or as homework, then returning for an intense marathon review session prior to a test, time-spaced learners study in several short sessions at intervals spread over a period of time. Give it a try! Select some difficult information you must learn for one of your classes, such as math formulas, verb conjugations for a language class, or names and dates for history. Create a 10 day time-spaced study plan using **flashcards, repetition at intervals, mnemonics, recitation, and self-testing.**

	MONDAY	TUESDAY	WEDNESDAY	THURSDAY	FRIDAY
WEEK 1					
WEEK 2					

Dear Parent or Caregiver,

Today I participated in my study skills class based on *The Middle School Student's Guide to Study Skills*. One of the best ways I can prepare for high school and college is to use good study skills whenever I am learning.

I learned:

1. Hermann Ebbinghaus created _____ which illustrates how quickly learned information is forgotten.

2. The sharpest decline in memory of learned content happens in the first _____ minutes after learning it.

3. Ebbinghaus discovered that _____and _____of material over time is the best way to learn, with the highest rate of retention. Today this is called _____ learning.

4. Time-spaced learning techniques are: _____, _____, _____, and _____-testing at intervals that move farther and farther apart. _____ more and more information over time until it is all learned.

5. Recitation can include _____ what you have learned to a brother, sister, parent or even your dog, so you can hear yourself say the concepts aloud. To self-test, make _____ with a word, sentence or mnemonic cue on one side and the information on the other. Try to recall the information from _____.

Ask me about the skills I learned today! Your support at home will help me make good study skills daily habit.

Thank you for all you do for me every day.

Sincerely,

_____

Name: _____

WHAT DID YOU LEARN ABOUT MEMORY AND RECALL STRATEGIES?

1. What is the purpose of a *mnemonic device*?

   _____

   _____

2. What is an *acrostic*?

_____

_____

3. What is an *acronym*?

_____

_____

4. How does a *name/trait* mnemonic help you recall learned information?

_____

_____

5. What topic was of interest to Herman Ebbinghaus in 1885?

   a. human emotion
   b. healthy children
   c. forgetting
   d. physical fitness

6. Why are intervals between reviews important for time-spaced learning?

   a. Spaced review makes the brain work harder to retrieve information and builds stronger synaptic patterns and connections to the information.
   b. The intervals allow time for group meetings
   c. The intervals allow students time to catch up on other homework
   d. none of the above

7. *Active recall* means:

   a. making your brain generate the answer
   b. pulling information from memory
   c. reciting the answer aloud (or writing it out)
   d. all of the above

8. What is *cramming* and why is it an inefficient way to study?

_____

_____

9. *Time-spaced* learning includes:

    a. review/repetition at intervals
    b. active recall generating the answer in your brain
    c. moving review/repetition intervals farther apart and adding bits of information until all is learned!
    d. all of the above

True or False:

10. _____ Crammers and time-spaced learners spend about the same amount of time studying, but cramming is a far more efficient use of time.

11. _____ Overall, time-spaced learning is more stressful than cramming and yields about the same results.

12. _____ You will use time-spaced learning instead of cramming because it is a good study skill and has been shown to greatly improve retention of learned content.

13. What does the graph below tell you about *forgetting*:

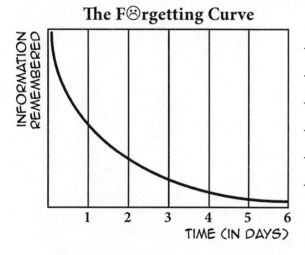

The F☹rgetting Curve

INFORMATION REMEMBERED

TIME (IN DAYS)

_____

_____

_____

_____

_____

_____

14. What does the graph below tell you about *remembering*?

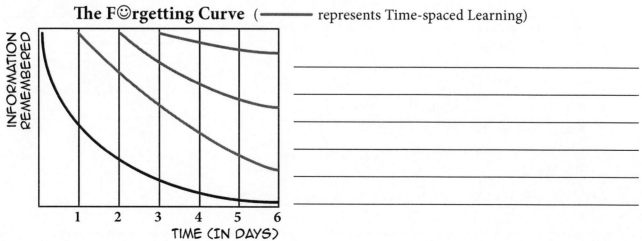

The F☺rgetting Curve (———— represents Time-spaced Learning)

INFORMATION REMEMBERED

TIME (IN DAYS)

_____

_____

_____

_____

_____

_____

SHORT ANSWER & ESSAY TEST TIPS

Back in chapter one, you learned that *learning is the acquisition, retention and ability to demonstrate knowledge.* Learning is measurable and, as a student, you are frequently required to demonstrate what you have learned so it can be measured by your teacher.

What are some ways students are required to demonstrate what they have learned? Tests and quizzes of course, and oral presentations in class. Tests and quizzes come in many forms. There are short answer tests, essay tests, multiple choice, and true/false tests.

All tests have unique challenges, but did you know that there's more to taking a test than knowing the right answer? You have many, many more tests in your academic future. Knowing correct test-taking strategies for all types of tests is a good study skill for middle school, high school and college. You can be a lean, mean test-taking machine!

In the next few chapters, you will learn test-taking skills and strategies for all types of tests. Let's get started with short answer and essay test skills…

Chapter 20 Learning Goals:

- ☐ describe six test-taking strategies for short answer tests.
- ☐ describe six test-taking strategies for essay tests.
- ☐ use basic symbols for proofing a written response.
- ☐ identify strategy errors in a series of sample short answers.

What are basic strategies for all tests and quizzes?

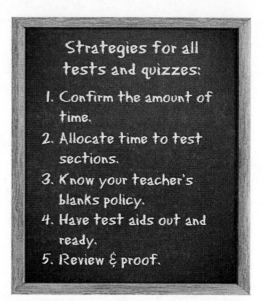

Strategies for all tests and quizzes:
1. Confirm the amount of time.
2. Allocate time to test sections.
3. Know your teacher's blanks policy.
4. Have test aids out and ready.
5. Review & proof.

Confirm time. Before starting a test or quiz, confirm how much time you have to complete it. It happens all the time—students think they have an hour to finish, but find out the hard way they have only 45 minutes. Listen for your teacher to tell you how much time you have to finish a test or quiz. **Before starting the test, look at the clock in your classroom and note when time will be up.** If your classroom clock is analog (that's the kind with the big and little hands pointing to numbers) but you're a digital kid, make sure you can recognize where the clock hands will be when time is running low.

Allocate time. When you start a test, make a quick preview of the parts of the test to form a rough plan for the allocation of your time. If you have one hour to complete five short answer questions, an essay and ten multiple choice questions, how will you allocate your time? **Allocate by difficulty or by point value**, but don't spend 15 minutes of a 45 minute test struggling to answer a question worth 5 points, then short- change an essay worth 25 points. Keep track of time to make sure you are working according to your time allocation. Try to work at a pace that allows you 5-10 minutes at the end of the test to check answers and proof your writing.

Blanks policy. Confirm your teacher's blanks policy before beginning the test or quiz. **Unless specifically directed to do so by your teacher, do not leave an answer blank or you will lose points.**

Test aids. If you are allowed to use a calculator, make sure it's powered up and on your desktop. If your teacher allows you to use notes, or if the test is open book, have those items on your desk top. Mid-test is not the time to go digging through your backpack for them.

Proof answers. Reserve time at the end of the test to check written responses for spelling, punctuation, grammar and clarity. **Use proofing symbols to keep changes or additions to your answer neat and legible.** ∧, called a *caret*, means to insert a letter, word or phrase. The symbol ‿, drawn through a word or phrase means to delete the word or phrase. The word *stet* written next to something you have crossed out means *"nevermind—leave it the way it was."* ⓈⓅ next to a word indicates that you are unsure of the spelling, and the symbol ¶ next to the beginning of a sentence indicates that you meant to start a new paragraph with that sentence.

What is an effective strategy for a short answer test?

In high school and college, short answer questions (also called *prompts*) are almost always on an exam. There are specific strategies for these types of tests.

1. **Confirm the test section.** Tests often have many different sections, including an essay, short answer and multiple choice section. In the jangle of nerves and rush to answer, students can get confused and mix up sections, answering the essay question with a short answer, and the short answer with an essay. Oops! **Don't start writing until you've confirmed the test section.**

2. **Read the question.** Read the question carefully, then read it again. **Resist the urge to assume you know what it asks,** or you may read what you assume, instead of what it actually asks.

3. **Underline key words.** Search the question for <u>key</u> words and underline them. **Key words tell you what you will write about**—usually a name, date or concept you studied.

4. **Circle action words.** While key words tell you *what* you will write about, **action words tell you *how* you will write about the key words**. Questions will ask you to present information in a particular way like "*define*", "*state*", "*list*", "*compare*", or "*name*." Questions often have more than one action word. For example, "*Name* the author of the following passage, and *list* three other works by that author." Circle each (action) word and address each in your response.

5. **Write 3-6 sentences.** How short is too short? How long is too long? Some teachers tell you up front how many sentences are too many and how many are too few, but generally **3-6 content rich sentences is about the norm.** Short answer questions generally ask for factual information, not a lengthy analysis. A short answer test may ask you to list items, dates, names or steps. Concise answers are best.

6. **No blanks!** If you can't answer a question, try scanning other questions and parts of the test. Something you see there may activate your schema and trigger enough recall for an answer. **Write down whatever you know that's relevant to the question:** a name, date, fact, place, related vocabulary word or event, and hope for partial credit.

What is an effective strategy for an essay test?

1. **Confirm the test section.** (See above)

2. **Read the question.** Read the question carefully, then **read it again.** Don't assume you know what the question's asking.

3. **Underline key words.** Underline the <u>key</u> words in the question. **Stick to the topic indicated by the key words.** Focus on what the question asks about the key words, and prepare a relevant response. The blank page can be intimidating, but resist the urge to include random ideas just to fill up space. Adding unrelated information can backfire, resulting in a loss of points. Do not begin a sentence with "I believe" or "In my opinion," unless the question clearly asks for your opinion, belief or personal interpretation.

4. **Circle action words.** While short answer questions generally ask for factual-type information, essay questions look for a deeper analysis and more thorough demonstration of knowledge. Typical essay question (action) words are "*analyze*", "*compare and contrast*", "*defend*", "*refute*", "*discuss and compare*", "*state the cause and effect of*", "*evaluate*", and "*summarize.*" **Develop a mental bank of words and phrases that support certain action words.** For example, for "compare and contrast" use phrases like "by contrast", "in comparison", "on the other hand", "likewise", or "similarly" in your response. Using supporting action word language in your response tells the reader (your teacher) that you understood what was asked, and that you structured your response as required by the action word.

5. **Brainstorm!** No matter how concerned you are about time, do not jump right in and start writing. "Stream of consciousness" writing usually ends up with the writer writing themselves into a corner, or failing to address the prompt. **Expositive essays require thought, organization and structure.** First, get your schema on! Brainstorm what you know about the topic. Jot down words, ideas and facts. **Reread the question and think through your answer, from introduction to conclusion.**

6. **Create a 5-paragraph essay outline.**
Expositive essays must have a structured, informative style. The easy-to-follow, five paragraph essay provides this. **Once you have brainstormed and thought through your answer, organize the ideas and facts into a basic RCNi outline.** Don't obsess over how neat it is. It's function is to provide structure and direction for your essay. Include an introduction with a one-sentence thesis statement and three subtopics. List supporting information and details for the subtopics. Conclude with a summary. That's simple!

BRAINSTORM	OUTLINE
words	I Introduction/Thesis
	A. Subtopic
	1. Idea
	2. Detail/Example
facts	B. Subtopic
	1. Idea
	2. Detail/Example
ideas	C. Subtopic
	1. Idea
details	2. Detail/Example
thoughts	II Conclusion

Note about the five-paragraph essay: The five-paragraph essay is adequate for middle school and high school writing. Practice, practice, practice your five-paragraph essay skills. **Once you are comfortable with the format, use it as a foundation for developing a more sophisticated and flexible writing style for college.**

7. **Get writing!** Fold the subtopics from your outline into your essay. Develop ideas and details more thoroughly, and provide examples. At the end of each subtopic paragraph, include a transition sentence leading the reader to the next subtopic. Conclude with a brief summary.

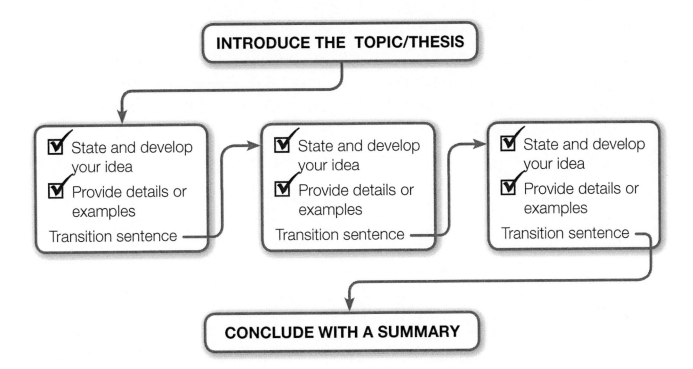

8. **Proof.** No matter how tired you are of writing, or how much you want to finish up and get out of there, proof your essay! **Check and correct spelling, grammar, and punctuation.** Check for clarity. If you run out of time, jot down the rest of your answer in bullet points. **Use proofing symbols to keep edits and additions neat and legible.**

Practice for your test-filled future

Over the next few years you will write many short responses and essays. **You must develop your ability to successfully demonstrate what you know in a timed writing situation.** Whenever you take an essay or short answer test, use your test-taking skills to improve your ability to successfully show what you know.

Name: _____

Short Answer Shenanigans

On a recent American History test, U.B. Smart Middle School students were asked:

What were the thirteen original colonies? List the colonies and identify which ones were founded primarily for religious freedom or purposes. (Value: 3 points)

Below are the students' responses. describe their short response strategy error(s) and award 0-3 points.

Alison's Answer: Pennsylvana, Massachusetts, New Hampshire, Virginia, Mariland, Delaware, South Carolina, North Carolina, Georgia, Rhode Island Connecticut New Jersey, and New York. Religion was very important in all of the colonies, especially in the New England colonies where the puritans lived.

What short answer test strategy errors did Alison make?

_____

_____

_____

_____ Pts. _____

Max's Answer: The original thirteen colonies are: Pennsylvania, Massachusetts, New Hampshire, Virginia, Maryland, Delaware, South Carolina, North Carolina, Georgia, Rhode Island, Connecticut, New Jersey, and New York. The colonies which were founded because of a quest for religious freedom or for a religious purpose are: Massachusetts, Connecticut, Rhode Island (Puritan/Protestant); Maryland (Catholic), and Pennsylvania (Quakers.)

What short answer test strategy errors did Max make?

_____

_____

_____

_____ Pts. _____

A.J.'s Answer: _____

_____

_____

_____

Answer test strategy errors did A.J. make?

_____

_____

_____

_____ Pts. _____

Jason's Answer: There were 13 colonies separated into the Middle Colonies, the Southern Colonies and the New England Colonies. In my opinion, religion had a very important role in the founding of all of the original thirteen colonies. Some colonies were mainly Puritan and some were mainly Baptist and Lutheran, but there were also Catholics, Jews and Quakers.

What short answer test strategy errors did Jason make?

_____

_____

_____ Pts. _____

Elena's Answer: The original thirteen colonies are: Pennsylvania, Massachusetts, New Hampshire, Virginia, Maryland, Delaware, South Carolina, North Carolina, Georgia, Rhode Island, Connecticut, New Jersey, and New York. The New England colonists were mainly Puritans. They led very strict lives. The Middle colonists were a mixture of religions, including Quakers who were led by a man named William Penn.

There were Catholics, Lutherans, Jews, and others located in various colonies. Southern colonies were home to many religions, including Baptists and Anglicans. French Huguenot settlers arrived in America around 1685, because they faced religious persecution in France under King Louis XIV. He revoked the Edict of Nantes that protected their religious freedom. After that, many Huguenots came to America and settled in New York and New Jersey.

Many of the outer colonies were safe havens for colonists who sought religious freedom. Catholics (also called Papists) were discriminated against and treated unfairly by the other colonists. I believe that treating any group unfairly because of their religion is just wrong!

What short answer test strategy errors did Elena make?

_____

_____

_____ Pts. _____

Name: _____

Dominate Short Answer and Essay Tests

There's more to taking a test than knowing the right answer! Test-taking strategies and techniques are important. Let's see what you've learned about short answer and essay test strategies.

1. The life science quiz begins at 10:05 on the dot. Your teacher is allowing 45 minutes for the quiz. What time will it end? _____

2. Draw the location of the classroom clock hands when there are just five minutes left on the quiz.

3. Key words will tell *what* you will write about. Action words tell *how* you will write about the key words. Circle the action words and underline the *key* words in the following essay and short answer prompts:

   • List three major diplomatic conferences of World War II and name the world leaders who attended.

   • State five noticeable changes in climate occurring in the past 50 years.

   • Name the six types of triangles and provide an example of a right triangle

   • Define "extinction" and identify three species at risk for extinction in the next 25 years.

   • Summarize the rights of a Roman citizen and compare by class and gender.

   • Define and discuss two forms of display for data sets.

   • Illustrate the proper safety procedures for handling an emergency in the science lab.

4. What can happen if you do not carefully read a question in its entirety, assuming you know what it is asking?

   _____

   _____

5. What is the purpose of a five-paragraph essay outline?

   _____

   _____

   _____

6. When Derek takes an essay test, he wastes a lot of time trying to make his outline look really good. What's your advice about this?

_____

_____

7. Write a short answer question containing two action words for any topic in Chapter 20 of *The Middle School Student's Guide to Study Skills*. Circle the (action) words and underline the <u>key</u> words, then write a response to your question.

Question: _____

_____

_____

Response: _____

_____

_____

8. Create an essay question with two action words for any topic in Chapter 20 of *The Middle School Student's Guide to Study Skills*. Circle the action words and underline the <u>key</u> words. Brainstorm, and create an outline below.

Question: _____

_____

_____

BRAINSTORM	OUTLINE

9. Even if you're exhausted from writing short answers and essays, you're not done with a test until you've gone back and _____ your responses.

10. *Proofing* means, searching for errors in:

    a. spelling
    b. punctuaton
    c. grammar
    d. clarity
    e. all of the above

11. Match the proof symbol to its meaning.

    ∧   new paragraph
    stet   keep it as it was
    ‿   not sure of spelling
    (sp)   insert text or letter
    ¶   delete a word or phrase

12. Below is Ali's short answer. Help her make the changes listed below by using the appropriate proofing symbol:

> The Compact, signed by 40 men, laid the foundation of the governing law in America. It states that settlers should have faith and belief in God, loyalty towards the King of England, equalaty among one another, and the ability to establish democratic law. 150 years later, many of the colonist had a common goal: to govern themselves and to have a say in how they were represented.

✓ Insert the word "Mayflower" between "The" and "Compact" in the first sentence.
✓ Delete the number 40 and change it to 41.
✓ Indicate that that the sentence starting "150 years later..." was intended to start a new paragraph.
✓ Indicate that Ali is uncertain of her spelling of *equalaty*.
✓ Delete the words "to have a say in how they were represented," then indicate that she changed her mind and wants to leave the sentence as originally written.

＊ Bonus: Key words tell *what* you will write about; action words tell *how* you will write about the key words. Below are 10 action words commonly found on high school and college test questions. Research the action word and explain how to put it into action. (Suggested search: "Action words for essays and tests.")

Action Word	What does it mean?
Analyze	
Compare	
Identify	
Define	
Discuss	
Critique	
Illustrate	
Contrast	
Summarize	
Explain	

Dear Parent or Caregiver,

Today I participated in my study skills class based on *The Middle School Student's Guide to Study Skills*. One of the best ways I can prepare for high school and college is to use good study skills whenever I am learning.

I learned:

1. Before taking a test, quiz or exam, confirm the amount of _____ the teacher has allowed for completion, and preview parts of the test to make a rough _____ of time to answer the questions.

2. Carefully _____ the short answer or essay test question, then _____ it; do not _____ you know what it is asking!

3. Key words tell you _____ you will write about; _____ words tell you *how* you will write about the keywords; a question can have one or _____ action words.

4. _____ essays require thought, organization and structure. Brainstorm, organize your ideas, and make an _____ for a _____ -paragraph essay; essay writing becomes easier with lots of _____!

5. Underline _____ words and focus your response on what the question asks about them; Even if you're stuck, resist the urge to include _____ ideas or facts which have little or nothing to do with the question. Don't state your personal _____ unless the question asks for it.

Ask me about the skills I learned today! Your support at home will help me make good study skills daily habit.

Thank you for all you do for me every day.

Sincerely,

_____

NOTES

SO MANY CHOICES, SO LITTLE TIME...

When your teacher announces that a test will be multiple choice, what's your reaction? Relief? Do you prefer a multiple choice test over an essay test? Many students do.

There's a perception among students that multiple choice tests are easier than essay tests. After all, multiple choice tests don't require a student to generate the answer in their brain. The answer to the question is right in front of them. All they have to do is find it, and check a box or bubble in a circle, right?

Wrong!

From knowing how to study for a multiple choice test, to using a scannable answer form, to deciding between two answers both of which seem right, multiple choice tests have their own unique challenges.

In this chapter, you'll explore strategies and techniques for success on multiple choice and true/false tests...

Chapter 21 Learning Goals:

☐ explain how to study for multiple choice tests.

☐ describe strategies for success on multiple choice tests.

☐ demonstrate how to avoid marking errors on a scannable answer form.

☐ explain strategies for segmented true/false tests.

How do you study for a multiple choice test?

When you find out that a test or quiz will be multiple choice, your first thought should be *How will I study for this test?* Studying for a multiple choice test is different, and sometimes more difficult than studying for an essay or short answer test.

Information focus. Generally, multiple choice tests won't ask you to analyze information, apply theories, or provide examples, but you will be expected to know **specific dates, names, vocabulary terms and definitions.** Multiple choice questions often test your knowledge of **orders of steps in processes, or a chronology of events.** Mnemonics are especially useful study techniques for multiple choice tests.

Study holistically. When preparing for a multiple choice test, don't make the mistake of studying only up to the point of being able to recognize the correct answer. On these kinds of tests, the correct answer is often found by *process of elimination.* The student eliminates wrong choices until settling on what they hope is the correct one. Studying for a multiple choice test requires a holistic approach. **Study with the broader goal of being able to recognize incorrect choices too.** For processes, steps or chronology of events, know the right sequence, but also be able to recognize when a date or step is out of sequence.

To study *holistically* means to be able to recognize answers that are:

- right
- wrong
- processes, sequences and events in and out of order
- not the best or most accurate choice
- right and wrong interpretations of graphs and tables

Graphs and tables. Multiple choice questions often ask students to compare, contrast, or interpret information or data from a graph, chart, or table. Typically, the graph or table is pretty similar to one from a textbook or example discussed in class. Don't ignore the graphs, tables and charts in your textbook. They're not there for decoration. Study them carefully. **Know right and wrong interpretations, and be able to label parts of the graph or table.**

Write out questions. Multiple choice questions are often based directly on information in your textbook. Outline the textbook chapter and, as you outline, anticipate questions your teacher might ask on a test, and how he or she might ask them. **Turn information from your textbook and class notes into test questions.** Know the answer to the question, as well as possible wrong or even slightly inaccurate answers.

What are strategies for identifying the right choice on a multiple choice test?

Note that all those pre-test strategies you learned in Chapter 20 also apply to multiple choice tests: Confirm the amount of time allowed for the test, confirm what test aids are allowed and have them on your desktop. Allocate time, work at a pace that assures you will get to every question, and allow time to check answers.

Read the stem carefully. The "question" part of a multiple choice question is called the *stem*. Often it is not a question at all, but a phrase or a statement you must complete by selecting a, b, c or d. Read the stem carefully. Students often make errors because they rush and miss important words. Don't assume you know what the stem says or you may read what you assume, not what it actually says. Read the stem with the answer choices covered. Before uncovering the choices, try to predict the answer. Uncover the choices and read each one carefully. Even if the first choice seems correct keep reading! **Remember, on multiple choice tests, you are looking for the best answer**. Another choice may be more accurate.

Decision dilemma. On a multiple choice test, incorrect choices are called *distractors*. A typical multiple choice question will have a stem, three distractors, and a correct choice. There's usually one choice which is obviously wrong and can be quickly eliminated. Students are often able to narrow the choices down to two options, then face a decision dilemma. That's when both answers seem (and may actually be) correct. The student reads back and forth between the choices hoping to eliminate one or the other, and ends up guessing. Here are some tips to help you find the best, most accurate choice in a decision dilemma:

> **Tip.** Read through the whole stem and answer choices as complete sentences. If a choice **does not grammatically agree with the stem**, eliminate it.

> **Tip.** Read through the whole stem and each answer choice. Consider which choice more completely addresses the question. If an answer is **only partly true, or is true only under certain narrow conditions**, it's probably not the best answer. You can eliminate it.

> **Tip.** Read through the whole stem and each answer choice. If you have to make assumptions, or read additional facts or conditions into the choice to make it work, it's probably not the correct choice. **Take choices on face value**; do not read additional information or facts into them.

All of the above/none of the above questions. If you are certain one of the statements is true don't choose "None of the above." If you are certain one of the statements is false don't choose "all of the above." The "all of the above" or "none of the above" choice is often a distractor. If you are sure that at least two of the answers are correct, choose "all of the above."

Absolutes. Pay special attention when an answer choice is stated in an absolute. Absolutes are words like: *never, always, just, only, none, not, must, solely, invariably, totally, every, entirely, no and all.* When an absolute appears in the stem, circle it. If it appears in the choice, read the stem and the choice as a single sentence. Ask yourself *Is this 100% the case 100% of the time?* **An absolute is often an indicator of a distractor.**

What if you really, truly cannot decide on an answer?

Strategic guessing. Sometimes, no matter how hard you studied, you really, truly cannot figure out the correct choice. You can't even narrow it down to two choices! In that case, you have to guess. Don't randomly guess "c" or close your eyes and point like some students do! You can significantly increase your odds of making the correct choice by guessing strategically:

➡ Try to identify the obvious distractor and eliminate it.

➡ Eliminate any choice using an absolute.

➡ Eliminate the "all of the above" or "none of the above" choices.

➡ Eliminate the choice that does not grammatically agree with the stem.

What are strategies for true/false tests?

Segmented true/false statements. In middle school, true/false tests questions (which are actually statements) are relatively simple and straightforward.

Example:
> T   F   *Scientists classify life forms in groups called kingdoms.*

In high school and college, true/false statements are more complex. They are longer and may contain multiple segmented parts, which can make it hard to determine the answer.

Example:
> T   F   *Scientists classify life forms in five kingdoms, Monera, Protists, Fungi, Plant and Animal, which are further classified into Phyla.*

When given a compound or complex statement on a true/false statement, **read each segment or part set off by a comma as an independent statement**. For the answer to be "true", **each segment must be true**. If any one part is false, the entire statement is false.

Example:
> T   F   *Secretary of State Hillary Rodham Clinton went to Columbia University and graduated with honors in 1966.*

For the answer to be true, *each* of the following must be true:

☐ she is/was Secretary of State   ☐ she graduated in 1966

☐ she went to Columbia University   ☐ she graduated with honors

(BTW the answer is false. She went to Wellesley College and she graduated in 1969. It is true that she graduated with honors and has served as Secretary of State.)

Absolutes. A true/false statement containing an absolute is suspicious. Absolutes often indicate a false statement.

What are tips for avoiding marking errors on a scannable answer form?

Until such time as all tests have gone digital, another test-taking challenge you'll face is having to use a scannable answer form where answers are either "bubbled-in" (●) or indicated by filling in a small horizontal rectangle (▬). Scannable answer forms can be confusing. (Check out the sample scan form on page 233) So many rows of numbers! So many tiny bubbles! Here are some tips for successfully marking your answers on a scannable answer form:

Preview the Scan Form. Take a minute before the test to familiarize yourself with the scan form sheet and how you'll move through it to mark your answers. If there 50 questions on the test, find answer line number 1. Put your index finger on line 1, then slide down the column through the rows of numbers (and over to the next column if you need to) until you get to answer line 50. You will move through the answer sheet in that direction.

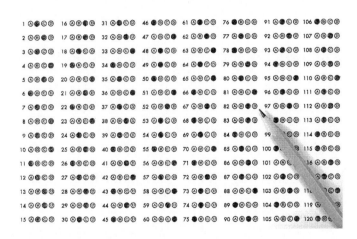

Use a #2 pencil. Most scannable answer sheets require number two pencils for an accurate scan. You need a good, clean eraser because dirty erasers can leave smears on the form. Thoroughly erase changed answers. Scanners are sensitive to rogue pencil marks.

Q&A Match Up. With so many columns, rows, numbers and letters, it takes concentration to stay on the answer line that corresponds to the question number. It's common for students to inadvertently skip or double-bubble a row, only to discover their mistake at the end of the test when the marked answers exceed or fall short of the number of questions. If you miss or double-bubble a row on a scan form, all subsequent answers will be incorrect. Ouch! Here's how to avoid this disaster:

→ Place the index finger of your free (non-writing) hand on the scan form, on the number of the question you're answering. Before bubbling-in your answer, look back at the question sheet. Make sure the question number and the "finger number" match. Bubble-in your answer, then scan the row to make sure there's only one answer bubbled-in. No double-bubbles! Slide your finger to the next number.

→ If the finger sliding/tracking method isn't for you, try pausing about every five answers to make a quick check to confirm that the number of the question you're answering matches the scan form row you're on. If they don't match up, you have a problem, but at least you won't have to go far to find the error.

→ Use a piece of blank binder paper or index card to cover up the filled rows as you work through the test. Each time you answer a question, move the paper down a row, so you do not inadvertently double-bubble a row. (Warning: Some test situations bar the use of any paper that could contain notes or answers. Get your teacher or proctor's permission before you use this method.)

→ If you're struggling with an answer and want to leave a row blank and return to it later, make a light pencil mark dash "–" on the scan form to the left of the question number. That tells you that it was intentionally left blank, and alerts you to return to that question later. Erase the dash after you bubble-in your answer.

Get into the multiple choice mentality

The next time your teacher announces that a test or quiz will be multiple choice, you may still be relieved that it's not an essay test, but don't kid yourself that it'll be easier. Use these strategies to do your best:

- Identify the information that will be on the test.
- Study holistically.
- Turn your textbook information and class notes into questions and answers including right, wrong, and slightly inaccurate choices.
- In a decision dilemma, use test-taking strategies to eliminate distractors and find the best answer.
- On true/false tests, be certain each segment is true before you circle T.
- When you take a multiple choice test on a scannable answer form, avoid disaster by practicing safe marking techniques.

Remember, you're a lean, mean multiple choice test-taking machine!

Name: _____

Conquer Decision Dilemma!

Questions 1-3 relate to the following question:

> The people of Canada
> a. a country located north of the United States.
> b. are all descendants of Nordic traders.
> c. honor Queen Elizabeth II as head of state.
> d. live in ten states and two territories.

1. What clue tells you **a** is a distractor?

   _____

2. What clue tells you **b** is probably distractor?

   _____

3. Select between **c** and **d**. Explain your choice and why you eliminated the other.

   _____

   _____

   _____

   _____

   _____

   _____

4. In the following true/false sample, list each fact which must be true in order for the answer to be true.

   > T   F   *The complementary base pairing of AT and CG is the basis of DNA replication, ensuring that both of the strands of DNA have exactly the same message contained in them.*

   _____

   _____

   _____

   _____

Question 5 relates to the following question:

> *Even prior to 1700, images of eagles can be found:*
> *a. on stamps*
> *b. on the U.S. government seal*
> *c. on business cards*
> *d. on coins*

5. Which is the obvious distractor and how did you recognize it? What other distractor(s) did you identify and how?

_____

_____

_____

Questions 6 and 7 relate to the following question:

> *From west to east, the major geographic features of the United States are:*
> *a. Rocky Mountains → Great Plains → Mississippi River → Appalachian Mountains*
> *b. Great Plains → Mississippi River → Rocky Mountains → Appalachian Mountains*
> *c. Rocky Mountain → Great Plains → Appalachian Mountains → Mississippi River*
> *d. Mississippi River → Appalachian Mountains → Pine Lake → Rocky Mountains*

6. Circle the key words in the *stem*.

_____

_____

7. What memory/study technique could help students recall the information necessary to select the correct answer on this question?

_____

8. List 10 *absolutes*:

_____

_____

9. When an *absolute* appears in a stem or question, what should you ask yourself?

_____

10. What does it mean to take choices *on face value*?

_____

_____

1. Ⓐ Ⓑ Ⓒ Ⓓ   26. Ⓐ Ⓑ Ⓒ Ⓓ   51. Ⓐ Ⓑ Ⓒ Ⓓ   76. Ⓐ Ⓑ Ⓒ Ⓓ

2. Ⓐ Ⓑ Ⓒ Ⓓ   27. Ⓐ Ⓑ Ⓒ Ⓓ   52. Ⓐ Ⓑ Ⓒ Ⓓ   77. Ⓐ Ⓑ Ⓒ Ⓓ

3. Ⓐ Ⓑ Ⓒ Ⓓ   28. Ⓐ Ⓑ Ⓒ Ⓓ   53. Ⓐ Ⓑ Ⓒ Ⓓ   78. Ⓐ Ⓑ Ⓒ Ⓓ

4. Ⓐ Ⓑ Ⓒ Ⓓ   29. Ⓐ Ⓑ Ⓒ Ⓓ   54. Ⓐ Ⓑ Ⓒ Ⓓ   79. Ⓐ Ⓑ Ⓒ Ⓓ

5. Ⓐ Ⓑ Ⓒ Ⓓ   30. Ⓐ Ⓑ Ⓒ Ⓓ   55. Ⓐ Ⓑ Ⓒ Ⓓ   80. Ⓐ Ⓑ Ⓒ Ⓓ

6. Ⓐ Ⓑ Ⓒ Ⓓ   31. Ⓐ Ⓑ Ⓒ Ⓓ   56. Ⓐ Ⓑ Ⓒ Ⓓ   81. Ⓐ Ⓑ Ⓒ Ⓓ

7. Ⓐ Ⓑ Ⓒ Ⓓ   32. Ⓐ Ⓑ Ⓒ Ⓓ   57. Ⓐ Ⓑ Ⓒ Ⓓ   82. Ⓐ Ⓑ Ⓒ Ⓓ

8. Ⓐ Ⓑ Ⓒ Ⓓ   33. Ⓐ Ⓑ Ⓒ Ⓓ   58. Ⓐ Ⓑ Ⓒ Ⓓ   83. Ⓐ Ⓑ Ⓒ Ⓓ

9. Ⓐ Ⓑ Ⓒ Ⓓ   34. Ⓐ Ⓑ Ⓒ Ⓓ   59. Ⓐ Ⓑ Ⓒ Ⓓ   84. Ⓐ Ⓑ Ⓒ Ⓓ

10. Ⓐ Ⓑ Ⓒ Ⓓ   35. Ⓐ Ⓑ Ⓒ Ⓓ   60. Ⓐ Ⓑ Ⓒ Ⓓ   85. Ⓐ Ⓑ Ⓒ Ⓓ

11. Ⓐ Ⓑ Ⓒ Ⓓ   36. Ⓐ Ⓑ Ⓒ Ⓓ   61. Ⓐ Ⓑ Ⓒ Ⓓ   86. Ⓐ Ⓑ Ⓒ Ⓓ

12. Ⓐ Ⓑ Ⓒ Ⓓ   37. Ⓐ Ⓑ Ⓒ Ⓓ   62. Ⓐ Ⓑ Ⓒ Ⓓ   87. Ⓐ Ⓑ Ⓒ Ⓓ

13. Ⓐ Ⓑ Ⓒ Ⓓ   38. Ⓐ Ⓑ Ⓒ Ⓓ   63. Ⓐ Ⓑ Ⓒ Ⓓ   88. Ⓐ Ⓑ Ⓒ Ⓓ

14. Ⓐ Ⓑ Ⓒ Ⓓ   39. Ⓐ Ⓑ Ⓒ Ⓓ   64. Ⓐ Ⓑ Ⓒ Ⓓ   89. Ⓐ Ⓑ Ⓒ Ⓓ

15. Ⓐ Ⓑ Ⓒ Ⓓ   40. Ⓐ Ⓑ Ⓒ Ⓓ   65. Ⓐ Ⓑ Ⓒ Ⓓ   90. Ⓐ Ⓑ Ⓒ Ⓓ

16. Ⓐ Ⓑ Ⓒ Ⓓ   41. Ⓐ Ⓑ Ⓒ Ⓓ   66. Ⓐ Ⓑ Ⓒ Ⓓ   91. Ⓐ Ⓑ Ⓒ Ⓓ

17. Ⓐ Ⓑ Ⓒ Ⓓ   42. Ⓐ Ⓑ Ⓒ Ⓓ   67. Ⓐ Ⓑ Ⓒ Ⓓ   92. Ⓐ Ⓑ Ⓒ Ⓓ

18. Ⓐ Ⓑ Ⓒ Ⓓ   43. Ⓐ Ⓑ Ⓒ Ⓓ   68. Ⓐ Ⓑ Ⓒ Ⓓ   93. Ⓐ Ⓑ Ⓒ Ⓓ

19. Ⓐ Ⓑ Ⓒ Ⓓ   44. Ⓐ Ⓑ Ⓒ Ⓓ   69. Ⓐ Ⓑ Ⓒ Ⓓ   94. Ⓐ Ⓑ Ⓒ Ⓓ

20. Ⓐ Ⓑ Ⓒ Ⓓ   45. Ⓐ Ⓑ Ⓒ Ⓓ   70. Ⓐ Ⓑ Ⓒ Ⓓ   95. Ⓐ Ⓑ Ⓒ Ⓓ

21. Ⓐ Ⓑ Ⓒ Ⓓ   46. Ⓐ Ⓑ Ⓒ Ⓓ   71. Ⓐ Ⓑ Ⓒ Ⓓ   96. Ⓐ Ⓑ Ⓒ Ⓓ

22. Ⓐ Ⓑ Ⓒ Ⓓ   47. Ⓐ Ⓑ Ⓒ Ⓓ   72. Ⓐ Ⓑ Ⓒ Ⓓ   97. Ⓐ Ⓑ Ⓒ Ⓓ

23. Ⓐ Ⓑ Ⓒ Ⓓ   48. Ⓐ Ⓑ Ⓒ Ⓓ   73. Ⓐ Ⓑ Ⓒ Ⓓ   98. Ⓐ Ⓑ Ⓒ Ⓓ

24. Ⓐ Ⓑ Ⓒ Ⓓ   49. Ⓐ Ⓑ Ⓒ Ⓓ   74. Ⓐ Ⓑ Ⓒ Ⓓ   99. Ⓐ Ⓑ Ⓒ Ⓓ

25. Ⓐ Ⓑ Ⓒ Ⓓ   50. Ⓐ Ⓑ Ⓒ Ⓓ   75. Ⓐ Ⓑ Ⓒ Ⓓ   100. Ⓐ Ⓑ Ⓒ Ⓓ

Name: _____

> As you move up into high school and college, multiple choice tests are more complex. Good test-taking skills include studying *holistically* for a multiple choice test, avoiding marking errors on a scannable answer form, and knowing how to recognize the best answer in the event of a decision dilemma.

1. On the scannable answer form above, put your finger on row one. Trace the rows from 1 to 100. What does this tell you?

   _____

2. There are four marking errors on the scannable answer form above. Find and circle each.

3. What is the consequence of any of the marking errors identified in question 2? What would the student have to do to fix the errors?

   _____

   _____

   _____

   _____

4. Marta is a using scannable answer form to take a test. She is distracted and confused by all of the bubbles and lines. Suggest some things she can do to minimize her confusion and ensure that her answers are synched with the question numbers.

_____

_____

_____

_____

_____

5. Write a true/false statement about yourself containing three segments, one of which is false.

_____

_____

6. If the statement you wrote in response to question 5 were on a true/false test, what *must* your answer be and why?

_____

7. What does it mean to study *holistically?* Why is this a good way to study for a multiple choice test?

_____

_____

_____

_____

8. On a multiple choice test, you are searching for the _____ choice.

   a. holistic
   b. correct
   c. best
   d. b and c

9. On a scannable answer form, how do you indicate that you intentionally left a row blank in order to return later to answer it? Mark the blank rows on the scanform on page 234 to indicate they were intentionally left blank.

_____

_____

10. If you absolutely do not know the answer on a multiple choice test, you may have to guess. What is **strategic guessing?**

_____

_____

_____

Dear Parent or Caregiver,

Today I participated in my study skills class based on *The Middle School Student's Guide to Study Skills*. One of the best ways I can prepare for high school and college is to use good study skills whenever I am learning.

I learned:

1. On a multiple choice tests, finding the correct answer is often by process of _____. Study holistically, with the goal of being able to recognize the right and _____ answers. Be able to recognize a _____ (wrong choice) which, even though it may be partly correct, is not the _____ choice.

2. On a scannable answer form it's common for students to inadvertently _____ or _____-bubble a row, only to discover their error at the end of the test.

3. The "question" part of a multiple choice question is called the _____, and often is not a question at all, but a phrase or a statement. Read it carefully with the choices _____. Try to _____ the answer.

4. Decision dilemma! Strategies for identifying the *best* of two seemingly correct choices are: Eliminate the choice that does not _____ agree with the stem; eliminate the choice which is only partly true, or true under narrow _____; eliminate the choice which requires you to make _____.

5. On true/false tests, _____ part of a statement (including parts set off by commas), must be _____ for the answer to be "true." If any part is _____, the answer is false.

Sincerely,

_____

HOW TO TRICK OUT YOUR ORAL PRESENTATION

Do you enjoy making a speech in class? Why or why not? What makes a speech successful? What makes a speech flop?

For a generation that's grown up on texting and Facebook, an oral presentation requiring eye contact and complete sentences can be a challenge. There are different types of speeches for different purposes and occasions. For example, an *impromptu* oral presentation is a short speech given with no preparation and little, if any, time for advanced thought, like when you are asked to introduce yourself at a meeting and tell about your interests or hobbies. An *extemporaneous* oral presentation is a presentation with limited preparation, such as addressing a topic in a speech competition or debate, presenting or receiving an award, or introducing a speaker.

Oral presentations in class are usually made for informative or persuasive purposes. They are expected to be prepared and practiced. Speeches aren't required as often as written tests, but when they're assigned, they almost always make up a significant portion of your grade in a class. Mastering the basic oral presentation is an important skill for high school, college, and career.

Chapter 22 Learning Goals:

☐ explain the process of preparing an oral presentation.
☐ tell speaking tips for making an effective oral presentation.
☐ make an extemporaneous oral presentation using speaking skills.
☐ critique oral presentation speaking skills.

WHY MEMORIZING YOUR ORAL PRESENTATION IS A BAD IDEA...

How to prepare an oral presentation

Review the rubric. Carefully read the oral presentation rubric or instructions. Understand your teacher's expectations and how the presentation will be graded. Search the rubric or instructions for key words, action words and presentation requirements. As with an essay, **the action and key words dictate the "what" and "how" of the presentation.** Determine the **purpose** of the oral presentation. (Is the purpose to inform, such as a book report? Is it to debate or persuade? Maybe the purpose is to inspire, honor or motivate, such as a speech to a team.) Note how much **time** you are expected to speak. Preparing a five minute presentation requires substantially more work than preparing a two minute presentation. Note whether you will be expected to include **visual aids** such as power points.

Write out your presentation. There's a saying that's popular with speakers: "Tell them what you're going to say, say it, then tell them what you said!" To prepare an oral presentation, write a rough draft of it in essay form. **A good oral presentation must have structure**. Include an introduction telling what you are going to say, a body saying it, and a conclusion telling what you said:

> **Introduction.** Tell your audience who you are and what you are going to talk about. The purpose of the intro is to get listeners interested in your presentation. Advise the audience of your thesis, the information that will be covered, and how it will be presented. Try to tell or show your audience something in the introduction that gets their attention and entices them to listen.

> **Body.** The body of the presentation is the longest part. It's where you present your main points and ideas. **Move from point to point by obvious and clear transition.** ("The next point I'd like to make is...") Try not to jump around or go back and forth between ideas. It confuses the audience. The number of ideas you present and how deeply you discuss them, depends on the amount of time you have for the presentation. Don't stuff so much information into a presentation that you have to rush to cover each point. On the other hand, don't make so few points that you end up without enough to say, and have to repeat points to fill time.

> **Conclusion.** A brief summary of the main points. If you have a message for the audience, such as the address of a website where they can find more information about the topic, or how they can help with a cause, tell them in the conclusion. Reserve a little time for questions from the audience. Finish your presentation by thanking the audience.

Make cue cards. Once you've written out your presentation and are satisfied with it, review the text and circle the main points. Make cue cards with main points condensed into key words and phrases. 3 x 5 index cards work great. Notes are acceptable too. Do not write the full text of the presentation on the cue cards. **You will not read from the cue cards, you will use them to prompt you to recall the main points in correct order.** If you've practiced your presentation well enough, the words and phrases on the cue cards should be sufficient to prompt your recollection of the content. Number the cue cards in case they get out of order.

Integrate visual/tech. In Chapter 14 you learned that *your eyes support your ears and your ears support your eyes*. **A good oral presentation includes visual aids.** Drawings, graphs, charts, pictures, comics, video clips, photos or maps make an oral presentation more effective and memorable. Select images that help your audience understand the points you're making. **If you are using slides, number them, and write the number on the coordinating cue card so the slides and the presentation stay in sync.** Do not read slides or other visual aids to your audience— *explain them*. Use bullet points instead of full sentences for text. Practice your entire presentation using the visual aids. Finally, tech is not infallible, so have a backup source for visual aids, like a copy on a flash drive or disk—even a hand out.

Tips for tricking out your presentation

It's a rare person who can make an oral presentation with little practice and actually do well. **Oral presentation skills are learned skills.** You can be sure that any speaker who appears to be relaxed, confident, and completely comfortable in front of an audience has put in long hours of practice. In fact, many excellent public speakers confess that they've never really gotten over stage fright, but because they practice their presentation many times and have developed speaking skills, the audience never suspects they're nervous. These tips will help you trick out your presentation to make you look like you are an experienced speaker:

Voice. Practice your presentation aloud several times, so you can hear your voice, volume, pace and intonation. When presenting, speak loud enough so the person in the back row will be able to hear you, but don't shout. Unless you're trying to put your audience to sleep, try not to speak in a monotone. **Voice intonation is a tool speakers use to emphasize a point, or signal the transition between points.** An active, intonated voice makes an audience pay attention and want to hear more.

> **How to look like an experienced speaker:**
> 1. Use your voice as a tool.
> 2. Watch the time.
> 3. Speak at a normal pace.
> 4. Use gestures for emphasis.
> 5. Use facial expression and eye contact.
> 6. Regain composure with cue cards.
> 7. Use appropriate vocabulary
> 8. Don't memorize.

Time. Time your presentation. Make sure you meet the requirements set by your teacher.

Pace. Nervous speakers often rush through their presentation. Resist doing this! **Speak at a normal pace.** Pause between main points to allow your audience a chance to absorb information and recognize transitions.

Gestures. Standing still with your hands at your sides in robo-speaker mode is not interesting to an audience. On the other hand, excessive gesturing is distracting and can make you appear nervous. **It's perfectly fine to use your hands or walk around a bit to emphasize points.** Just don't get carried away with movement. Don't put your hands in your pockets or fiddle with your hair during a presentation.

Facial expression and eye contact. This is no time to master your deadpan delivery. **Facial expression is important!** It draws your audience in. If you look bored, your audience will be bored. If you look sincere and interested, your audience is more likely to be interested in what you have to say. Make eye contact with audience members—not with your shoes or the ceiling. Don't stare at your cue cards. Look around at all of the audience, not just at one or two people, or at the front row.

Pauses. If you get stuck or lose track of where you are in your presentation, try not to mutter "ummmm" or giggle nervously. Pause, and look at your cue card to find your place. **Take a breath, regain your composure and move on.** The pause may seem like an eternity to you, but audiences are pretty tolerant and will barely notice.

Vocabulary. When you give an oral presentation, you must appear to be an expert. **That requires seriousness of purpose and use of appropriate vocabulary.** Do not demean your role as expert by infusing the presentation with middle school student jargon like "awesome," "sucks," or "ya know?"

Memorization. Novice presenters are often tempted to memorize their entire presentation, then recite it from memory. Do not do this. Memorization is a technique for acting. You are speaking, not acting. **Memorization is a poor oral presentation technique because it does not allow for flexibility.** More often than not, memorization backfires because the speaker forgets part of the speech, gets confused, and has to backtrack through the speech to prompt their memory. Memorizers often speed through delivery ending up with a presentation that sounds unnatural, and falls short of the time mark. It's truly much easier to make a good presentation with practice and reliable cue cards, than to memorize it.

How to develop speaking skills

If you plan to pursue a leadership position in a high school club or association, or are interested in a college major or career requiring oral communication, good speaking skills are essential. In high school, you will have many opportunities to develop speaking skills. The debate team is an excellent place to hone skills, as are clubs like Youth in Government (YIG), Model United Nations (MUN), Junior Statesman of America (JSA) and Junior Toastmasters. Developing your public speaking skills through one of these fun associations also goes a long way toward improving your ability to make an effective informative or persuasive oral presentation in the classroom. Developing competence as a public speaker is a good skill for high school, college, and career.

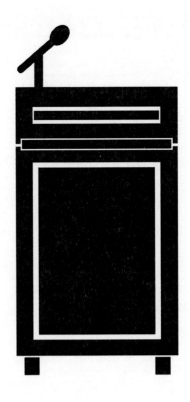

Name: _____

The One Minute Presentation

You will prepare a one minute oral presentation on a topic selected at random. Include an introduction, body and conclusion. Focus on using your voice, intonation, and facial expression. Use your hands to emphasize points. Watch your pace. If you lose concentration, try not to say "ummm" or giggle. When you conclude, thank your audience and refer them to the chart on page 245 to critique your presentation. (Use this page as your cue card.)

Topic: _____

Introduction

_____

_____

Body

Point 1

_____

_____

_____

Point 2

_____

_____

_____

Point 3

_____

_____

_____

Conclusion

_____

_____

_____

ORAL PRESENTATION CRITIQUE CHECKLIST

SPEAKING SKILL	CRITIQUE		NOTES
Volume	Volume was adequate.	Too soft or too loud.	
Gestures	Gestures were appropriate and used to emphasize points.	Too few or too many. Hands in pockets or fiddled with hair, etc.	
Pace	Good pace.	Too fast or too slow.	
Eye contact	Good eye contact. Looked around at the audience, not just at the front row.	Looked up or down, but made little/no eye contact; stared at one or two people.	
Time	On time.	Under/over 1 minute.	
Intonation	Used voice to emphasize points and indicate transitions.	Monotone – could use a little vocal variety.	
Pauses/loss of concentration	Handled well; looked at cue cards and got back on track.	Said "ummm" "uhhhh" giggled, looked around, or gave up.	
Facial expression	Used facial expressions to draw in audience; looked interested in their own message.	Deadpan delivery. Could use a little more facial expression.	
Vocabulary	Used "expert-appropriate" language	Too much slang or informal language. (i.e. "awesome" "ya know" "and like" etc.)	
Introduction	Introduced themselves, the topic and thesis.	No introduction; dove into presentation without telling the audience about their topic or thesis.	
Body of presentation	Points were clearly stated; transitions clearly made.	Points not clearly made; transitions not clearly indicated; jumped around between ideas.	
Conclusion	Summarized their presentation. Asked for questions. Thanked the audience.	Ended abruptly. Didn't thank the audience or allow questions.	

Name: _____

Awesome Advice for A.J.

> A.J., a student at U.B. Smart Middle School, has to make a three minute oral presentation in Miss Loveless' literature class. Knowing that you're an expert on oral presentations, he's asked your advice.

1. "I have to give a 3 minute oral presentation in my literature class on Friday. My teacher, wants us to argue for or against a particular 20th century author as the most influential on modern American literature. What kind of presentation is that?"

   _____

2. "I'm a pretty good talker, and have a basic idea of what I want to say. I think I can wing it. What do you think?"

   _____

   _____

3. "If I don't wing it, how should I prepare for my oral presentation?"

   _____

   _____

   _____

   _____

4. "What are cue cards and how do I use them?"

   _____

   _____

   _____

   _____

5. "Should I memorize my presentation?"

   _____

   _____

6. "I feel totally awk standing up and talking in front of people, even if it is just a bunch of my classmates. What speaking skills can help me overcome this, or at least appear less nervous?"

_____

_____

_____

_____

_____

_____

_____

_____

7. "When I'm talking in front of an audience I don't know what to do with my hands so I shove them in my pockets. Is that ok?"

_____

8. "When I lose track of my place in my presentation or I get confused, I sometimes say "ummm" or start laughing. It's totally embarrassing. What should I do if that happens?"

_____

_____

_____

9. "Should I thank the audience for listening? If so, when? What should I say?"

_____

_____

_____

10. "I am using Power Points for my presentation. There's a lot of text on them. Is it cool if I just read the slides to the audience?"

_____

_____

_____

Dear Parent or Caregiver,

Today I participated in my study skills class based on *The Middle School Student's Guide to Study Skills*. One of the best ways I can prepare for high school and college is to use good study skills whenever I am learning.

I learned:

1. An _____ speech is an oral presentation given with a little time to prepare, such as in a debate, introduction of a speaker or acceptance of an award. Most oral presentations students make in school are to inform or persuade, and are expected to be _____ and _____!

2. _____ is a poor oral presentation technique because it does not allow for flexibility. It can cause a speaker great distress if they forget a part.

3. *"Tell them what you're going to say, say it, then tell them what you said."* A good oral presentation needs _____, including a(n) _____, a _____, and a _____.

4. Oral presentation skills are learned skills. To appear to be an experienced and confident speaker, use _____ intonation to signal transitions, speak at a _____ pace, do not make excessive _____, make _____ contact with the audience and try not to say _____ when you pause.

5. Oral presentation skills are a must for any academic or career leadership role. In high school, consider joining the _____ team, Model _____, Youth in _____, Junior Statesmen of _____, Junior _____, or any other club or activity to develop your speaking skills.

Ask me about the skills I learned today! Your support at home will help me make good study skills daily habit.

Thank you for all you do for me every day.

Sincerely,

_____

TAMING TEST ANXIETY

Do you get stressed out before a test? Have you ever blanked out on a test and been unable to answer a question, even though you knew the material? Why does this happen and what can you do about it?

Almost everyone gets a little nervous before a test. It's perfectly normal. But for some students, a bout of nerves can get so severe it causes them to have trouble concentrating, or even blank out on answers. This is called *test anxiety*. It's not the kind of stress you logically (and deservedly) feel when you've blown off studying for a test. Students who suffer from test anxiety often do poorly on tests in spite of the fact that they studied and are well prepared. Some students begin to feel nervous days or even weeks before a test. That's called *anticipatory test anxiety*. For others, the nervousness happens during the test. That's called *situational test anxiety*.

If you suffer from text anxiety, don't let it defeat you. Take action! Test anxiety can be tamed. Let's learn how…

Chapter 23 Learning Goals:

☐ explain types of test anxiety.

☐ tell tips to relieve anticipatory test anxiety.

☐ tell tips to relieve situational test anxiety.

Where does test anxiety come from?

The physical symptoms of test anxiety—the racing heart, tense muscles, queasy stomach etc., come from a stress hormone called *adrenaline* which the body produces when it's in a scary situation and wants o-u-t! The more important a test, the more severe a reaction can be. There are a lot of opinions about why students become anxious before tests. Some experts believe it may be a learned behavior resulting from a prior bad test experience. Others think it affects students who are inclined toward perfectionism and have a fear of failure. **The fact is, test anxiety is quite common.** It just affects students to a greater or lesser degree. If it begins to interfere with your performance on tests, it's time to tame the test anxiety beast!

Time to tame the test anxiety beast!

How do you control anticipatory test anxiety?

Make a plan. Do you feel anxious days before a test? Do butterflies in your stomach flutter their wings when you think about an upcoming test? **That's called anticipatory test anxiety, and experts say that our old nemesis procrastination may be at the root of it.** For some students, the very thought of a test makes them so uncomfortable that they ignore it and "stick their head in the sand." Later they have to cram to prepare, which adds to the stress. To quell anticipatory anxiety, take control. Wage all out war against procrastination. Face test preparation head on. **Create a good study plan, organize a study schedule, and stick to it. Planning, routine, and preparation go a long way toward controlling anticipatory test anxiety.**

Use your study skills. Build your test-taking confidence by using the study skills you've learned in this course, including **time-spaced learning, anticipating test questions, and self-testing.** The good study skills you have learned in this course have made you a faster, more efficient and effective learner. You should be confident in your ability to adequately prepare for any test.

Visualize success. Thinking positively about the outcome of the test helps control anticipatory anxiety. Don't let your mind wander to the dark side, seeing yourself failing the test and imagining all sorts of horrible consequences. **Replace negative thoughts or visions of failure with positive ones of you confidently taking the test and achieving a good outcome.**

How do you control situational test anxiety?

Expect a little anxiety. In an academic world addicted to tests and test scores, many students struggle with situational anxiety. It hits when they're taking or about to take a test. Sure, it would be great not to feel nervous at all, but how realistic is that? If you begin to feel a little nervous, don't be surprised by it. **Understand that it's normal. Don't focus on it.**

Have confidence in your test taking skills. Make a preemptive strike on situational anxiety by reminding yourself of your awesome test-taking skills. You know how to read a test question for action and key words. You know how to allocate your time on a test. You can brainstorm and activate your schema. You have essay and short answer skills, and if you run into trouble on a multiple choice test, you know strategies to help you select the correct answer. Remember: you're a lean mean, test-taking machine!

Relax and breathe. If you feel anxiety creeping up on you during a test, tell it "no" and push it away with your mind. **Take slow, deep breaths.** Relax your shoulders and neck—that's where muscle tension often builds. Don't think about it or give into the feeling. Visualize yourself doing well on the test.

Assess the threat. Anxiety is the body's reaction to a perceived threat. It starts pumping out adrenaline to charge up the muscles to either fight, or get the heck outta there! Ask yourself *What danger am I in here? What will really happen to me if I don't do well on this test? Is this a life-threatening situation? Aren't I overreacting a little?* It helps to remind yourself that, while failing a test is an inconvenience, and has obvious negative consequences, it won't actually kill you.

Ignore students who finish ahead of you. A test is not a race. There's no reward for finishing first and there's no penalty for finishing last. Take your time. Focus on doing your best. **The fact that other students finish before or after you has no significance.** Don't read anything into it.

Sacrificing sleep to study is a gamble.

Get your zzzzzz's! Shakespeare nailed it when he wrote "sleep knits up the ravell'd sleeve of care." It's important to get enough sleep the night before a test. Too little sleep can leave you edgy and irritated, adding to the adrenaline dump and making you feel more anxious. Sacrificing sleep to study for a test is a gamble. You may think you're learning, but you could actually be sabotaging your test performance. **Get a good sleep the night before a test.** When you wake up, spend a few minutes thinking about what you studied and **recalling information.**

Eat! Hydrate! Oxygenation, hydration and carbohydrates are the fuel that makes your brain work. Carbohydrates are transformed into glycogen which fuels the brain. Do you know your brain uses 50% of your body's glycogen? Brainy needs even more when it's stressed out and working hard on a test. **Do not go into a test hungry.** Eat breakfast in the morning. Grab a healthy snack and a glass of H20 before a test.

Write your fears away. Researchers at the University of Chicago recently discovered that students who are prone to test anxiety improved their test scores when they were allowed a few minutes before the test to write about their fears. Apparently, dumping anxieties onto a piece of binder paper frees up brainpower normally occupied by worries about the test. If you suffer from situational test anxiety, it's worth a try. Arrive a few minutes early to the classroom. **Write a paragraph addressing your fears about the test.** Visualize the anxiety moving out of your brain, down your arm, to your hand, and on to the paper.

Talk to your teacher. Test anxiety is fairly common, but if you feel it's affecting your test performance, talk to your teacher or counselor about it. They can help.

Name: _____

NOTHING IS SO FATIGUING AS THE ETERNAL HANGING ON OF AN UNCOMPLETED TASK.

HEY KIDS! HE MEANS THAT PROCRASTINATION CAUSES A LOT OF STRESS!

PROCRAST-O-METER

Anticipatory anxiety is the nervousness a student feels days or weeks before a test. **Procrastination** is often at the root of it. To tame test anxiety, wage all out war against procrastination! Create a study plan, organize a study schedule, and commit to it. Procrastination can be conquered!

William James

Bill Skillsworth

Take this survey then check your score on the **Procrast-o-meter.**
Scoring guide: **10 = No, never! 1= Yes, totally!**

← NO, NO NEVER! — YES, TOTALLY →

1. **I put low priority tasks ahead of high-priority tasks.**

    10   9   8   7   6   5   4   3   2   1

2. **I blow off important tasks and responsibilities to do fun stuff instead.**

    10   9   8   7   6   5   4   3   2   1

3. **I blame my "poor time management skills" when I fail to complete an assignment or adequately prepare for a test.**

    10   9   8   7   6   5   4   3   2   1

4. **My typical reaction to being assigned a project or report, or needing to study for a test is** *"Why do today what I can put off until tomorrow?"*

    10   9   8   7   6   5   4   3   2   1

5. **I delay working on a project or studying because I work more productively under pressure.**

    10   9   8   7   6   5   4   3   2   1

6. **I put off working on a project or studying because I'm more creative under pressure.**

    10   9   8   7   6   5   4   3   2   1

7. **My way of coping with the prospect of studying for a test or quiz is to stick my head in the sand and hope the test or quiz goes away.**

   10   9   8   7   6   5   4   3   2   1

8. **I can't start studying or working on a project until everything is "just right" (ie. I'm comfortable, organized, not hungry, not thirsty, in the right mood to start working, etc.)**

   10   9   8   7   6   5   4   3   2   1

9. **I have to rush to complete projects and assignments by the due date.**

   10   9   8   7   6   5   4   3   2   1

10. **I cram.**

    10   9   8   7   6   5   4   3   2   1

60 50 70 40 80 30 90 20 100 10

Mild procrastinator status. Figure out why and when you procrastinate. Do you really believe you're more creative, or study better at the last minute? That attitude can backfire in high school and college! Break the procrastination habit before it becomes a serious problem. When you're assigned a project or need to study for a test or quiz, make a study plan and stick to it!

Congratulations! You are not a procrastinator. You face projects, reports and test preparation head-on, without delay. The words "I'll do it later" are not even in your vocabulary! Keep up the good work.

Serial procrastinator status. You miss deadlines and due dates. You cram to prepare for tests. You waste a lot of time. Your procrastination has become a bad habit and it's affecting your grades. Conquer procrastination now, or one day it may take you down.

PROCRAST-O-METER

Name: _____

Taming Test Anxiety

1. With regard to test-taking, what are the differences between *anticipatory* anxiety and *situational* anxiety?

   _____

   _____

2. You're half way through a test. Most of the students have already handed in their tests and left. Should you be worried? What does it mean?

   a. Those students are smarter than you.
   b. You must have been given a different, harder test.
   c. Don't worry. It means nothing. Ignore them.
   d. They probably couldn't answer the questions and gave up.

3. Glycogen fuels the brain, so it's important to _____ before a test.

   a. glyke up
   b. chant
   c. eat something healthy, duh.
   d. study

4. To control *anticipatory* test anxiety it's helpful to:

   a. create a thorough study plan
   b. organize a study schedule
   c. stick to the plan and schedule
   d. all of the above

5. Some tips for controlling *situational* test anxiety are to:

   a. expect a little anxiety
   b. have confidence in your test taking skills.
   c. relax your muscles and take deep slow breaths
   d. all of the above.

6. According to researchers at the University of Chicago, how might writing about test-taking fears before the test reduce situational anxiety?

   _____

   _____

   _____

Create a PROCRASTINATION acrostic telling why procrastination is a bad habit and how you will conquer it.

P _____

R _____

O _____

C _____

R _____

A _____

S _____

T _____

I _____

N _____

A _____

T _____

I _____

O _____

N _____

Dear Parent or Caregiver,

Today I participated in my study skills class based on *The Middle School Student's Guide to Study Skills*. One of the best ways I can prepare for high school and college is to use good study skills whenever I am learning.

I learned:

1. _____ anxiety is not the kind of stress you logically (and _____!) feel when you blow off studying for a test. Students with this problem often do poorly on tests in spite of the fact that they have _____ and are well prepared.

2. Feeling nervous days or even weeks before a test, is called _____ anxiety; feeling nervous during the test is called _____ anxiety.

3. Strategies for controlling anticipatory test anxiety include making and sticking to a study _____ and _____; Anticipatory test anxiety is often the result of _____.

4. If anxiety creeps up on you while you are taking a test, tell it "_____!", push it away with your mind and take slow, deep _____; remind yourself that you have excellent test taking skills and strategies.

5. Students prone to test anxiety may be able to control their nervousnes if they _____ about the causes of their fears just before the test; unloading anxiety frees up _____ normally occupied by worries about the test.

Ask me about the skills I learned today! Your support at home will help me make good study skills daily habit.

Thank you for all you do for me every day.

Sincerely,

_____

Name: _____

WHAT DID YOU LEARN ABOUT TEST-TAKING TIPS & STRATEGIES?

1. In a short answer or essay test question, what is an *action* word? Why are action words important?

   _____

   _____

   _____

2. Circle the *stem* of this multiple choice question:

   It is warmer at the equator than at the North Pole because _____

   a. the equator has a larger area than the North Pole.
   b. the equator is closer to the Sun than the North Pole.
   c. the equator receives more direct sunlight than the North Pole.
   d. the equator has more hours of daylight per year than the North Pole.

3. Circle the obvious *distractor* on this multiple choice question.

   George Washington was:

   a. a General in the United States Army.
   b. the first President of the United States of America.
   c. a peanut farmer from Georgia.
   d. signed the Declaration of Independence.

4. By using a *process of elimination* to find the answer to question 3, you may eliminate **d** as a distractor. What clue tells you **d** is wrong?

   _____

   _____

5. Anticipating questions and choices your teacher might include on a multiple choice test is a good way to study. When you do this, include:

   a. wrong, better and best choices
   b. choices with processes and steps
   c. choices with chronology of events
   d. all of the above

6. Always reserve a few minutes at the end of a test to proof and edit your essay. To keep your edits neat, and your essay legible, use proofing symbols:

   ^ = _____   (sp) = _____

   stet = _____   ¶ = _____

   ℮ = _____

7. Decision dilemma! On a multiple choice test, when deciding between two choices which both seem correct, eliminate the choice that:

    a. grammatically agrees with the stem.
    b. is true only under certain narrow conditions
    c. needs additional facts read into it (or assumed) to make it work
    d. b and c

8. How can *voice intonation* be used effectively in an oral presentation?

    _____

    _____

9. How can the speaker's *facial expression* add to their message in an oral presentation?

    _____

    _____

10. In an oral presentation, what are *cue cards* used for?

    _____

    _____

11. When an action word tells you to *analyze* a key word, concept or idea, what should you do?

    _____

    _____

12. In the following sentence, state every fact that must be true in order for the answer to be "true."

    Transferases are enzymes that transfer molecules and trigger the transfer of a functional group.

    _____

    _____

13. The debate team is an excellent place to develop oral presentation skills, as are clubs like Youth in Government (YIG), Model United Nations (MUN), Junior Statesman of America (JSA) and Junior Toastmasters. Go to your future high school's website. What opportunities does the school offer for students to develop public speaking skills?

    _____

    _____

14. What is your strongest test-taking skill? What test-taking skills do you need to improve?

    _____

    _____

    _____

SO CLOSE YET SO FAR... DISTANCE LEARNING

Ready or not, here it comes! Distance learning ("DL") is headed your way. DL has many aliases: *"Online courses," "online learning," "virtual classroom," "distance education," "e-learning,"* and *"web-based learning."* DL is a program or class delivered over the internet instead of in a traditional classroom.

The proliferation of smart devices such as iPads, cell phones, tablets, and laptops means that education is increasingly tech-based. Have you ever wondered what it would be like to take an entire course online? What would you like about it? What problems might you encounter?

DL is a fast-growing trend in American education. In high school and college, you will take one, or even several DL courses. Along with the many benefits of DL come a few challenges. The ability to work successfully online is an important study skill.

In this chapter you'll explore distance learning, and check out its benefits and challenges...

Chapter 24 Learning Goals:

☐ define distance learning.
☐ identify the benefits and challenges of distance learning.
☐ state strategies for a successful online learning experience.
☐ observe the navigation of a distance learning course.

How does distance learning work?

There are thousands of online DL courses, covering just about every subject. In high school and college, teachers and administrators select the DL courses students may take for credit. In high school, students take DL courses designed by an online company or publisher. In college, DL courses are often created by professors. In a DL course, students are supervised and graded by a teacher, professor or "course facilitator" at the high school or college. Course materials, including all reading, study guides, worksheets, and quizzes are accessed through the course website. For example, lots of high school students take a popular online American Government course. The course appears on their schedule as a regular class, but with no assigned period. Students go to the course website and set up a student account with a user name and password. From that point on, all of their course work is completed online, through the website.

What are the benefits of distance learning?

Anytime, anywhere! An obvious benefit of DL is freedom! Students can choose when and where to "go to class." As long as they have a computer, tablet or digital device with internet access they can access their course account and work from anywhere in the world 24/7. Another benefit: No dress code! Jammies and slippers are acceptable attire.

A big advantage of DL: You can attend class from anywhere, anytime!

Materials included. No more toting around heavy textbooks. Online courses are taught in *modules*, which are like lesson units. All the materials students need for a module are on the course website. The downside is, there may actually be more required reading than a traditional classroom course. DL students often underestimate the amount of time needed to complete the reading and other assignments in a course module.

Virtual and interactive experiences. DL courses are interactive, allowing for a rich sensory learning experience. A well-designed DL course includes links to audio and video resources such as music or other audio, film clips, and slides to improve comprehension and engagement with the course content.

Participation. DL coaxes students out of their shell and encourages participation in class. As distance learners, everyone's on equal footing. Since participation is generally by discussion board or chat, everyone gets a say, not just the talkative overachievers. "Classmates" can also be grouped for online projects.

Do-overs. Unlike the one-shot at information you get in the classroom lecture, DL enables students to read and reread materials, and listen over and over again to a lecture. Some courses allow students several attempts at a quiz, and provide instant feedback on errors and scores. There are however, limits to do-overs. For example, in March you probably can't access a module assignment or quiz you were supposed to complete in February. **Like a traditional class, there are deadlines and due dates.**

Upward mobility. DL enables students to take courses at a level of study more advanced than their current grade level. **With approval from their counselor, high school students can take college level courses or study subjects not offered at their school, such as a world language or advanced math course.** Because you can set your own schedule, it's not hard to take a DL course in addition to your regular courses.

Remediation and Credit Recovery. DL is popular option for students who need to repeat a class for **credit recovery**, or **remediate skills** before moving to the next level in a subject.

What are the challenges of distance learning?

System requirements. Obviously, students need access to a computer or smart device with a reliable internet connection. In a few rural areas in the U.S., the internet connection is still spotty, but those problems should resolve as broadband expands into even the remotest of locations. Most DL courses require

DL courses can be delivered through most mobile devices, as long as there's internet access.

the user to download a plugin. Most DL courses can also be delivered through mobile devices including smart phones, tablets and iPods. In fact, virtual delivery of content is getting so popular that many high schools are turning to BYOD or BYOT (Bring Your Own Device/Tech) programs, allowing students to use their mobile device in class to access digital content.

Program navigation. In a traditional classroom, students walk in, sit down and have a pretty good idea of how the lesson will be presented, and what is expected of them. Not so with DL programs. There isn't a standard DL course design. Some programs can be trickier than others to navigate. **When you enroll in a DL program, plan on spending some time learning your way around it.** Take the tutorial. Watch the demo. Check for download and system requirements. Try out the links, access the discussion board, learn how to post a message and contact the instructor. Know how to file an essay, take a quiz, track grades, and get the instructor's feedback. Fumbling around a DL program when you need to do your reading or post an assignment can make the DL experience frustrating.

Avoid losing your work in cyberspace by creating and saving extended responses outside the DL Program.

Submitting work. Have you ever accidentally deleted a document, or lost your work in cyberspace? DL programs suffer occasional tech glitches. Users can be timed out sooner than expected, or by going back a page, inadvertently delete their work. **To avoid this, compose extended responses or essays in a word processing program outside of the DL program, then copy and paste the response into the response window.** Some DL programs have a dropbox feature enabling students to file papers and essays by attachment. **Before you click "submit" always save copies of written work or posts.**

Submitting work outside of the DL program. Students may be required to submit papers, reports or essays outside of the DL program through a professional online submission service such as *TurnItIn.com*. **Build in additional time for this task, because it often does not go as smoothly as hoped.** Students must first create an account and password. Users may need to download a plugin or application. Users can encounter file format errors, file size limitations, or other problems uploading a document. **Allow plenty of time before a deadline to upload your work.**

Attendance. Guess what? The instructor or course facilitator is able to track exactly how often and for how long students log on, what files or pages they access, and when they log off. **If you don't "show up for class" for several days the instructor will know.** Regular attendance is important! Since students are able to log into their account using any mobile device with internet access, there's no excuse for poor attendance.

Time Management. DL classes can be surprisingly time-consuming. **In fact, they often require more time and more work than on-site classes.** After all, reading a lecture takes more time than listening to it. There's often a great deal of required participation and writing. Before starting a module, preview all of the required reading and assignments. Make an estimate of the amount of time it will take to complete the module work. Schedule the assignments in your planner. If you miss an assignment, don't count on being able to make it up. **Generally, when a due date passes, the assignment link in the module is taken down, and the student receives a zero for the assignment.**

Keyboarding. Would it be stating the obvious to say that strong keyboarding skills are important? Most DL courses require quite a bit of writing. **The ability to type with speed and accuracy makes an online class easier and more enjoyable.**

Logins and PWs. A minor hurdle, but accessing your DL account requires a student ID number, user name, and password. Select a user name and password that is secure, but easy to remember. Record your user name and password somewhere secure in the event you forget them. Being locked out of your account, or searching for a user name and password is stressful, and can result in a **missed deadline.**

Procrastination. Procrastination is a huge challenge for some DL students. No bell rings to tell them it's time for class. No campus security sends students to the office for a tardy slip. No classmates remind them of due dates or deadlines. **Students who are procrastination-prone and need structure, should be extra-vigilant about establishing a homework routine and sticking to it. Log in to your DL course at regular intervals as part of a normal homework routine.** Track DL course due dates and responsibilities in your planner or e-calendar as you would any other class.

Isolation. Students who enjoy interacting with other students in a traditional classroom might find DL a lonely experience. To combat the isolation from peers, some DL courses incorporate video conferencing. Others use a blended model, combining online learning with periodic classroom instruction or field trips with DL classmates.

The Flipped Classroom

A form of instruction called The Flipped Classroom is gaining popularity with middle and high school teachers. Under this model, students learn at home by watching a brief 5-10 minute video created or selected by their teacher. It may be a video of their teacher's lecture, or other online resource. Students watch the video, then write down questions and thoughts about it. The following day in class, they participate in a lab or practice activity related to the video. Flipped learning leaves more time for practice and individualized instruction from the teacher.

Be prepared for your future!

Distance learning has lots of benefits, but also quite a few challenges. When you are assigned to a distance learning program, don't get tripped up by the challenges! Take time to get to know the DL course program. Anticipate problems. Expect a lot of work. Preview modules in order to estimate time to completion. Log on at regular intervals as part of your normal homework routine. The ability to succeed in a distance learning program is an important study skill for high school and college.

Name: _____

DL Navigation Demo

Distance Learning ("DL") is becoming a popular format of American education. In high school and college, you will take one or several DL courses. The ability to work successfully online is an essential study skill. Your teacher has selected a DL course for you to review. Check it out and answer the questions below.

What is the title of the DL course? (ie. Government and Economics 101)

_____

How do students access the DL course? (What is the URL?) Do you log in through a link on teacher's web page?

_____

Does the DL course require a student number, user name and/or password?   yes   no

What downloads or plugins are needed for this course?

_____

Is there a course syllabus?   yes   no

Is there a tutorial or demo to help students learn how to navigate the DL progam?   yes   no

How do students communicate with the instructor/course facilitator? How do students communicate with each other?

_____

_____

Is there a course schedule?   yes   no

Can students view the course schedule or calendar by month?   yes   no

Can students view the course schedule or calendar by week?   yes   no

Is the course schedule interactive (links to assignments, downloads to iCal, etc.)?   yes   no

Can students view their grades and course progress?   yes   no

Is the course organized in modules? If so, how many?   yes   no   Number of modules: _____

How do students access module assignments posted by the instructor?

_____

Is there a video conferencing capability/link?   yes   no

Is there a discussion board?   yes   no

Is there a chat room?   yes   no

Are there links to content outside the program?   yes   no

Decribe two of the linked resources. (i.e. video? document? audio? slides? topic?)

_____

_____

How do students submit written work? Is there a dropbox?

_____

_____

Sample course readings or assignments for one module. Estimate the amount of time it would take you to complete the reading or assignments.

_____

_____

Are there any classroom or peer activities for students enrolled in this course? If so, describe:

_____

_____

In your opinion, is this DL program easy to navigate?   yes   no

What makes this program easy (or difficult) to navigate? How can it be improved?

_____

_____

Do you think you would succeed in this class as a distance learner? Why or why not?

_____

_____

Name: _____

So Close Yet So Far... Distance Learning (DL)

1. List the benefits of DL:

   _____

   _____

   _____

   _____

   _____

   _____

   _____

Could this be your classroom?

2. Which two benefits of DL do you find most appealing and why?

   _____

   _____

   _____

   _____

3. What are the challenges of DL?

   _____

   _____

   _____

   _____

4. For you, what are the two biggest challenges of DL? What specific things will you do to overcome these challenges in order to be a successful DL student?

   _____

   _____

   _____

   _____

5. What happens if a student misses a DL assignment deadline?

_____

_____

6. DL classes require students to actively participate in discussions, chats and message boards. Are you an active participant in the traditional classroom answering questions and contributing to discussions? Would your participation level increase or decrease in a DL class? Discuss.

_____

_____

_____

_____

7. Online programs suffer occasional operational glitches, and a student's work can be lost or deleted. When a DL course requires you to submit an extended written response, what should you do to protect yourself from loss of data?

_____

_____

_____

_____

8. Your teacher has decided to teach in a Flipped Classroom model. What does that mean?

_____

_____

_____

_____

9. What's your vote on The Flipped Classroom Model?   Sounds great!   Not for me.   I'd have to try it first

10. What's your keyboarding wpm (words per minute)? _____

    7th graders should be able to type about 35 wpm. If you haven't reached that goal, practice!

✽ Your friend Bella has just signed up for a DL course. She says she really likes DL because she can ignore the class most of the time, and get all the assignments done at the end of the month. What's your advice?

_____

_____

_____

_____

Dear Parent or Caregiver,

Today I participated in my study skills class based on *The Middle School Student's Guide to Study Skills*. One of the best ways I can prepare for high school and college is to use good study skills whenever I am learning.

I learned:

1. *Online courses, virtual classroom, distance education, e-learning,* and *web-based learning* are all names for _____.

2. DL is a course, program or class delivered over the _____ instead of in a traditional _____ setting.

3. List five advantages of distance learning:

   _____

   _____

   _____

4. List ten challenges of distance learning:

   _____

   _____

   _____

   _____

5. To avoid inadvertently losing written work, _____ documents and written responses in word processing outside of the DL program; _____ the response into the response window. Before you click "submit" or upload an attachment to the _____, _____ a copy of your work.

Ask me about the skills I learned today! Your support at home will help me make good study skills daily habit.

Thank you for all you do for me every day.

Sincerely,

_____

COGNITO ERGO SUM.

OUCH MY BRAIN HURTS! CRITICAL THINKING SKILLS

About 400 years ago, the great French philosopher René Descartes declared *"Cogito ergo sum."* (I think, therefor I am.) For hundreds of years historians and philosophers have debated the meaning of this famous statement. What does it mean to you? Have you ever heard of *critical thinking*? By the end of this chapter, you will declare:

*I think **critically**, therefore I am an awesome student!*

In 1956, some cognitive psychologists got together in a group headed by Dr. Benjamin Bloom to consider how to classify education objectives. They didn't examine *what* students should know. They considered *how* they should know. The result of their studies is a famous classification of learning objectives called *Bloom's Taxonomy* which guides the development of higher order thinking skills in students: *knowledge, comprehension, application, analysis, synthesis,* and *evaluation.* The ultimate goal is for students to become critical thinkers.

Critical thinking doesn't mean criticizing someone or something. It is a *process of thinking* that leads the thinker to the right conclusion or solution. Learning to be a critical thinker is an important skill for high school, college, and career.

Chapter 25 Learning Goals:

☐ list higher order thinking skills.
☐ explain the process of critical thinking.
☐ demonstrate critical thinking skills.

Why are higher order thinking skills important?

Knowledge is not static. It grows. It changes. It's flexible. There are many levels and dimensions to thinking. People can think conceptually, make assumptions, draw inferences, consider implications, argue different points of view, etc. **Developing higher order thinking skills is like moving beyond one dimension, fact-and-recite thinking, to thinking in 3-D.**

Can students learn to be higher order thinkers?

Yes and no. The ability to use higher order thinking skills is partly developmental. While the average first grader has the ability to learn the letters and sounds of the alphabet, it would be ridiculous to expect them to be able to reflect on the development of the alphabet and analyze its impact on western society over the past 2000 years. As your brain matures, it develops the ability to think at higher levels. Piaget (remember him from Chapter 12?) believed that thinking develops in stages, and that around the age of 12-16 the brain is mature enough to think critically.

How are higher order thinking skills demonstrated?

➔ **Knowledge.** Why do you suppose the first level of Bloom's hierarchy of thinking skills is *knowledge*? **Gathering knowledge is important, because it's impossible to think if you have nothing to think about!** Knowledge is the foundation of higher order thinking skills, so gather a lot of it. Read fiction and nonfiction books, study a variety of subjects, study maps, get a hobby, get up to date on developments in science and tech, listen to news and political commentary. Cut down on reality T.V. and celebrity gossip. You are not too young to gather knowledge about the world. Be a curious, engaged person and an active learner.

➔ **Comprehension.** To *comprehend* means to grasp the meaning of something or the importance of a fact. For example, the exclamatory sentence: "OMG, she has no clue!" read literally means that the subject *does not have the information she needs to solve a problem or a mystery*. However, your comprehension skills tell you that there is an alternate meaning to this statement. Comprehension is on the lower level of the thinking skills hierarchy, but still an important step toward critical thinking. Active reading, active listening, taking-notes, and outlining chapter textbooks are study skills that improve comprehension.

➔ **Application.** What good is knowledge if you don't use it? The *application* of knowledge means **to use what you know to understand situations and solve problems.** To be a successful student, you must apply knowledge to create solutions and solve problems. For example, if you know a little about history, apply that knowledge to try to understand what is going on in the world now. Use what you know about science to understand the environment, climate change, or other current issues in science.

→ **Analysis.** *Analysis means to distinguish among parts and ideas, know and recognize relationships among concepts and processes.* For example, you may be asked to analyze a pattern of behavior, or a character's motive. You may be asked to extrapolate and interpret data. **Analysis requires you to separate ideas, issues, or matter into parts for separate study, then explain how they relate to one another.** In high school and college it will not be enough to simply regurgitate facts. You must be able to analyze them.

Analysis separates ideas for study.

→ **Synthesis.** In terms of the hierarchy of thinking skills, *synthesis* is up near the top. It is sort of the flip side of analyze. It means *to combine separate elements or substances to form a coherent whole.* **Synthesis requires you to combine what you know to create, invent, design, build, compose or construct something.** In high school and college you will be expected to synthesize information and concepts from a variety of subjects and sources: the classroom, textbooks, labs and experiments, and the real world outside of the classroom.

Synthesis combines ideas or concepts to create a whole.

→ **Evaluation.** Higher order thinking skills culminate in *evaluation.* The ability to successfully evaluate something requires *critical thinking.* **Critical thinking is a process that applies logical reasoning, objective thought, and unbiased judgement to reach a conclusion.** When the process is followed correctly, the thinker is lead to a well-reasoned and accurate conclusion. There's nothing mysterious about critical thinking, but it does require effort, discipline and practice. In high school you will be expected to exhibit basic critical thinking skills. In college and career, deeper and more complex critical thinking skills will be required of you.

Critical Thinking for Beginners

Gather Information

Approach any problem project, paper, or report by gathering knowledge about the topic. Read. Research. Gather facts and data. Work holistically, keeping an open-mind. Don't exclude information that challenges beliefs, or contradicts ideas or opinions.

Assess Information

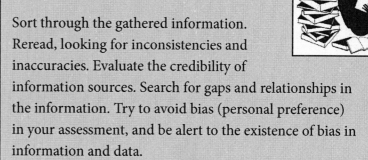

Sort through the gathered information. Reread, looking for inconsistencies and inaccuracies. Evaluate the credibility of information sources. Search for gaps and relationships in the information. Try to avoid bias (personal preference) in your assessment, and be alert to the existence of bias in information and data.

Apply Logic

Compare the information. Discriminate between ideas. Determine *fact vs. opinion*. A fact is *based on evidence and can be verified*. An opinion is a belief or conclusion that is not supported by evidence or fact. Beliefs are often presented as fact, so always look for supporting evidence. Reflect on the information you have gathered, and apply reason to make a judgement, reach a conclusion or find a solution.

Formulate a Thesis

A thesis is a simple statement of what you will prove, show or conclude from the information you have gathered, assessed and logically reviewed.

Make Your Argument

Base your evaluation on facts and evidence, not on feelings or beliefs. Refer back to the facts and evidence to prove your point. When writing or presenting any evaluation, avoid subjective language like "I believe", "I think..." or "My opinion is." Use logic jargon such as "Based on the evidence, I have concluded that...," "The weight of the facts indicates that...," or "The research best supports the conclusion that..."

Impress your teachers with your critical thinking skills!

In high school and college, teachers talk a lot about critical thinking, and frequently direct students to "use their critical think skills." Applying critical thinking skills in written and verbal exchanges will impress your teachers. When you are assigned a project, or even when you're just discussing a problem or issue in class, don't jump at a conclusion. **Ask questions about the problem or issue. Gather facts and information. Make a careful assessment of the information. Is a critical piece of information missing? Is there inconsistency or bias in the information? Verify evidence that claims to support a fact. Note when a fact is merely an opinion.** When you present your conclusion, leave emotion and personal opinion out. Demonstrate for your teacher how the facts and evidence support your conclusion. Show your teacher that you are a critical thinker.

Name: _____

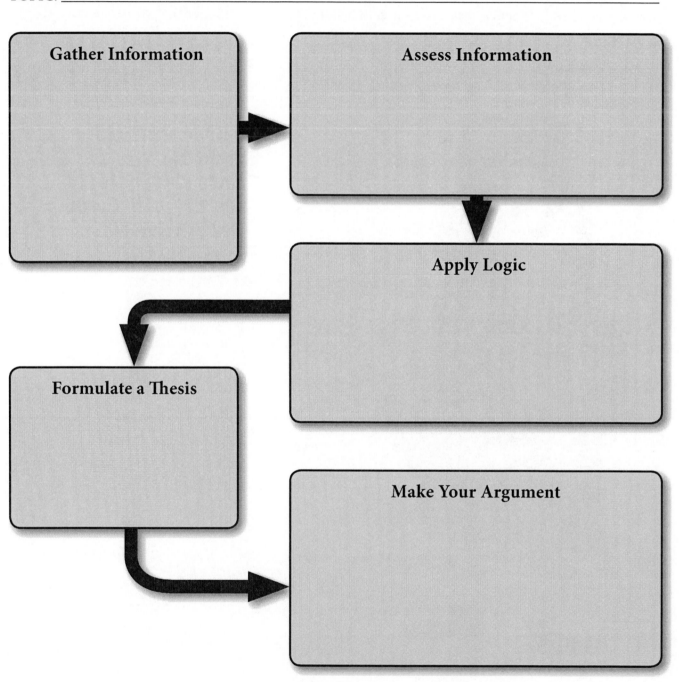

I Think (Critically), Therefore I am an Awesome Student!

Thinking critically means gathering and analyzing data, and setting aside personal bias or preconceptions to apply **logical reasoning, objective thought,** and **unbiased judgement.** Select a topic from page 283. Use this worksheet to follow the steps of critical thinking. Prepare a thesis and make a logical argument based on verifiable fact.

TOPIC: _____

Gather Information

Assess Information

Apply Logic

Formulate a Thesis

Make Your Argument

TOPICS: *I Think (Critically), Therefore I am an Awesome Student!*

1. Some middle schools have banned students from reading *Harry Potter* novels on the basis that they promote wizardry and sorcery, and that middle school students are too young and impressionable to read about such things. *Harry Potter* censorship: Right or wrong? Is there ever a benefit to censorship?

2. Padma and Lara have been friends since second grade. Padma's birthday was Saturday. She had a party but didn't invite Lara. When Lara found out she was devastated. She confronted Padma who explained "I'm really sorry, Lara, but my mom arranged for a party at the zoo. I know that being around animals triggers your asthma attacks, so I thought it was best if I didn't invite you." Lara accused Padma of being a bad friend. What is friendship? Padma: Good or bad friend?

3. Colin has been accused of cheating on a test. Here's how it went down: Colin's cousin Dominic is in the same grade at a different school. His school doesn't use that particular test any more so Dominic's teacher gave students a copy of the test as a study guide. Colin saw it on Dominic's desk and asked for a copy. Colin's teacher found out that he used it to study for the test. Colin's school is very strict about academic dishonesty so he's been suspended. Fair or unfair?

4. Which Disney princess best represents the ideals of a modern American teenage girl? What are the ideals of the modern American teenage girl?

5. Kenisha loves animals. She wants to be a veterinarian when she grows up. Her science teacher assigned a project requiring students to compare the pros and cons of using animals in medical experiments. Kenisha is 100% opposed to animal experimentation. She believes that animals have a right not to be used in medical experiments. Is she right about animal rights?

6. Avi and Emil have had it in for each other since kindergarten. It's gotten worse as they've gotten older. Today they had a fist fight in the cafeteria. Now the school counselors and parents are involved and the boys are in big trouble. Is it ever ok to fight?

7. Should middle school cafeterias be banned from serving cookies, or sugary foods other than fruit? Should a school be allowed to tell students what they can and cannot eat at school?

8. Use these lines to write down a topic assigned by your teacher:

    _____

    _____

    _____

    _____

Name: _____

Step Up to Critical Thinking

HIGHER ORDER THINKING SKILLS MOVE YOUR BRAIN BEYOND ONE DIMENSION, FACT-AND-RECITE THINKING. SUMMARIZE THE HIERARCHY OF THINKING SKILLS IN THE STEPS BELOW. THEN DRAW YOURSELF MOVING UP THE STEPS TO BECOME A CRITICAL THINKER.

EVALUATION:

SYNTHESIZE:

ANALYSIS:

APPLICATION:

COMPREHENSION:

KNOWLEDGE:

Dear Parent or Caregiver,

Today I participated in my study skills class based on *The Middle School Student's Guide to Study Skills*. One of the best ways I can prepare for high school and college is to use good study skills whenever I am learning.

I learned:

1. Dr. Benjamin Bloom's 1956 study didn't examine *what* students should know; it considered _____ students should know. Higher order thinking skills include: _____, _____, _____, _____, _____, and _____.

2. The foundation of higher order thinking is _____, so gather plenty of it! Cut down on _____ and _____.

3. Critical thinking applies _____ reasoning, _____ thought, and _____ judgement to reach a _____.

4. Beliefs or _____ are often presented as fact. Remember, however, that *fact* is based on evidence that can be _____.

5. Critical thinking is a process. Critical thinkers reach conclusions or find solutions based on _____ and _____; this requires them to discriminate between ideas, look for inconsistencies and inaccuracies, and determine fact vs. _____.

Ask me about the skills I learned today! Your support at home will help me make good study skills daily habit.

Thank you for all you do for me every day.

Sincerely,

_____

RAMP UP YOUR RESEARCH SKILLS

Go ahead—pat yourself on the back! You have the great fortune of being born into an era when most information is right at your fingertips. A mere generation earlier, research required the tedious tasks of going from library to library, culling through card catalogs, filling out form after form to check out books, and waiting (often weeks) for a book to be returned by another borrower. Information searches were made page-by-page. Copying required standing at a temperamental machine feeding it a nickel per page. It was a slow and painstaking process.

Isn't it ironic that, in spite of how easy it is to research these days, one of the biggest problems faced by first year college students is their lack of basic research skills? Many students assume that because they have good tech skills, they also have good research skills. These skills are *not* the same. The ability to use a computer, surf YouTube, instant message, share photos, use Facebook, download music and games, and upload a video, makes you *digital literate* not *information literate*.

Don't wait until you get to college to learn information literacy. Students who mistake digital literacy for information literacy can end up learning the hard way, through a failed class, or mandatory and costly remediation, that they need to ramp up their research skills!

Chapter 26 Learning Goals:

☐ compare digital vs. information literacy.
☐ list information literacy skills students need for basic college readiness.
☐ identify bias, relevance, accuracy, credibility, and currency in a sample article.

What is Information Literacy?

The National Forum on Information Literacy ("NFIL") is the go-to group for information literacy. Experts there say that to be information literate a student must be able to *identify, locate, evaluate,* and *effectively use* information for the issue or problem at hand. Information literacy is such an important 21st century skill, it's even the subject of a presidential proclamation:

> *"Every day, we are inundated with vast amounts of information… Rather than merely possessing data, we must also learn the skills necessary to acquire, collate, and evaluate information for any situation. This new type of literacy also requires competency with communication technologies, including computers and mobile devices that can help in our day-to-day decision making. [There is a need for] all Americans be adept in the skills necessary to effectively navigate the Information Age."*
>
> *President Barack Obama, 2009*

What is Information?

Seems like a simple question, but information is actually a complex concept. **Information comes in many forms.** The NFIL categorizes information as *factual, analytical, subjective,* and *objective*:

→ **Factual information** consists of short facts or statements, without explanation or elaboration. It's the type of information you find in reference materials like encyclopedias, dictionaries, and almanacs. It includes facts like dates, names, places, or statistics. Government agencies produce a lot of factual information.

→ **Analytical information** interprets or analyzes factual information. It is often published by experts, such as an automotive association analyzing the gas mileage statistics of various car models, or an association of healthcare professionals analyzing a report on disease control.

→ **Subjective information** is information presented from one point of view, such as an opinion piece in a magazine, newspaper or blog. Movie, restaurant, and fashion reviews are subjective information. Political and news blogs are subjective information because they are written from the point of view of the blogger.

→ **Objective information** encompasses many points of view, presenting all aspects of an issue or story with factual accuracy, and without judgement or opinion. Objective information includes fact-based, informative journalism that recounts important events and newsworthy issues, such as a war, elections, or natural disasters.

To develop college-ready research skills, whenever you receive information, whether by reading, hearing or watching, get into the habit of asking yourself: What type of information is this? Factual, analytical, subjective, or objective?

How do you locate information?

Sources of information

In high school and college you may be restricted to using primary sources for a report. Will you know what those are and how to find them?

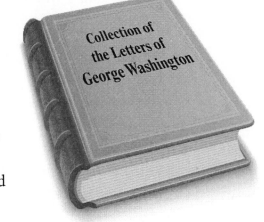

→ **Primary sources** can be difficult to find online because they are **original materials**. They include historical documents such as a handwritten letter, pages of a diary, an original recording of a news event, a newspaper article written at the time of the event, photographs, and original research reports. Copies are often maintained in a library or historical association's online archive, which is like a file that must be accessed and searched to find the source.

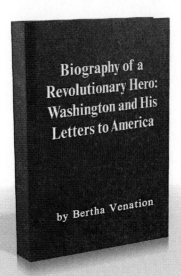

→ **Secondary sources** are papers, books, magazine articles, journals analyzing, interpreting, or evaluating a primary source.

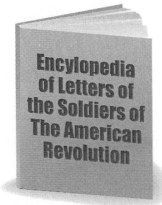

Tertiary sources are lists, compilations, digests, indexes or encyclopedia. Research often begins at the tertiary source, like a Wikipedia or encyclopedia article, then works inward to secondary sources, such as an article or book about the subject, then to the primary sources themselves.

To develop college-ready research skills, know the difference between primary, secondary, and tertiary sources. Get into the habit of thinking about a source as you read, watch or listen. Ask yourself: Is this a primary, secondary, or tertiary source?

Searching for information

Don't jump into a search. Choose search words carefully because they determine what kind of information is returned, and whether it is relevant to your topic. Think for a few moments about your research topic. Jot down key words and concepts. **Adding key words to a search makes it more specific to your topic and increases the chance that the search will return relevant information.** Cast a wider information net by including alternative terms or synonyms in your search. For example, if you are researching "types of cats" also search "feline breeds." If you are researching "ocean pollution clean up," also try "marine environmental remediation." If you can't think of alternative terms, include a "syn." next to the key words your search will bring up reference material including synonyms.

How do you evaluate online information for reliability?

You were just told how lucky you are to have so much information available to you with little effort, but there's a dark cloud to every silver lining, and this is it: Before the internet existed, information was pretty much limited to printed resources. All books and articles went through a publication process where they were reviewed, edited, and analyzed for accuracy by many people before being made available to the

Online information needs careful evaluation.

public, or allowed on a library shelf. The internet however, is a completely different animal. It is a *public forum*, which means anyone, anywhere can digitally publish any information, story or article, and make it immediately available for public consumption. Anyone can claim to be an "expert." Remember those critical thinking skills you learned in the last chapter? This is one place they definitely apply! Use your critical thinking skills to evaluate the *reliability* of online information:

Purpose. Personal websites are maintained by people with a **personal interest** in a topic. Special interest sites are maintained by groups of people with a **common interest**. Professional sites are maintained by institutions or **professional organizations**. There are news and journal sites, commercial/business sites, and government sites. Verify the *purpose* of a site or source before you use it.

Currency. You live in the Information Age. The world generates and circulates information at incredible speed. As a result, **information becomes stale and outdated pretty quickly, particularly in areas like science, tech, and medicine.** If you're researching a topic that requires current information, such as a state-of-the-art stadium design, or discoveries in biology, check the date of publication. Be sure your information is *current*.

Credibility. An author should **state their credentials** telling you why they are qualified to write a particular piece, or state an opinion on a topic. Credentials include affiliations and memberships, educational background, length of time in the field or industry, reputation, and other publications they have written. Verify *credibility* before you use information.

Bias. The ability to determine *bias* of sources is a big part of information literacy. Bias reflects **a preference for, or a prejudice against something or someone.** As a middle school student, you may not yet have enough life experience to immediately recognize bias in a source, but you certainly have enough intelligence to understand that sources can be (and frequently are) biased. Use your critical thinking skills. Be doubtful. Scrutinize. Investigate the writer's relationships or associations. Analyze the words chosen by the writer. Are they inflammatory or informative? Bias can be very subtle, or hidden under many layers of information.

Relevance. Information you use must be relevant to your specific topic. If you are researching "cat breeds," and you find an article on crazy cat tricks, it may be interesting, but it's not *relevant*.

Accuracy. When using quantitative research (such as statistics or measurements) check for *accuracy*. Scrutinize the research. Does it measure what you think it is measuring? Was the data collection procedure is reliable? Poor data collection practices may invalidate data. Generally, U.S. government agency reports are always considered accurate, reliable, and citeable sources.

Get into the habit of using your critical thinking skills to evaluate the reliability of digital (and print) information. Ask yourself: What's the purpose of this? Is it current? Is it accurate? Is there a possibility of bias? Is it relevant? Could it be inaccurate?

Are there restrictions on using information?

Plagiarism. Don't copy. Whenever you use a quote, paraphrase or summarize information from any source other than directly from your own brain, and use it in a paper, essay or in other writing, tell your reader about the source, otherwise you are taking credit for someone else's work. When you research, keep track of your sources and give them proper credit.

Citation. You know how credits run at the end of a movie? You must credit helpful sources at the end of a paper, report or essay. This is done by a sort of fussy arrangement of details called *citation* which includes the name of the author, title of the publication, date of publication, etc. There are three common citation styles: **MLA (Modern Language Association)**, **CTA (Chicago Citation)** and **APA (American Psychological Association.)** Different styles are used for different subjects. Teachers tell students which style they prefer. There are citation rules for all sources of information: books, journals, articles, audio recordings, websites, even blogs! Citation credits the author with the work, and tells your readers where they can find the sources you used. Free online resources can help you master citation styles. When you write a paper or essay, don't guess at the citation. Consult *citationmachine.net, easybib.com,* or *bibme.org.*

To be college-ready, understand that there are a variety of citation styles, know the basics of each, and know how to locate online citation resources.

What about using information from blogs?

Verify. A blog is an online journal or diary where people can express their opinion on just about anything. These days it seems like everyone, everywhere is blogging about everything and anything! Blogs are increasingly cited as information sources, but there are restrictions on their use: You must be able to *verify (1) who wrote the blog, and (2) that the blogger is a credible source.* Blogs that are part of, or connected to a news agency, magazine, university, professional association, online publication, or other credible site (like a sports expert who blogs for ESPN) are considered reliable, citable sources. As a general rule, self-published blogs (not connected to a credible site), are not considered reliable, citable sources. However, many experts and professionals are now quite active in the world of independent blogging, and since information literacy is an evolving and adapting field, **a self-published blog, written by a credible professional blogger within their field or profession, and under their real name, may be considered a citable source**.

What about Wikipedia?

Wikipedia is the ultimate public forum. Anyone can add to or alter information on a page. That impacts its reliability as a source. In fact, Wikipedia has experienced several accuracy errors in recent years. As a result, it is not considered to be a citable source. Many high schools, and most colleges follow a strict "Look-but-don't-cite" Wikipedia policy. Wikipedia is a great way to jump-start research, check basic facts, or find sources, but it is a tertiary source at best. **Do not cite Wikipedia in a paper.** Over-reliance on Wikipedia will impede your development of college-ready research skills.

Help! Where can students learn information literacy skills?

Don't be fooled by the unassuming demeanor of a school librarian. Librarians, also called "information technicians," have mad research skills. **Your best source for learning college-ready research and information literacy skills is a librarian.** If you are not taught information literacy in school, make an effort to learn it on your own. Many public universities have research skills information and tutorials on their website. Check your local public library for classes. Information literacy is an essential college readiness skill.

Librarians have mad research skills!

U.B. Smart Middle School's
FIGHTING OWL NEWS

MIDDLE SCHOOL STUDENT BITTEN BY SPARK-L-TEETH SCANDAL

Elena, a popular U.B. Smart Middle School student, is caught up in a dispute between rival toothpaste companies. Her science fair project compared Spark-L-Teeth toothpaste against Dental D'Light toothpaste to determine which brand is more effective in whitening teeth. Elena's research concluded that Spark-L-Teeth's product is superior to Dental D'Light's.

Popular student is under investigation.

Science fair officials have learned that Dental D'Light is suing Spark-L-Teeth for making false claims about Spark-L-Teeth's toothpaste. Since Elena's report relies on information from Spark-L-Teeth, her project is under investigation.

The Spark-L-Teeth/Dental D'Light conflict began over a recent advertisement. In the ad, ordinary smiling people vouch for Spark-L-Teeth toothpaste, claiming that since using it, they have 20% fewer cavities. One of these people, L.I. Arpants, claims her teeth "are 20% brighter." All of the smiling people received a case of Spark-L-Teeth for participating in the advertisement.

"We love Spark-L-Teeth!" people claim.

Elena's research also relies on information received from Spark-L-Teeth user and ex-NASA astronaut Col. Pho Nee, who writes a popular blog about space travel. He blogged that his teeth "shine like stars in outer space." He states that, in his expert opinion, he's had 15% better luck with the ladies because of Spark-L-Teeth.

Spark-L-Teeth spokesperson Pearl E. White, confirms that Spark-L-Teeth has the data to back up their sparkle superiority complex. She cites a 2001 U.S. Department of Smiles test confirming that an ingredient similar to the one used in Spark-L-Teeth is 15% more effective in whitening teeth.

Buck Tuth, President of the Tooth Fairies Association ("TFA"), and noted dental industry expert, is skeptical. "We believe the government data is flawed," he said, "Our fairies report that teeth from children who use Spark-L-Teeth are no easier to find in the dark than teeth from children who use

Buck Tuth is skeptical of Spark-L-Teeth's superiority claim.

other products. Our fairies note no difference at all."

Spark-L-Teeth and the TFA haven't always seen eye-to-eye, (or tooth-to-tooth!) Spark-L-Teeth recently mouthed off about the tooth fairies' refusal to leave money under the pillows of children with cavities. Dental D'Light has referred all questions to their law firm Dewey, Cheatem and Howe.

Name: _____

Help Elena respond to the Science Fair Committee's inquiry!

SCIENCE FAIR COMMITTEE

Dear Elena,

Thank you for participating in the U.B. Smart Middle School Science Fair. Due to the dispute between Dental D'Light and Spark-L-Teeth, the Science Fair Committee is asking you to confirm that your sources are unbiased, credible, current, accurate, and relevant. Please answer the questions below.

Thank you,

X. Perry Ment

Dr. X. Perry Ment
President, The Science Fair Committee

1. The people from the advertisement claim that since using Spark-L-Teeth, they have had 20% fewer cavities. Is this information *relevant* to your science project?

   _____

   _____

   _____

2. Ms. L.I. Arpants says her teeth are 20% brighter. Silly name aside, is Ms. L.I. Arpants' information *accurate*?

   _____

   _____

   _____

3. Are the "ordinary, smiling people" in the ad *unbiased* sources?

   _____

   _____

   _____

4. What type of information is the U.S. Dept. of Smiles statistics report?

   _____

5. Are U.S. government agency reports generally considered to be *unbiased, reliable* and *credible?*

   _____

6. Is the U.S. Department of Smiles report a *primary, secondary* or *tertiary* source?

   _____

7. What kind of website/blog does ex-Astronaut Pho Nee maintain?

   _____

8. You relied on information from ex-Astronaut Pho Nee's blog that Spark-L-Teeth improves romantic relationships. Is ex-Astronaut Pho Nee's opinion about the effect of whiter teeth on relationships *credible?*

   _____

   _____

   _____

9. For what topics of information would ex-Astronaut Pho Nee be a *credible* source?

   _____

10. Do you have *currency* or *relevancy* concerns about Pearl E. White's statement that the U.S. Department of Smiles report supports Spark-L-Teeth's claim?

    _____

    _____

    _____

11. What kind of organization is the TFA?

    _____

12. What type of information is the TFA report that analyzes the government data?

    _____

13. Is Buck Tuth a *credible* expert on tooth whiteness and dental matters?

    _____

    _____

    _____

14. Is there any evidence that Buck Tuth's opinion is *biased?*

    _____

    _____

    _____

Name: _____

> Your science class is studying energy. You must write a report on "The Future of Solar Energy in America."

1. What's your basic *search strategy*?

   _____

   _____

   _____

   _____

   _____

2. What are some *alternative search terms* for solar energy? How can you find *synonyms*? Find them and list them here.

   _____

   _____

3. You found a good article about a solar energy experiment. It is in a respectable online science journal. The authors are the very scientists who conducted the experiment! Is this a *primary, secondary* or *tertiary source*?

   _____

4. You found a 2012 report produced by the U.S. Department of Energy comparing the efficiency of solar energy with other forms of energy. Is this a *reliable* and *current* source?

   _____

5. You found information about a Colorado solar energy project in a blog written by an amateur scientist who calls herself "Solar Barb." She has written many blog entries discussing factors influencing the growth of solar energy in America. May you cite it?

   _____

   _____

   _____

6. You found an online video interview with a scientist who conducted solar energy experiments just like the experiments that are the topic of your paper. In the video, he discusses the results of other scientists' experiments. Is this a primary, secondary or tertiary source? May you use it?

   _____

   _____

   _____

7. You found an October 2007 article in *Newsweek* magazine titled *"The Power of the Sun."* What kind of information is this?

    _____

8. Is the *Newsweek* article a primary, secondary, or tertiary source?

    _____

9. Your teacher has instructed students to use MLA Citation format for your paper. How would you cite the *Newsweek* article? What website could you go to for help with the citation?

    _____

10. You found an online article arguing that there are several political factors influencing the future of a solar energy policy in America. You have searched and searched, but are unable to confirm the authorship. May you cite the article?

    _____

11. You found a report that is particularly informative and you would like to use it and cite it in your paper, but need to confirm the author's *credibility*. Which of these will you check?
    a. affiliations and memberships
    b. educational background and other publications
    c. reputation in the field or industry
    d. all of the above

12. You found a very convincing article by O.L. Wells, arguing that there's no future in solar energy in America. You almost altered your thesis, but remembering what you learned in your study skills class, decided to check the author's credentials for the possibility of bias. You discovered that O.L. Wells is a member of an association called FFF which stands for Fossil Fuels Forever, and has served as a lobbyist (paid advocate) for the petroleum industry. He is a noted energy development expert. Explain your strategy about how you will deal with this article?

    _____

    _____

    _____

    _____

    _____

    _____

✻ **Bonus:** May you cite a website?

    _____

Dear Parent or Caregiver,

Today I participated in my study skills class based on *The Middle School Student's Guide to Study Skills*. One of the best ways I can prepare for high school and college is to use good study skills whenever I am learning.

I learned:

1. Your impressive tech skills do not mean you are _____ *literate*, or have college-ready _____ skills.

2. The National Forum on Information Literacy ("NFIL") says that to be *information literate* a student must be able to "_____, _____, _____ and _____ information for the issue or problem at hand."

3. The NFIL categorizes *information* as _____, _____, _____ and _____. Because the internet is a _____ forum, any information obtained online must be carefully evaluated for _____.

4. Combine _____ words in a search, so the results you get are more relevant to your topic; use _____ search terms, (like synonyms) to cast a wider search net.

5. When evaluating information, use your _____ thinking skills to determine: _____ (whether the information is up-to-date), _____ (whether the author has a preference or prejudice), and _____ (whether the author is qualified.)

Ask me about the skills I learned today! Your support at home will help me make good study skills daily habit.

Thank you for all you do for me every day.

Sincerely,

_____

NOTES

GOOD CITIZENS! PERFECT PARTICIPANTS!

The importance of classroom participation and citizenship is often overlooked by middle school students. After all, there's no quiz on these skills right? These skills make up a percentage of your final grade in a class, so they deserve your attention. As you move up into high school and college, the level and quality of your classroom participation and citizenship skills are increasingly important to your success as a student.

Most middle school students would define participation as *raising your hand and answering your teacher's questions*. That's partly right. Answering questions, engaging in discussions, and volunteering ideas is important. Participation is also demonstrated by *active listening*. When students focus, make eye contact with their teacher, and take notes during a lecture, they are demonstrating good participation skills.

Other ways to participate include coming to class prepared, and enthusiastically engaging in a class activity or small group discussion, instead of sitting on the sidelines contributing nothing. Participation is also demonstrated by taking a leadership role in a team exercise or group activity.

Let's take a look at how and why to participate in class...

Chapter 27 Learning Goals:

☐ describe ways to effectively participate in the classroom.
☐ list the benefits of good classroom participation skills.
☐ assess classroom citizenship and participation skills in a skit.
☐ make a plan to improve your participation and citizenship skills.

Four good reasons to participate in class

Do you participate in class? What's the hardest part about participating? Why participate if the teacher already has all the answers? There are many good reasons to participate in class:

1. **Participation impacts your final grade.**

   Some teachers assign a hefty weight to participation – up to 20% of a student's final grade a class. Some teachers don't assign a weight, but instead award an "S" for Satisfactory or "U" for Unsatisfactory at the end of the term. Always review the class syllabus to determine the weight your teacher has assigned to participation, because it definitely impacts your final grade to some degree. **At the end of the grading term, a solid participation history might just provide the bump you need to get your grade up to a higher letter.**

> **Why Participate in Class?**
>
> 1. Participation impacts your grade.
> 2. Participation is good for the classroom community.
> 3. Participating helps you learn.
> 4. Participating is good practice for high school and college readiness.

2. **Participate because the classroom is a community.**

   Why go through a whole year of school without your teachers and classmates realizing what an awesome person you are? **A classroom is a community, and every student brings a unique and important perspective to it.** When every student participates, the community thrives. Besides, it gets boring hearing from the same students all the time. Class participation is also important because it enables a teacher to make a quick check of the depth and breadth of their students' understanding of the topic under discussion, and make adjustments to the lesson if needed.

3. **Participation is a good learning skill.**

   Generating thoughts in your head, organizing ideas, verbalizing your ideas and hearing yourself express them is an important part of learning. **Participation improves comprehension, retention of content, and speaking skills.**

4. **Participating is good practice for your future.**

   In high school and college, participation expectations are high. Verbal response and active commentary in classroom discussions are a common means of measuring a student's achievement. **In college, you will take classes called *seminars* where participation can count for up to 50% of your grade! You must be able to engage in intelligent discourse about an academic topic.** Participating now is excellent practice for a successful academic future.

How can students demonstrate good classroom participation skills?

Prepare. Questions and discussions usually key off of homework or the prior night's reading. If you haven't done the homework or assigned reading, you won't have much to say. Sitting in class hoping your teacher won't call on you can be pretty uncomfortable. **Prepare. Do the homework. Do the reading.** It's much easier than the constant stress of trying to hide in plain sight.

Anticipate. When doing homework or assigned reading, try to anticipate questions your teacher will ask, or discussion topics they might raise. **Prepare answers. Jot down notes.** Run through answers in your head or say them aloud. Pretend you're preparing for an interview. When a question is asked or a discussion starts, your notes will prompt you to recall the answer.

Be Relevant. Comments should be relevant to the point under discussion. Establish relevancy by linking back to the reading, or to a comment made by another student. **If you don't have a relevant comment to make, try asking a relevant question.** If you've prepared for class, you should be able to answer most questions. If you can't answer a question when asked directly, politely say "I don't know." Redeem yourself later by answering another question. It's better to make one relevant comment and ask one relevant question, than ten pointless or irrelevant ones.

Don't be Judgemental. Don't expect greatness right away. **The ability to effectively participate in class develops over time, with patience and practice.** Set a goal to participate twice in every class. Keep at it. Don't worry if your answer comes out less-than-perfect, if your voice cracks, or you're nervous. Don't go all judgemental on yourself (or others.) Confidence builds with effort and practice. Your skills will improve.

A special note to the introverted student

Ever notice how some students can jump right into a conversation and answer questions without hesitation, yet others stammer and stall even when they know the answer? An estimated one in four people are introverts. Introverts are not just "shy" students, and they are not afraid of participating. **They are thoughtful, often gifted people, who need a bit more time to process a question and formulate a verbal response.** Unfortunately, their delay can be interpreted as a lack of preparation or inability to answer. If you're an introvert, take notes when you're doing the reading and homework. Have your notes handy in class. Let your teacher know that when called on, you need a moment to formulate your response.

The rules of engagement: Good Citizenship

→ **Be polite.** Listen attentively when classmates speak. Don't look around the room, tap your pencil, roll your eyes, or make a disparaging comment or noise. Never scoff or laugh at a speaker and do not judge them as cool or uncool, smart or dumb. To do so would reveal the extent of your immaturity. In a classroom discussion, it's ok to disagree, but don't let a disagreement get personal. Don't bring schoolyard animosities into the classroom.

→ **Don't hog the floor.** It's great that you're an enthusiastic participant, but don't dominate the discussion. Let other students have a turn at voicing opinions and practicing skills. Don't interrupt when others speak.

→ **Elevate the discussion.** One problem with classroom discussions, particularly in middle school, is that students are hesitant to take or represent an uncool or contrary viewpoint, and the discussion stagnates. For the benefit of classroom citizenship, and to generate a meaningful discussion, offer to take an alternative or unpopular viewpoint. You might even come to enjoy being the classroom "Devil's Advocate."

→ **Compliment.** A simple "Good point!" or "Well said!" helps create an atmosphere of acceptance. Coaxing more students to participate will make your classroom community more vibrant. Be especially patient and encouraging when you encounter a student with limited English skills.

→ **Speakers.** If your class is lucky enough to have a guest speaker, listen actively. When they conclude, it is your duty as a good classroom citizen to ask at least one relevant question— two if no one else steps up. Thank the speaker for coming.

As a middle school student, participation and citizenship skills may not be at the top of your list of essential skills, but as you move up into high school and college, your participation and citizenship skills are increasingly important to your success as a student. Take the time and make the effort now to work on these skills. The more you participate, the easier it gets!

Name: _____

> Observe **The Not-So-Perfect-Participants of Room 141**. Consider each student's preparedness, speaking, behavior, and involvement in activities. Use the Classroom Participation and Citizenship rubric on page 308 to assess and score their skills.

Student 1 Score: _____. AKA: _____

What are Student 1's participation and citizenship errors?

_____

_____

How can Student 1 improve his/her participation and citizenship skills?

_____

_____

Student 2 Score: _____. AKA: _____

What are Student 2's participation and citizenship errors?

_____

_____

How can Student 2 improve his/her participation and citizenship skills?

_____

_____

Student 3 Score: _____. AKA: _____

What are Student 3's participation and citizenship errors?

_____

_____

How can Student 3 improve his/her participation and citizenship skills?

_____

_____

Student 4 Score: _____. AKA: _____

What are Student 4's participation and citizenship errors?

_____

_____

How can Student 4 improve his/her participation and citizenship skills?

_____

_____

Participation and Citizen Rubric

Skill	Excellent	Good	Unacceptable
Preparedness	Brings materials to class. Does reading and homework. Fully prepared for class discussion. Anticipates questions/discussions and prepares in advance of class. **3 pts.**	Usually brings materials to class. Usually does reading and homework. Usually prepared for class discussion. **2 pts**	Preparation is inconsistent. Student is rarely or never prepared. Rarely/ never brings materials to class. **0 pts.**
Speaking	Regularly participates in discussions; makes thoughtful, insightful comments relevant to the reading or topic under discussion. Consistently exhibits interest in the discussion topic. Doesn't dominate the discussion. **3 pts.**	Usually participates in discussions; Comments are basic, but accurate and moderately insightful. Comments are usually relevant to the discussion topic or reading. Exhibits moderate interest in the discussion topic. **2 pts.**	Rarely or never participates in discussion. If so, comments are inaccurate and irrelevant. Indicates little thought, insight, or interest in the discussion topic. Dominates the discussion **0 pts.**
Behavior	Actively listens to teacher and classmates. Does not interrupt when others are speaking. Engages respectfully with classmates. Encourages the participation of other students by exhibiting interest in comments and opinions. Polite to classmates and teacher. **3 pts.**	Usually listens actively to teachers and classmates. Is occasionally distracted; Sometimes interrupts speaker. Usually voices disagreement respectfully and is tolerant of other students' comments and opinions. Usually polite to classmates and teacher. **2 pts.**	Does not use active listening skills. Engages in disrespectful behavior when other students are speaking. Such as eye rolling or making disrespectful noises. Impolite. Argues with classmates and interrupts. **0 pts.**
Activities	Always engages enthusiastically in class activities and exercises. Always takes a leadership role and encourages other students. **3 pts.**	Usually engages enthusiastically in class activities and exercises. Sometimes takes a leadership role. **2 pts.**	Never/rarely engages in class activities and exercises. Avoids taking a leadership role. **0 pts.**

Name: _____

Are You a Good Citizen and a Perfect Participant?

In high school and college, **participation and citizenship skills are important to your success.** Do you regularly participate in classroom discussions and activities? Assess your skills, and make a plan for becoming a good citizen and a perfect participant.

CLASSROOM PARTICIPATION AND CITIZENSHIP SKILLS

- Prepare for class by doing the reading and homework
- Prepare notes as cues to answer questions
- Ask relevant questions
- Encourage others to speak
- Be polite to classmates
- Don't judge yourself others as cool or uncool
- Speak respectfully to your teacher
- Don't interrupt
- Be respectful of other's opinions
- Set daily participation goals
- Leave schoolyard animosities out of the classroom

- Ask questions when you have a guest speaker
- Make relevant comments
- Don't hog the floor
- Elevate the discussion
- Compliment another speaker
- Anticipate teacher's questions/ discussions
- Take a leadership role in an activity
- Be patient when others speak
- Listen actively
- Make eye contact with your teacher
- Thank a guest speaker

1. What is your most difficult class? _____

2. Review *The Participation and Citizenship Rubric* on page ___. With regard to the class you identified in question 1, what score would you give yourself for *preparedness?* _____.

3. What score would you give yourself for *speaking?* _____.

4. What score would you give yourself for *behavior ?* _____.

5. What score would you give yourself for *activities?* _____.

Use the **Classroom Participation and Citizenship Skills Chart** for questions 6-9.

6. Select two things from the chart that you will do to improve your *preparedness* skills in each of your classes:

   _____

   _____

7. Select two things from the chart that you will do to improve your *speaking* skills in each of your classes:

   _____

   _____

8. Select two things from the chart that you will do to improve your *behavior* skills in each of your classes:

   _____

   _____

9. Select two things from the chart that you will do to improve your *engagement in activities* in each of your classes:

   _____

   _____

10. In which of your classes are you most comfortable participating? In which class are you least comfortable participating? Discuss and compare what makes you feel comfortable participating in a class, and what inhibits your participation. Confirm your goal to participate twice in every class.

   _____

   _____

   _____

   _____

   _____

   _____

   _____

   _____

Dear Parent or Caregiver,

Today I participated in my study skills class based on *The Middle School Student's Guide to Study Skills*. One of the best ways I can prepare for high school and college is to use good study skills whenever I am learning.

I learned:

1. Demonstrating good participation skills includes answering your teacher's questions, engaging in the classroom discussion, using your _____ listening skills, _____ notes, coming to class _____, and taking a(n) _____ role in a team exercise or group activity.

2. Even if your teacher assigns a low weight to participation, or awards a "satisfactory/unsatisfactory" mark, participation definitely _____ your final grade to some degree.

3. In high school and college, participation expectations are _____; In college, you will take a class called a _____ where participation can account for up to 50% of your grade!

4. Good participation skills take confidence, which is earned over time with plenty of _____ and _____; set a goal to participate _____ in every class.

5. Good classroom citizenship skills mean that when your class has a guest speaker, it is your _____ to listen actively and ask at least _____ relevant question.

Ask me about the skills I learned today! Your support at home will help me make good study skills daily habit.

Thank you for all you do for me every day.

Sincerely,

_____

THE BENEFITS OF FAILURE

Do you know there are scientists who study only *failure?* They are called *failure analysts.* It's their job to figure out why something failed, such as the collapse of a building or bridge. Failure analysts systematically gather and review data to identify the root cause of a failure, hoping to prevent future failures.

Almost every industry uses failure analysts. In business they study why a product isn't selling. The military uses failure analysts to understand why a strategy did not succeed.

The principles of failure analysis apply to academics too. How you deal with failure is important. When you experience failure, don't let it defeat or define you. Gather and review data, determine why you failed, and how you can succeed in the future.

And remember, while failure is never fun, there are some potential benefits to it. Knowing how to analyze, correct, and benefit from your failure is not only a good study skill—it's a good life skill.

Chapter 28 Learning Goals:

☐ compare "failure" vs. "set back".
☐ set grade goals for success.
☐ recognize the relationship of poor study skills to a failure to meet grade goals.
☐ list three benefits of failure.

What is failure?

A simple definition of failure is a *lack of success*. But isn't *success* a subjective concept? Your notion of success could be quite different from your friend's. One student may consider passing a very difficult math class with a C+ and their sanity intact, as a great success. On the other hand, a student who accepts nothing less than straight A's would consider that grade closer to failure. *Failure*, like success, is a subjective concept. For students, a useful definition of failure is **not meeting your personal goals for success in school**. (Yes, that means you need to set goals for academic success.)

How to analyze failure.

Set grade goals!

To analyze failure, you must first know what you wanted to achieve. That, of course, requires setting goals. **For starters, you need a grade goal for every class.** Without a grade goal, your successes and failures as a student are hard to measure. Don't just pick a grade goal out of the air. **A grade goal is the final grade you can expect to receive by making your very best effort in a class.** Don't set grade goals so high as to be unattainable, because that will make failure inevitable. On the other hand, never set a grade goal too low. Always challenge yourself to be the very best student you can be.

Action steps = study skills.

The path to your grade goal is paved with many **action steps**. Those are the study skills and strategies you learned in this course, which you must use everyday to meet your grade goal. Sticking to a homework routine, thinking about your thinking, using time-spaced learning to study for tests and quizzes, preparing for every class, exhibiting good citizenship and participation skills, taking notes in class, using your critical thinking skills, etc. are the action steps that will lead you to success. **Sometimes students focus only on their grade goal for a class, and overlook the constant daily effort and diligence it takes to reach it.**

Find the root cause of the failure.

Keep your eyes on your grades. **Grades and scores are external indicators of your progress toward your grade goal.** Don't just shrug off a poor grade or score with a vague vow to "do better next time." When your grade in a class starts heading south, morph into failure analyst mode and get to the root cause. A falling grade in a class is a warning sign that you are not completing one or more of the many action steps to your goal. **Focus your investigation on your study skills.** Analyze your performance and you will find that somewhere in the process of learning, studying, or taking a quiz or test, you made one or several action step (study skills) errors. Ask yourself: *Did I not actively read the textbook chapter? Did I not actively listen in class? Did I cram instead of study* over time? Would using mnemonics have helped me master the information? Should I have used a supplemental or tutorial resource, or outlined the chapter? Did I fail to use good test-taking strategies? Did I not put in enough effort? Once you identify the root cause (or causes) of a failure, apply the appropriate study skills so you do not repeat it.

What is not failure?

Failure ≠ Not succeeding. True and permanent failure is rare. We mostly experience **setbacks** by not succeeding on a first, second, or even third try. It often takes more than one attempt to succeed at something. Think about the first time you tried to swim the full length of the pool, or ride a bike. When you didn't succeed on the first try, did you say "What a failure! I'll never try that again!"? Of course not! Success is incremental. **For most things in life, including learning, it takes sustained effort, and sometimes several setbacks before success is achieved.**

Whaaaa! I'll never try that again!

Failure is not rejection. Ouch! Sometimes failure hurts. People often equate failure with rejection, or as judgement of their value as a person. **When you get a poor grade on a paper, project or test, or experience any other set back in school, it is not rejection of you or a measurement of your value as a person.** It's an indication that somewhere in the process of learning, or completing a project or paper, or preparing for or taking a test, you made one or more errors.

Failure is not *you*. Failure does not define you. In fact, out of failure often emerges a stronger, smarter, and more resilient student. The only failure that defines you is the kind of failure that results from not caring about learning, not making an effort to learn, and not trying again (and again and again) to succeed at learning.

Failure is not the end of the world. Some things in life (or school) come with a do-over, some don't. When you encounter the latter, **accept responsibility and the consequence of the failure. Take your lumps and move on.** Look forward to the many more opportunities to learn and succeed that will come your way.

Will you fail?

Yes. You are going to fail. At some point in your life as a student you will suffer a set back that you consider a failure. It might be a terrible grade on a paper or project, it could be failing a test, even a class. It could be in high school, college, or graduate school. It could happen more than once. It could be a big failure. It could be a small failure. **No one wants to fail, but when you do fail, how you handle it is important.** Believe it or not, there are some potential benefits to it.

What are the benefits of failure?

→ **Self-sufficiency.** Failure provides you with an opportunity to learn how to fix something yourself. When you suffer a failure or setback, own it. Don't pass it off on someone else. Don't blame your teacher. **Ask your parents *not* to intervene to cover your every failure or constantly smooth the road ahead of you.** They mean well, but when you get to high school, college and career, you'll be glad you learned to handle small failures and setbacks on your own.

→ **Resilience.** Students who have experienced failure understand that while unpleasant, it will not kill you. Students who have pulled themselves up from the pit of failure once or twice understand that **the experience can be sort-of like a failure vaccine enabling them to recover faster and stronger from subsequent failures.**

→ **Clarity.** Some of the world's greatest inventors, innovators, leaders and athletes have suffered epic and occasionally very public failures. Thomas Edison, J.K. Rowling, Steve Jobs, and Abraham Lincoln all failed several times before achieving success. **Each recovered from failure with a clearer and stronger vision of their goal.**

→ **Perspective.** Failure puts success in proper perspective. These days too many people expect immediate success, and when it doesn't happen right away, they give up. **Failure provides the perspective that success is a *process*.**

A final word about failure (and success)

Success is rarely instantaneous. Most success in life takes time, a great deal of effort, and several setbacks. At this stage in your life, academic success is your primary goal. Set grade goals that reflect your best efforts. Know what you want to achieve. Actively monitor your progress toward your grade goals. *You have the skills it takes to be a successful student in middle school, high school, and college.* Never let the prospect of failure prevent you from going big and bold, and trying your very best to do whatever it is you want to do. Develop a personal philosophy for dealing with failure. How you handle failure is not only a good study skill, it's a great life skill!

Name: _____

The Benefits of Failure

Harry Potter author, J.K. Rowling, came from an impoverished background in Britain. She suffered many failures before achieving great success. In a famous 2008 Harvard University commencement speech, "The Fringe Benefits of Failure," she shared her insights into failure. Watch the video (mins. 1-12), then answer questions 1-4 below:

1. What does Ms. Rowling mean when she says *"failure means a striping away of the inessential"*?

   _____

   _____

   _____

   _____

2. What does Ms. Rowling mean when she says *"Rock bottom became the solid foundation upon which I rebuilt my life"*?

   _____

   _____

   _____

   _____

3. According to Ms. Rowling, how is *failure* related to *achievement*?

   _____

   _____

   _____

   _____

4. Ms. Rowling told the graduates that *"there is an expiry date for blaming your parents for steering you in the wrong direction."* Comment.

   _____

   _____

   _____

   _____

5. Why is *failure* a topic in your study skills course?

_____

_____

_____

_____

_____

Below are some famous quotes about *failure*. **Read them, and select a quote that you find particularly meaningful. Discuss why it appeals to you. Then create your own quote about the meaning of** *failure*. **Share your quote with your classmates.**

"Success is not final, failure is not fatal: it is the courage to continue that counts."
– Winston Churchill

"It is impossible to live without failing at something, unless you live so cautiously that you might as well not have lived at all - in which case, you fail by default."
– J.K. Rowling

"Failure is simply a few errors in judgment, repeated every day."
– Jim Rohn

"I can accept failure, everyone fails at something. But I can't accept not trying."
– Michael Jordan

This quote is meaningful to me because:

_____

_____

_____

_____

My personal quote about failure:

_____

_____

_____

_____

APPLICATION OF SKILLS

Name: _____

Get'n Your Grade Goals On

Students should have a grade goal for every class. Don't just pick one out of the air! A grade goal is the final grade you can expect to receive **for making your best effort in a class**.

1. List each of your classes, then write the grade *you expect to receive for making your best effort in the class.*

Name of Class	Grade Goal
_____	_____
_____	_____
_____	_____
_____	_____
_____	_____
_____	_____

2. Grade goals are reached through many action steps, including making good study skills a daily habit. Do all assigned reading and homework, prepare for class, establish (and stick to) a study routine, participate in class, use SQ3R active reading skills, limit breaks when you study, etc. Select one of the classes above and list your *study skills action steps* for meeting your grade goal:

_____

_____

_____

_____

3. How do study skills failures impact long term grade goals?

_____

_____

_____

4. Review each chapter of *The Middle School Student's Guide to Study Skills.* List the study skills you have learned which will help you successfully reach your personal grade goals.

_____

_____

_____

_____

_____

_____

_____

_____

_____

_____

_____

_____

_____

_____

_____

_____

_____

_____

_____

_____

_____

_____

5. In Chapter 1 you learned that the term *study* skills is misleading, because study skills apply to all aspects of learning. How have you applied the skills you have learned in this class to all aspects of your learning?

_____

_____

_____

_____

_____

6. In Chapter 1, you learned that good study skills make you a *faster, more efficient and effective student.* How are you a faster, more efficient and effective student since learning good study skills? Provide examples.

_____

_____

_____

_____

_____

7. In Chapter 1 you identified your three worst study habits. Have you replaced your poor study skills and habits with productive habits? Provide examples.

_____

_____

_____

_____

_____

8. What grade would you give your current study skills and habits?

A+   A   A-   B+   B   B-   C+   C   C-   D+   D   D-   F

✳ **Bonus:** When you notice that your grade in a class is falling, what should you do?

_____

_____

_____

_____

Dear Parent or Caregiver,

Today I participated in my final study skills class based on *The Middle School Student's Guide to Study Skills*. One of the best ways I can prepare for high school and college is to use good study skills whenever I am learning.

I learned:

1. _____ analysts study failure, systematically gathering and reviewing data to identify the root cause of a failure, hoping to prevent _____ failures.

2. True and permanent failure is rare. We mostly experience _____. It takes sustained effort and often several attempts to _____.

3. A falling grade in a class is a warning sign that in some way, you are failing to meet your _____ steps (ie. not consistently using the study skills and strategies learned in this class.) When that happens, morph into failure analyst mode and get to the root _____ of the problem.

4. The skills and strategies you've learned in this study skills class provide you with all of the _____ (skills and strategies) you need to meet your grade goals.

5. While no one enjoys failure, there are some potential _____: failure provides an opportunity to develop self-_____ skills (the ability to handle something yourself); overcoming failure builds _____ (the ability to recover from setback), and often provides a _____ vision of your goals.

Ask me about the skills I learned today! Your support at home will help me make good study skills daily habit.

Thank you for all you do for me every day.

Sincerely,

_____

Name: _____

WHAT DID YOU LEARN ABOUT WRAPPING UP FOR COLLEGE READINESS?

1. Why is perfecting your classroom participation skills important for high school and college readiness?

   a. High school and college teachers have higher expectations of the level and quality of students' participation.

   b. In college *seminars,* participation can count toward up to 50% of your grade

   c. If you don't participate in high school and college classroom discussions, you will not graduate.

   d. a and b

2. State five Rules of Engagement for *good citizenship* in the classroom:

   _____

   _____

   _____

   _____

   _____

3. Good strategies for preparing for a classroom discussion are:

   a. do the homework and reading.

   b. avoid making eye contact with by your teacher until you are sure of your answer.

   c. anticipate questions or discussion topics your teacher may ask and jot down notes.

   d. a and c

4. How is the classroom a community? What responsibilities do members of the classroom community have to one another? Discuss:

   _____

   _____

   _____

   _____

   _____

5. Which of the following is <u>not</u> a benefit of distance learning:

   a. Schedule flexibility: Students can attend class 24/7

   b. Upward mobility: Students can take classes at advanced grade levels

   c. Online classes require less time.

   d. Course enrichment: Most DL classes link to interesting resources.

6. What's your advice to a procrastination-prone student who enrolls in a DL course? Be specific:

_____

_____

_____

_____

_____

7. Anika's progress report in algebra shows that her grade in the class is a C-. She's told her mom that she "will work harder," but doesn't understand why her grade is so low. What's your advice?

_____

_____

_____

8. What are the difference between a *fact* and an *opinion?*

_____

_____

9. According to the National Forum on Information Literacy (NFIL), an information literate student must be able to do each of these, *except:*

   a. identify information
   b. make up information
   c. evaluate information
   d. effectively use information

True or False:

10. _____ As a middle school student, you may not yet have enough life experience to recognize *bias* in a source, but you certainly have enough intelligence to understand that sources can be (and frequently are) biased.

11. _____ There are no benefits to failure.

12. _____ Critical thinking is a process of gathering and assessing information, reflecting on and comparing information, discriminating between ideas, facts and opinions to reach a well-reasoned conclusion.

13. _____ Good study skills should be used everyday, as part of your normal routine.

14. _____ Higher order thinking skills recognize the static and inflexible nature of thinking.

15. _____ You have the study skills and strategies you need to be high school and college ready—provided you use the skills every day.

Certificate of Super Study Skills

CONGRATULATIONS!

THIS IS TO CERTIFY THAT _____
(print your name here)

HAS COMPLETED THE LESSONS AND ACTIVITIES IN

THE MIDDLE SCHOOL STUDENT'S GUIDE TO STUDY SKILLS,

HAS LEARNED SKILLS AND STRATEGIES

FOR HIGH SCHOOL AND COLLEGE READINESS,

AND IS A TOTALLY AWESOME MIDDLE SCHOOL STUDENT!

DATE: _____

_____
STUDY SKILLS TEACHER

_____

_____

_____

_____

_____

_____

_____

_____

_____

_____

_____

_____

_____

_____

_____

_____

_____

_____

_____

_____

Blackwell, Lisa S., Kali H. Trzesniewski, and Carol S. Dweck. "Implicit Theories of Intelligence Predict Achievement Across an Adolescent Transition: A Longitudinal Study and an Intervention." Child Development, 78.1 (2007): 246-263. Web. 16 June 2012. www.stanford.edu/dept/psychology/cgi-bin/drupalm/system/files/

Hamilton, Jon. "Think You're Multitasking? Think Again." NPR. National Public Radio, 2 Oct. 2008. Web. 1 July 2012. www.npr.org/templates/story/story.php?storyId= 95256794

Schraw, Gregory, and Rayne S. Dennison. "Assessing Metacognitive Awareness." Contemporary Educational Psychology 19 (1994): 460-475. Print.

Souza, David. How the Brain Learns. 3rd ed. Thousand Oaks: Corwin Press, 2006. Print.

"Metacognition - Thinking about thinking - Learning to learn." Holistic Education. Holistic Education Network, 20 Sept. 2004. Web. 16 June 2012. www.hent.org/world/rss/files/metacognition.htm

Aubrey, Allison. "I.Q. Isn't Set In Stone, Suggests Study That Finds Big Jumps, Dips In Teens." Shots: NPR's Health Blog. NPR, 19 Oct. 2011. Web. 12 Sept. 2012. www.npr.org/blogs/health/2011/10/20/141511314/iq-isnt-set-in-stone-suggests-study-that-finds-big-jumps-dips-in-teens

Dweck, Carol S. Mindset: The New Psychology of Success. New York: Random House, 2008. Kindle.

Dweck, Carol S. "Caution—Praise Can Be Dangerous." American Educator 23.1 (1999): 4-9. Web. 12 Sept. 2012. www.aft.org/pdfs/americaneducator/spring1999/PraiseSpring99.pdf

Gardner, Howard. Frames of Mind: The Theory of Multiple Intelligences. New York: Basic Books, 1993. Print.

Graham, Emily. "What Is Your Child's Learning Style?" School Family. School Family Media Inc., n.d. Web. 16 June 2012. www.schoolfamily.com/school-family-articles/article/826-what-is-your-childs-learning-style

Moreno, Roxana, and Richard Mayer. "Multimodal Learning Environments: Special Issue on Interactive Learning Environments: Contemporary Issues and Trends." Educational Psychology Review 19.3 (2007): 309-326. Web. 16 June 2012. www.springerlink.com/content/v5414u250220511r/

Prashnig, Barbara. "Learning Styles vs. Multiple Intelligences (MI): Two Concepts for Enhancing Learning and Teaching." www.teachingexpertise.com 9 (2005): 8-9. Web. 16 June 2012. www.creativelearningcentre.com/downloads/LS vs MI TEX9_p8_9.pdf

Ramsden, Sue, Fiona M. Richardson, Goulven Josse, Michael S. C. Thomas, Caroline Ellis, Clare Shakeshaft, Mohamed L. Seghier, and Cathy J. Price. "Verbal and non-verbal intelligence changes in the teenage brain." Nature 479.7371 (2001): 113-116. Web. 19 June 2012. www.nature.com/nature/journal/v479/n7371/full/nature10514.html

Sankey, Michael, Dawn Birch, and Michael Gardiner. "Engaging students through multimodal learning environments: The journey continues." Proceedings ascilite Sydney 2010: curriculum, technology & transformation for an unknown future (2010): 852-863. Ed. University of Queensland. Web. 16 June 2012. ascilite.org.au/conferences/sydney10/procs/Sankey-full.pdf

Hansen, Katharine. "MyCollegeSuccessStory.com: The Course Syllabus: Know It, Love It, Understand It, Benefit From It." MyCollegeSuccessStory.com: Empowering Academic and Career Success. EmpoweringSites.com, n.d. Web. 16 June 2012. www.mycollegesuccessstory.com/academic-success-tools/course-syllabus.html

Porter, Karla. "Strategies to Activate Prior Knowledge." WSU Teachall. WSU Development Team, n.d. Web. 16 June 2012. departments.weber.edu/teachall/reading/prereading.html#StrategiesPriorKnowledge

Taylor A. & Gousie, G. (1988) The Ecology of Learning Environments for Children. (EFPI Journal, 26 (4) 23-28

Ergonomics.org: posture, motion & ergonomics. Alexander Technique Nebraska and Toronto, and Care for your Parents, Care for Yourself Coaching, n.d. Web. 16 June 2012. www.ergonomics.org

"Constructivism as a Paradigm for Teaching and Learning." Concept to Classroom. Educational Broadcasting Corporation, 2004. Web. 16 June 2012. www.thirteen.org/edonline/concept2class/constructivism/index.html

Scheid, Karen. Helping Students Become Strategic Learners: Guidelines for Teaching.

"SQ3R - A Reading and Study Skill System." Cook Counseling Center. Cook Counseling Center, Virginia Tech, 26 Aug. 2004. Web. 16 June 2012. www.ucc.vt.edu/stdysk/sq3r.html

Sticht, Thomas G. "The Reading Formula that Helped Win World War II." Reading Today 20.2 (2002): 18. Print. Cambridge: Brookline Books, 1993. Print.

Nell, Victor. "The Psychology of Reading for Pleasure: Needs and Gratifications." Reading Research Quarterly 23.1 (1988): 6-50. JSTOR. Web. 1 July 2012.

Thayer, Kathleen D. "How Can I Organize My Textbook Reading? Or Unraveling The Textbook Maze." Purdue University. Purdue University, n.d. Web. 16 June 2012. www.cla.purdue.edu/students/asc/documents/textbook.pdf

"Note Taking – Symbols and Abbreviations." ilile: Institute for Library & Information Literacy Education. Institute for Library & Information Literacy Education, n.d. Web. 8 Sept. 2012. www.ilile.org/events/past/Seminar_08_03/lesson_plans/Wheelersburg/NoteTakingSymbolsandAbreviations.htm

Rohrer, Doug, and Harold Pashler. (2007). "Increasing Retention without Increasing Study Time." Current Directions in Psychological Science 16 (2007): 183-186. Web. 21 June 2012. escholarship.org/uc/item/6061k9j5

Thalheimer, Will. (2006, February). Spacing Learning Events over Time: What the Research Says. Feb. 2006. Web. 21 June 2012. www.leerbeleving.nl/wp-content/uploads/2011/11/Spacing_Learning_Over_Time__March2009v1_.pdf

Beilock, Sian, Choke: What the Secrets of the Brain Reveal About Getting It Right When You Have To. New York: Free Press, 2010. Print

Boyle, Emily, The Great Debate Over the Five-Paragraph Essay - Academic Help or Creative Hindrance? Yahoo, 2007

Ramirez, Gerardo, and Sian L. Beilock. Writing About Testing Worries Boosts Exam Performance in the Classroom. Science 331.6014 (2011): 211-213. Web. 26 Aug. 2012. www.sciencemag.org/content/331/6014/211.abstract?sid=df05d946-2962-4fc8-8dc6-e9d137ffa918

Taking Multiple Choice Exams www.uwec.edu/geography/ivogeler/multiple.htm

Toastmasters International. Toastmasters International, 2012. Web. 9 Sept. 2012. www.toastmasters.org

Bloom, Benjamin S. Taxonomy of Educational Objectives Book 1: Cognitive Domain. 2nd ed. Boston: Addison Wesley, 1984. Print.

Laney, Martin O. The Introvert Advantage - How to Thrive in an Extrovert World. New York: Workman Publishing, 2002. Print.

NFIL. National Forum on Information Literacy, 2012. Web 13 August 2012 infolit.org

Eissinger, Richard. "Library Research Skills and New College Students." Online slide show. SlideShare. SlideShare Inc., 2008. 9 Sept. 2012. www.slideshare.net/eissinger

Flipped Learning. Flipped Learning Network, 2012. Web. 9 Sept. 2012. flippedclassroom.org/video

Tween Publishing is a little company on a big mission: to provide engaging, innovative curriculum for teaching essential college readiness skills. With Tween's classroom-ready series it's easy to teach:

- *Work habits, time management, & organizational skills*
- *Super study skills*
- *Confidence on the path to college*

Why select Tween Publishing's college readiness series for your students?

✓ Tween's resources are the only comprehensive college readiness skills programs designed specifically for 11-14 year olds.

✓ Tween's resources deliver content in a fun, easy-to-follow "how to" format that appeals to, and works for this age group.

✓ Tween's resources are classroom-ready, easy to teach, and affordable.

✓ Tween's programs eliminate the haphazard, inconsistent approach many schools take to teaching these important skills. From work habits, time management and organizational skills, to study skills, and getting students confidently on the college path, your school can provide consistent, progressive skills instruction in grades six through eight.

✓ Free extras! Audio podcasts, webslides, downloadable materials, consultations, links, tips, articles. Tween is committed to supporting your college readiness program.

✓ Teachers love it!

✓ Students love it!

✓ Parents love it!

✓ Your students' success is our success!

Titles from Tween Publishing

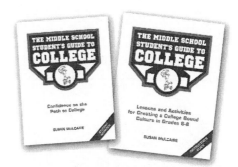

The Middle School Student's Guide to Ruling the World!
Work Habits &
Organizational Skills
Student Workbook $11.95
Instructor's Guide $45.95
(Recommended for Grades 5/6/7)

The Middle School Student's Guide to Study Skills
Student Workbook $15.95
Instructor's Guide $69.95
(Recommended for Grades 7/8/9)

The Middle School Student's Guide to College
Student Workbook $11.95
Instructor's Guide $45.95
(Recommended for Grades 7/8/9)

Tween Publishing

College Readiness Begins in Middle School

**Prices apply 2015 - 2016. Fax form to 949-209-1871 or
email to info@middleschoolguide,com**

TITLE	PRICE	X	QUANTITY	
The Middle School Student's Guide to Ruling the World! Work Habits & Organizational Skills (Student Workbook) 0-9785210-0-5	$11.95			
The Middle School Student's Guide to Ruling the World! Work Habits & Organizational Skills (Instructor's Guide) 0-09785210-1-3	$45.95			
The Middle School Student's Guide to Study Skills! (Student Textbook) 9785210-6-6	$15.95			
The Middle School Student's Guide to Study Skills! (Instructor's Guide) 9785210-5-9	$69.95			
The Middle School Student's Guide to College! Confidence on the Path to College (Student Workbook) 978-0-9785210-3-5	$11.95			
The Middle School Student's Guide to College! Lessons & Activities for Creating a College Bound Culture in Grades 6-8 (Instructor's Guide) 978-0-9785210-4-2	$45.95			
The 21st Century Student's Guide to Financial Literacy Student textbook/workbook. 978-0-9785210-9-7	$15.95			
The 21st Century Student's Guide to Financial Literacy Instructor's Guide 978-0-9785210-8-0	$71.25			
SUBTOTAL				
USPS Media Mail. Allow 7-10days for delivery. S&H $7.50 for the first 2 books; $1.00 per book thereafter.				
Tax (for sales within CA only) include 8.0%on merchandise.				
TOTAL				

SHIP TO

Name: _____

Street: _____

City & State: _____

Attn: _____

Zip/Postal: _____

Country: _____

Contact (email address and phone)

VISA   MASTERCARD   AMEX

Card Number: _____

Expiration Date: _____

Purchase orders accepted.

**Tween Publishing/c21 Student
PO Box 8677
Newport Beach CA 92658
www.middleschoolguide.com
949-723-5131**